OBOR: China's Alternate Indo-pacific Policy

OBOR: China's Alternate Indo-pacific Policy

Ashutosh Kumar

PRASHANT PUBLISHING HOUSE
DELHI-110094

Published by :
Prashant Publishing House
C-34, 28 Foota Road, Gali-3,
West Karwal Nagar, Delhi-110094
Phone : 011-22963970, Mob. : 9810396373
e-mail.: prashantpublishinghouse@gmail.com

OBOR: China's Alternate Indo-pacific Policy

Reserved
First Published 2018

ISBN 978-81-938012-0-8

PRINTED IN INDIA
Published by Mr. R.K. Jha M/s Prashant Publishing House and Published at H.S. Offset House Press, Delhi.

Contents

Preface

The Belt and Road Initiative is a way for win-win cooperation that promotes common development and prosperity and a road towards peace and friendship by enhancing mutual understanding and trust, and strengthening all-round exchanges. The Chinese government advocates peace and cooperation, openness and inclusiveness, mutual learning and mutual benefit. It promotes practical cooperation in all fields, and works to build a community of shared interests, destiny and responsibility featuring mutual political trust, economic integration and cultural inclusiveness.

Plans for OBOR were first outlined by Chinese President Xi Jinping during a visit to Kazakhstan in September 2013. One strand of OBOR includes the "21st century Maritime Silk Road", which is to go from China's coast to Europe through the South China Sea and the Indian Ocean in one route, and from China's coast through the South China Sea to the South Pacific in the other.

Reflecting at the land and sea routes of the old Silk Road linkages, the OBOR has land and sea dimensions that converge at certain points, which together constitute an extraordinary seamless connectivity that embraces all of Eurasia and the Indian Ocean littoral. The Eurasian land connection, known as the "New Silk Road Economic Belt" or simply the "Belt," is made up of railways, highways, oil and gas pipelines, and major energy projects.

The PLAN's attempt to develop the capability to safeguard China's maritime interests along the western SLOCs is a source of anxiety for some in Asia. There is apprehension that China's infrastructure investments, particularly port developments, while commercial in nature is a furtive strategic attempt to advance PLAN access across Asian ports to safeguard China's energy security interests and SLOC access.

There is also concern that the rise of China as a maritime power could result in the loss of ASEAN centrality in Asian affairs. It is concluded that a key source of distrust stems from the fact that China remains embroiled in territorial and maritime boundary disputes with other Asian neighbours.

The process of travelling the Silk Roads developed along with the roads themselves. In the Middle Ages, caravans consisting of horses or camels were the standard means of transporting goods across land. Caravanserais, large guest houses or inns designed to welcome travelling merchants, played a vital role in facilitating the passage of people and goods along these routes.

Found along the Silk Roads from Turkey to China, they provided not only a regular opportunity for merchants to eat well, rest and prepare themselves in safety for their onward journey, and also to exchange goods, trade with local markets and buy local products, and to meet other merchant travellers, and in doing so, to exchange cultures, languages and ideas.

This is a reference book. All the matter is just compiled and edited in nature, taken from the various sources which are in public domain.

The present book is serve the very purpose meaningfully and give a fresh impetus to the scientific community for further research on geographical aspects on OBOR, which we could not cover in this book due to its limited scope.

—*Editor*

1

Introduction

ONE BELT, ONE ROAD

The Silk Road Economic Belt and the 21st-century Maritime Silk Road, otherwise called The Belt and Road (shortened B&R), One Belt, One Road(abbreviated OBOR) or the Belt and Road Initiative is an advancement technique and structure, proposed by Chinese president Xi Jinping that spotlights on availability and collaboration among nations basically between thePeople's Republic of China and whatever is left of Eurasia, which comprises of two principle parts, the area based "Silk Road Economic Belt" (SREB) and oceangoing "Sea Silk Road" (MSR).

The procedure underlines China's push to play a greater part in worldwide issues, and its need to fare China's generation limit in territories of overproduction, for example, steel fabricating. It was uncovered in September and October 2013 in declarations uncovering the SREB and MSR, individually. It was likewise advanced byPremier Li Keqiang amid the State visit in Asia and Europe.

Infrastructure networks

The coverage area of the initiative is primarily Asia and Europe, encompassing around 60 countries. Oceania and East Africa are also included. Anticipated cumulative investment over an indefinite timescale is variously put at US$4 trillion or US$8 trillion. One Belt, One Road has been contrasted with the two US-centric trading arrangements, the Trans-Pacific Partnership and the Transatlantic Trade and Investment Partnership.

Silk Road Economic Belt

When Chinese leader Xi Jinping visited Central Asia and Southeast Asia in September and October 2013, he raised the initiative of jointly building the Silk Road Economic Belt and the 21st-Century Maritime Silk Road. Essentially, the 'belt' includes countries situated on the original Silk Road through Central Asia, West Asia, the Middle East, and Europe. The initiative calls for the integration of the region into a cohesive economic area through building infrastructure, increasing cultural exchanges, and broadening trade. Apart from this zone, which is largely analogous to the historical Silk Road, another area that is said to be included in the extension of this 'belt' is South Asia and Southeast Asia. Many of the countries that are part of this belt are also members of the China-led Asian Infrastructure Investment Bank (AIIB). North, central and south belts are proposed. North belt goes through Central Asia, Russia to Europe. Central belt goes through Central Asia, West Asia to the Persian Gulf and the Mediterranean. South belt starts from China to Southeast Asia, South Asia, the Indian Ocean. Central belt is spoken down due to complex religion problems and separation movement along the belt.

Maritime Silk Road

The Maritime Silk Road, also known as the "21st Century Maritime Silk Road" is a complementary initiative aimed at investing and fostering collaboration in Southeast Asia, Oceania, and North Africa, through several contiguous bodies of water – the South China Sea, the South Pacific Ocean, and the wider Indian Ocean area.

The Maritime Silk Road initiative was first proposed by Xi Jinping during a speech to the Indonesian Parliament in October 2013. Like its sister initiative the Silk Road Economic Belt, most countries in this area have joined the China-led Asian Infrastructure Investment Bank.

East Africa

This region of Africa (In particular Zanzibar) will form part of the MSR after improvement of local ports and construction of a modern standard-gauge rail link between Nairobi and Kampala.

Closely related networks

The China Pakistan Economic Corridor (CPEC) and the Bangladesh-China-India-Myanmar (BCIM) Economic Corridor are officially classified as "closely related to the Belt and Road Initiative". In coverage by the media, this distinction is disregarded and the networks are counted as components of the initiative. The CPEC in particular is often regarded as the link between China's maritime and overland silk road, with the port of Gwadar forming the crux of the CPEC project.

Financial institutions

AIIB

The Asian Infrastructure Investment Bank first proposed by China in October 2013, is a development bank dedicated to lending for projects regarding infrastructure. As of 2015, China announced that over one trillion yuan ($160 billion US) of infrastructure projects were in planning or construction. On 29 June 2015, the Articles of Agreement of the Asian Infrastructure Investment Bank (AIIB), the legal framework was signed in Beijing. The proposed multilateral bank has an authorized capital of $100 billion, 75% of which will come from Asian and Oceanian countries. China will be the single largest stakeholder, holding 26% of voting rights. The bank plans to start operation by year end.

Silk Road Fund

In November 2014, Xi Jinping announced plans to create a 40 billion USD development fund, which will be distinguished from the banks created for the initiative. As a fund its role will be to invest in businesses rather than lend money for projects. The Karot Hydropower Station in Pakistan is the first investment project of the Silk Road Fund, and is not part of the much larger CPEC investment.

Oversight

The Leading Group for Advancing the Development of One Belt One Road was formed sometime in late 2014, and its leadership line-up publicized on February 1, 2015. This steering committee reports directly into the State Council of the People's Republic of China and is composed of several political heavyweights, evidence of the importance of the program to the government. Vice-Premier Zhang Gaoli, who is also a member of the 7-man Politburo Standing Committee, was named leader of the group, with Wang Huning, Wang Yang, Yang Jing, and Yang Jiechi being named deputy leaders.

In March 2014, Chinese Premier Li Keqiang called for accelerating the "One Belt One Road" initiative along with the Bangladesh-China-India-Myanmar Economic Corridor and the China-Pakistan Economic Corridor in his government work report presented to the annual meeting of the country's legislature.

Role of Hong Kong

On the eve of his 2016 policy address, Hong Kong chief executive CY Leung's announced his intention of setting up a Maritime Authority aimed at strengthening Hong Kong's maritime logistics in line with Beijing's economic policy. Leung mentioned the "one belt, one road" no fewer than 48 times during the policy address, but the amount of small detail presented in addition to the macro-economic measures related to "one belt, one road" which commentators considered to be irrelevant to Hong Kong people because it skirted over matters of importance to them.

Leung's apparent overemphasis was seen as a sycophantic promotion of Xi Jinping's concept, and was widely lampooned.

The anchor ofTVMost, Dong Fong-sing, satirised it using a Chinese homonym – "one covered, one exposed" instead of "one belt, one road"– in a photograph of him half-wearing a brassiere in which one of his nipples was exposed. An op-ed in *Wen Wei Po* said CY Leung was "horrendously scandalised" by the picture, which was considered obscene.

INDIA AND "ONE BELT ONE ROAD (BRI)": IMPLICATIONS

According to various experts from different countries from east coast of Africa to Northeast Asia, India's role in BRI has been acknowledged and seen essential. Indian Ocean is vital for pursuing the economic and strategic interests of China. However, unlike most of the ASEAN and South Asian countries who have welcomed the idea of BRI, India has not. For India, the proposal to build BRI is vague and does not give surety as to how serious Beijing is about opening up trade and cultural exchanges along the Himalayan barrier. The project has several implications for India.

Impact on Security

India, in order to balance China's North-South connectivity to South- East Asia, has been promoting East- West Connectivity through Myanmar, Thailand and Vietnam. India however is concerned about the Bangladesh- China- India- Myanmar (BCIM) Economic Corridor which links Yunnan with North-east part of India.

Through the OBOR, China is countering the strategies of India and is promoting its greater presence in the North-Eastern region of India, part of which China claims as its own territory. These along with China's plan to supply eight type 039 A submarines to Pakistan have made India anxious of China's policy of 'balanced' South Asia. With China's aid to Pakistan and launch of BRI, such submarines will be more than doubled. India, on the other hand only has 13 aging conventional subs which could result in India- China arms race and geopolitical rivalry in the India ocean region.

Further, the China- Pakistan Economic Corridor (CPEC) which is a part of the BRI passes through Pakistan Occupied Kashmir. According to the document released at the Bao Forum Conference in March 2015, the creation of maritime facilities with China's aid will have an obligation for the host country to serve Chinese interests including strategic interests (Rajan 2014) .This is worrisome for India as Chinese will eventually increase their military presence in Indian Ocean and will reshape the economic arrangement in the regions. Further, the railway route planed under BRICS expected to link Pakistan and China via Pakistan occupied Kashmir will be of strategic importance in the event of conflicts with India and will facilitate China to supply missiles and spare parts to Pakistan. This might have serious consequences on India's power to negotiate with China on the territory of Ladakh and further cause tensions at border.

Impact on Trade

The Silk Road Economic Corridor initiative is similar to that of BCIM and the CPEC Corridor. India has direct and indirect presence in all the three economic corridors. BCIM gives India greater presence in the region as it is the formal member. India pursues its soft power in the Silk Road Economic Corridor that outvie the economic and political development. The CPEC would link to the larger India market in order to reach its full economic potential. This corridor will open up the flow of trade between India and Pakistan which presently has to be routed through third-countries instead of receiving them directly. Further, India does not enjoy much leverage to guide ocean trade markets despite having proximity to sea and strong navy. Through OBOR project India will get access to more business in an environment which will promote business friendly reforms.

Although, China is the largest trade partner with most of the countries involved in BRI projects, India's also is significant trading partner especially with African, South Asian and South East Asian countries. India will have economic implication once the BRI project is launched. The port development in Myanmar, Bangladesh, Sri Lanka, Maldives and Pakistan which is incorporated in the BRI project have the potential to change the bilateral equation of India further to its disadvantage (Sibal 2014) as it favors China's trade flows through the Indian Ocean. This also will lead to trade diversion of Indian goods and services. China and India export some of the similar set of goods to the countries like Thailand, Myanmar Cambodia in South East Asia region, Sri Lanka, Pakistan and Nepal in South Asia, few countries in Western Europe and Central Asia.Once the BRI is built the countries might divert their trade from India to China because of the easier accessibility to Chinese goods and currency exchange.

Why India should join?

China has a tradition of using the "Cheque book" policy against India. And under maritime silk route (MSR)China is developing ports in Bangladesh, Sri Lanka and Pakistan and is trying to enlarge its sphere of influence using its economic might in the Bay of Bengal, Arabian Sea, thus MSR is nothing but an economic disguise to the "string of pearl" theory. China is investing huge amount of monies in India's immediate neighbors and these south-east Asian countries tend to use the "China card" against India that is try to play with the India-China mistrust in order to further their development and economic agenda. With more south East Asian nations coming under China's sphere of influence would result in a serious setback to India's traditional concept of the subcontinent as its privileged sphere.

Further, the project, though an informal channel at present, offers an alternative against the US –led Trans- Pacific Partnership (TPP) in the Asia- Pacific and Transatlantic Trade and Investment Partnership between the European Union and United States. These Mega Free Trade agreements through their policies and rules of global trade particularly where multilateral level consensus is more necessary will make it difficult for the government to regulate the market and will have economic implications on India's trade.

Moreover, India and China are members of the BRICS Bank which aims to offer financial support for infrastructure projects and sustainable development. By refusing to be the member of BRI, India's infrastructure needs may get neglected. This may further interfere with the economic cooperation among the BRICS countries and may cause conflicts. Once the issue relating to strategic and economic implications is judiciously analyzed, India could benefit from being the BRI partner. Most importantly, from a strategic perspective, India's involvement in OBOR will help the country, better implement and integrate its "spice route" and the "Mausam project". Beside tangible benefit of physical connectivity, the integration of these projects will also invigorate a climate of mutual trust, stability and prosperity between the member countries. Additionally, India could also expedite the progress on the Chahbahar port on the Iranian coast which will give India access to Afghanistan and Central Asia. This would enable India to be a major player in the overland Silk Route.

India's participation in OBOR will give a new start and a new bright spot in India- China cooperation as it will foster policy coordination, increase trade and investment and ensure people to people connect and most importantly integrate the financial system. For India MSR could prove to be a boon and help enhance its regional and bilateral cooperation. India does not have the same economic might as China has, but investing in neighboring littoral countries will help in reducing china's sphere of influence to some extent.

Challenges

The huge grandiose plan of OBOR has been painted as everything from a response to home-grown economic problems to a masterful reshaping of the regional economy. However the complete realization of the project as estimated will take about 35 year which will mark the 100thanniversary of the foundation of People's Republic of China in 2049. Though the project has met with skepticism from its neighbors, it has huge potential across regions.

However the plan is yet to finalise its strategic vision. The success of the project depends on addressing both internal and external challenges being faced by the Chinese economy.

Chinese are expecting quick results. As the project involves large scale infrastructure development, the plan needs to be given at least ten year time frame for success which means that expectation should be revised. Since China is planning continuous investment in infrastructure in the countries that are less developed and unstable, there is a potential for a debt crisis and limited returns. Moreover China presently is grappling with its own economic issues and slowdown can also have implication on its OBOR strategy. Therefore serious planning would be essential.

China has allocated $ 40 billion to its Silk Road Fund and established $100 billion AIIB. According to few analysts, the actual fund needed for the plan might exceed three or four time the amount allocated. The additional requirement will have to be met either by issuance of special bond and low-cost finance by the China Development Bank. China has to be vigilant of the financial challenges or else the ambitious project could end up as expensive boondoggles.

OBOR has also received criticism and skepticism from many member countries, particularly ASEAN. They see this project as an attempt by China to dominate its neighboring region and therefore are facing coordination problems.

Further regional and territorial disputes of China can interfere with the project. Additionally, Chinese failure in considering regional politics and non-interference policy can expose the project to political risks from both local opposition and competing regional power.

China's OBOR dream can also get affected because of the presence of underdeveloped and immature market along the route. Terrorism can further add to the risk. The potential of conflicts and geopolitical tension with the United and the unbalanced trade relations between China and Russia can further act as a hurdle. India may also challenge OBOR as the initiative is seen more of a threat to the country rather than opportunity.

Therefore, it's the adequate planning and coordination between the member countries that will be required for successful implementation of the OBOR initiative.

Conclusion

In sum, the OBOR initiative is a centerpiece of China's foreign policy and domestic economic strategies. It is aimed at rejuvenating two ancient trade routes and further opening up markets within and beyond the region In order to make the OBOR successful, China is keen to offer more economic and financial assistance to countries on the route and beyond through connectivity program, technical exchanges and the building of infrastructure. China has already started taking several initiatives by investing in infrastructure projects and seeking a comprehensive engagement with member countries. However better planning will be essential.

From an Indian perspective, it is apparent that the One Belt One Road initiative of China will seriously hamper India's efforts in increasing its share in global trade and commerce, if India chooses to stay out. Not only is India likely to lose existing and prospective markets, but also see its share in global capital inflows come down. In such a situation, it becomes imperative for policymakers in India to plan out strategies that not only mitigate adverse impacts of the OBOR Project, but also enables the country to reap benefits from the same.

China has repeatedly reached out to India and other countries of the region to partner her in the implementation of the OBOR corridor. India should therefore not miss the bus and strive to gain maximum economic and geopolitical advantage out of the Corridor. To begin with, India should seek to add more Indian nodes in the existing plan of the OBOR Scheme. The Belt is planned to pass through Pakistan Occupied Kashmir (PoK). India should seek to make the route pass through the Indian portion of the region of Kashmir. This would help her not only economically revive Kashmir, but also ease tensions and build mutual trust on both sides of the border. Similarly along the Maritime Road, India should attempt to make the route pass through another port like Kochi or Mumbai. Such a measure would augment India's own infrastructure development efforts by attracting foreign capital and technical expertise.

It is evident that India needs to actively engage in the development of the project, right from the beginning. She needs to heed China's call to participate in the project geographically, politically and financially. The OBOR Project provides India a perfect opportunity to attract foreign capital to develop a significant proportion of her requirements. Simultaneously India has the opportunity to tap new markets and make good economic returns by investing in infrastructure and industrial corridors along the Belt and the Road. India can also enhance her international prestige by playing the role of an international mediator between an aggressive China and a suspicious West. India thus has a lot to gain from the One Belt One Road Project, provided India sheds its inhibitions about the same and participates actively in its implementation.

THE IMPACT OF CHINA'S ONE BELT ONE ROAD INITIATIVE ON DEVELOPING COUNTRIES

In autumn 2013, President of the Peoples Republic of China (PRC), Xi Jinping, announced the One Belt, One Road (OBOR) initiative, comprising of the land-based "Silk Road Economic Belt" and the "Maritime Silk Road of the 21st Century".

OBOR will see the development of six major economic corridors. Building transport and information infrastructure will beget the development of energy and industrial clusters along these economic corridors.

China's OBOR initiative will boost the construction outlooks for many developing countries along the route through the development of substantial transportation and associated physical infrastructure. Crucially, OBOR will facilitate financing of such growth, providing alternative sources of funding to traditional public finance. The initiative will be driven largely through Public Private Partnerships (PPPs), with the standard OBOR financing model of Chinese loans paying for Chinese contractors.

The Chinese government is keen to emphasise that OBOR comes without any political strings attached. However, while this may strictly be the case, the investment is *de facto* building political and economic ties between China and the host government. OBOR will serve to facilitate greater market access to economies along the trade routes for Chinese companies, secure natural resources for China, expand and strengthen Chinese hegemony, and provide an outlet for China's investment-led growth model to continue.

As China has developed economically, its global political strength has also increased. The Chinese government has facilitated outbound investment in the form of equity stakes in projects and physical assets across the globe, particularly to secure access to resources.

The massive inflow of investment across the construction industries will bring with it greater technical capacity for the less developed countries along the Silk Road as: transport infrastructure standards become harmonised, easing cross-border trade; higher technical standards improve the quality of buildings and other construction projects; and the latest technology and innovative building methodologies are utilised.

The initiative has already hugely boosted trade and investment. Trade between China and countries along the OBOR routes constitute a quarter of China's total trade value, exceeding US$1 trillion in 2015. Indeed, Chinese exports to these countries exceed those to the US and the European Union, China's top two export destinations. This trend will continue as ongoing investment in supporting infrastructure encourages trade flows.

Many countries along the OBOR need to improve their infrastructure stock. Pressures on the existing stock continue to mount as populations rise, urbanisation continues, and ongoing industrialisation and economic development requires supporting infrastructure. These factors, combined with the need to catalyse future economic growth with high quality infrastructure, necessitate ongoing investment. However, many countries along the OBOR lack the financial capacity to develop their infrastructure through public coffers, and the private sector is unable to meet the shortfall.

Better integrating the private sector into the construction industry, rather than relying predominantly on the public sector, can bring a number of benefits, including mitigating the financing burden placed on the government; increasing productivity and improving the quality of public services; and facilitating knowledge transfer and sharing of best-practice experience and expertise from the private to public sector.

A greater number of such financing arrangements can be expected for construction projects across the Silk Road. Indeed, the financing model employed will be particularly well suited to building capacity and undertaking the required infrastructure development.

The private sector across many of the developing countries along the Silk Road is relatively nascent, and many firms lack the capacity or resources to properly implement the large construction projects proposed. Relying on domestic companies may limit the participation of the private sector and hamper growth, but the OBOR financing model is for loans from Chinese banks that pay for Chinese contractors. Utilising such firms will: utilise excess capacity of Chinese companies; bring in expertise; utilise the high technical capacity of firms; facilitate greater Chinese control of projects; create economic benefit for China (sending money back to Chinese firms and suppliers); and develop the capacity of domestic private sector firms.

There are a number of necessary conditions for private sector financing to work alongside public money. These include transparency around the way the money is allocated, an appropriate balance between the public funding and the private funding, clear returns, a strong regulatory system that is able to work across borders, and conduct that everybody can recognize as being close to market principles. Without these conditions, the private sector may be reticent to invest, dampening the spill-over effects.

Many developing countries have a great deal to gain from such an initiative, but there are a number of risks in investing in such markets, including: foreign exchange volatility; risk of recession; price instability; 'crowding-out' of private sector investment; legal and regulatory issues; dearth of pre-existing basic infrastructure; corruption; bureaucratic issues; and poor transparency.

Among the various developing countries along OBOR routes, there are some with relatively strong governance (such as India, Indonesia, and Vietnam) which will be hard for China to unilaterally dictate to and control. Such countries will most likely not want to accept large numbers of Chinese workers or take on high levels of debt. Other countries along the OBOR (such as Cambodia and Pakistan), however, have relatively weak governance systems. China may be in a better position to dictate terms to these countries, but operating risks are higher in such environments, project management could be fraught, and the financial returns hampered.

Due to the OBOR funding arrangements, China benefits from both the financing and construction of infrastructure projects, while the recipient countries must bear the financial risk. When trade volumes are high the arrangement will be mutually beneficial, and that may not matter, but when it is not, it could become a source of concern for the recipient country.

The OBOR is positive for developing countries, and an opportunity to improve their physical infrastructure stock. The initiative will also serve to strengthen the private sector in many countries, create positive spill-over effects beyond the initial projects, and facilitate further investment. Risks abound, however, particularly if trade volumes decrease and the terms are no longer competitive.

2

China's OBOR : Analysis from Indian Perspective

The development of China has been noteworthy since it embraced changes in 1978 and China is at present the second biggest economy on the planet notwithstanding having surpassed Japan. With a specific end goal to manage this improvement, the idea of the Silk Road was proposed. The restored activity of the Belt and the Road is proposed to adapt up to the significant changes and difficulties that rise over the span of improvement. The pompous thought is established in history with the new Silk Road monetary belt and the 21stcentury Maritime Silk Road (MSR) which prior connected the significant civic establishments in Asia, Europe and Africa for quite a long time.

As per the official record titled "Vision and Actions on Jointly Building Silk Road Economic Belt and 21st Century Maritime Silk Road", the undertaking plans to make an open, comprehensive and adjusted provincial monetary participation with basic philosophy that advantages every one of the nations required in the activity. The vision mirrors the interest from significant nations for discharging foundation bottlenecks and enhancing availability with expansive markets in Asia and Europe and also the requirement for China's own improvement and security.

To achieve its objective, a new "Silk Road Economic Belt" will link China to Europe that cuts through mountainous regions in Central Asia and the "Maritime Silk Road" that links China's port facilities with the African Coast and then pushes up through the Suez Canal into the Mediterranean Sea (Minnick2015). The MSR will extend from the Quanzhou province in China, heading south to Malacca Strait, from Kuala lampur it will head to Kolkata, crossing the northern Indian Ocean to Nairobi, Kenya.

Therefore it offers a tremendous opportunity to connect resource and commodity rich west and Central Asia to emerging South and South East Asian countries along the Road which has a huge potential consumer market. To facilitate this development, China has set up a US $40 billion Silk Road Fund.

CHINA'S ONE BELT ONE ROAD INITIATIVE

President Xi Jinping propelled China's "One Belt, One Road" (OBOR) activity in 2013 with the expressed expect to interface significant Eurasian economies through framework, exchange and venture. The activity was later indicated to contain two worldwide exchange associations: The area based "Silk Road Economic Belt" and oceangoing "Sea Silk Road."

The "Belt" is a system of overland street and rail courses, oil and characteristic gas pipelines, and other framework extends that will extend from Xi'an in focal China through Central Asia and at last reach similarly as Moscow, Rotterdam, and Venice. As opposed to one course, belt passages are set to keep running along the real Eurasian Land Bridges, through China-Mongolia-Russia, China-Central and West Asia, China-Indochina Peninsula, China-Pakistan, Bangladesh-China-India-Myanmar.

The "Street" is its sea comparable: a system of arranged ports and other beach front framework extends that dab the guide from South and Southeast Asia to East Africa and the northern Mediterranean Sea. At this stage, the idea, extension and nature of the activity are still liquid and the state of OBOR is liable to develop after some time. Since it was propelled by President Xi, the activity is prone to be unmistakable in China's abroad venture all through his term in office.

How big is it? OBOR can be big, indeed. In its largest definition, OBOR would include 65 countries, 4.4 billion people and about 40 percent of global GDP. China is backing the plan with considerable resources, setting up a New Silk Road Fund of $40 billion to promote private investment along OBOR. The New Silk Road Fund is sponsored by China's foreign exchange reserves, as well as government investment and lending arms.

In addition, the Asia Infrastructure Investment Bank is widely expected to support the initiative with a considerable share of its $100 billion in lending, and the China Development Bank reportedly said it would invest almost $900 billion into more than 900 projects involving 60 countries to bolster the initiative. The Economist magazine reported that $1 trillion in "government money" would be spent on the initiative.

More than infrastructure

The vision document for OBOR goes well beyond infrastructure, envisioning closer coordination of economic development policies, harmonization of technical standards for infrastructure, removal of investment and trade barriers, establishment of free trade areas, financial cooperation and "people to people bonds" involving cultural and academic exchanges, personnel exchanges and cooperation, media cooperation, youth and women exchanges, and volunteer services.

What could be the impact of the initiative? OBOR could stimulate Asian and global economic growth and make it more sustainable. In particular, countries along the corridor — especially those with underdeveloped infrastructure, low investment rates, and low per-capita incomes — could experience a boost in trade flows and benefit from infrastructure development. China would be able to better secure its energy and raw materials supply — which now predominantly gets shipped through the Strait of Malacca and the South China Sea.

Why OBOR? Some consider the initiative China's plan to ensure markets for its growing excess capacity in the construction industries as economic expansion and domestic investment slow. While it is true that the New Silk Road needs a lot of investment, even the highest estimates would constitute a relatively modest share of China's $5 trillion annual investments back home. Investments of $1 trillion over 10-15 years is not going to absorb a lot of China's overcapacity.

There are at least four reasons why OBOR can succeed better than individual countries fending for themselves: network effects, finance, leadership and China's current stage of economic development.

On network effects, benefits to individual countries accrue if each part of the Belt and Road gets built. It simply does not pay for individual countries to move forward on their own. In addition, the initiative helps individual countries align with each other, and China's finances and leadership provide vital credibility.

In my view, China's current stage of development further bolsters the credibility of OBOR. In the past decade, China has become a major player in foreign investment based on natural resources development. As China's domestic economy is now changing, its overseas investment is gradually shifting toward manufacturing rather than just natural resources. There are good reasons for this transition: at home, China faces rising labor costs and increasing environmental demands on production. Shifting some of its production base overseas makes sense — as long as the infrastructure exists to move the goods produced there. Chinese investment through OBOR provides countries along the Road and Belt an added incentive to join the initiative.

Will it work? China's top planning body, the National Development and Reform Commission, has issued a document on its vision for OBOR that discusses strengthening bilateral cooperation and improving existing regional cooperation mechanisms. However the document stops short of "multilaterilazation" of the initiative, such as a formal treaty or partnership.

The question is whether OBOR would need a more formal agreement at some point — covering trade, investment and business climate issues — to maximize its benefits. For now, countries along the Belt and Road have highly diverse development conditions, and some have challenging governance environment that has made investment in infrastructure hard.

So using the initiative to help countries improve their investment climate, technical standards and customs and logistics procedures through a formal agreement could bring major benefits. If a more formal agreement were to ensue, it would be among the largest of its kind, and similar in size to the just-concluded Trans-Pacific Partnership Agreement (TPP).

INDIA'S MARITIME STAKES IN THE SOUTH ASIAN LITTORAL

Lately, two advancements including India have assimilated dialogs inside oceanic circles. In the first place, the Indian Navy situated a guided rocket frigate, the INSKarmuk, off the Andaman and Nicobar Islands, prompting theory that New Delhi is executing arrangements to secure the eastern Indian Ocean. The Straits Times even proposed that India is bracing the Bay of Bengal to keep Chinese submarines from going by the Indian Ocean locale (IOR). A couple days after the fact, amid U.S. guard secretary Ashton Carter's visit to New Delhi, India and the United States consented to sign a logistics trade agreement in the coming months. The assention—a key foundational agreement went for operationalizing India-U.S. sea collaboration in the more extensive Asian hall—drove some political reporters to presume that New Delhi has assented to banding together with Washington in an oceanic coalition went for countering China.

Speculation surrounding India's real intentions in the Indian Ocean—though overblown—is not entirely off the mark. India's efforts to reclaim its maritime space have been evident since January, when New Delhi positioned two P-8I maritime reconnaissance aircraft in the Andaman Islands following reports that a Chinese submarine tender had ventured close to the strategic archipelago. Last month, the Indian Navy deployed another P-8I maritime surveillance aircraft, this time to the Seychelles, for surveillance missions and antipiracy patrols. The trigger for the move, analysts claim, was again growing concern in New Delhi that a Chinese submarine support ship had come too close to the Andaman and Nicobar Islands, suggesting the presence of a People's Liberation Army Navy (PLAN) submarine in the region.

While there have been clear signs of India's consolidation of its naval power in the Andaman and Nicobar Islands, some analysts see the recent developments as part of a larger strategic design in the wider eastern littoral. It is not happenstance, for instance, that India's new aircraft carrier, the INS *Vikramaditya*, visited ports in Colombo, Sri Lanka, and Malè, Maldives, in January; it is rare for an Indian aircraft carrier to visit two South Asian littoral states in the same deployment.

Nor is New Delhi's expansion of maritime aid to smaller Indian Ocean states in the past twelve months purely coincidental. Recent gestures of naval assistance, including sending a high-end patrol vessel to Mauritius in February 2014 and two advanced light helicopters to Maldives last week, underscore India's security stakes in its maritime neighborhood. Unsurprisingly, the Indian Navy's operations in the western Indian Ocean now involve top-end capabilities and high-value strategic platforms assigned diplomatic messaging missions. Some see this pattern of deployments as a clear illustration of New Delhi's ambition for a larger maritime profile in the IOR.

More importantly, India appears to be fine-tuning its combat machinery in the South Asian littoral. Impelled perhaps by China's growing naval forays into the Indian Ocean, New Delhi has been strengthening its Andaman and Nicobar Command for a more robust defense of the near littoral. In an amphibious exercise conducted in April, the three arms of the Indian military combined seamlessly to practice defensive missions in the strategically located islands. The Indian Navy, which commissioned an air base on the southern tip of the island chain in 2012, has now proposed the Maritime Infrastructure

Perspective Plan to transform smaller naval detachments at the Lakshadweep and the Andaman and Nicobar Islands into larger maritime hubs. Meanwhile, New Delhi has also signed agreements to develop an island in both Mauritius (Agalega) and Seychelles (Assumption). To this end, India is undertaking infrastructure projects that would, among other things, enhance the capabilities of the regional defense forces—hinting at greater strategic synergy in regional maritime endeavors. Despite actively seeking maritime influence in the regional commons, however, India has desisted from projecting combat power in its near seas. The Indian Navy's operational approach has been, to the contrary, remarkably collaborative, with increasing attempts to improve tactical coordination with regional maritime agencies in the protection of vital sea lanes and crucial trade chokepoints. The navy's flagship endeavor in South Asia is still the Milan exercise—a cooperative meeting of regional navies in Port Blair every two years with a singular focus on humanitarian operations. Furthermore, India's naval leadership continues to promote the Indian Ocean Naval Symposium, a collaborative endeavor that addresses the complex operational challenges faced by regional navies, such as floating armories and illegal acts of violence by on-board security personnel at sea.

India's effort to expand security cooperation with the United States underscores the country's realistic appreciation of Asia's evolving maritime architecture. Despite being the most capable maritime force in South Asia, the Indian Navy does not have the capacity to underwrite security in the South Asian littoral—especially with rising transnational crime and environmental degradation. Since 2011, India, Sri Lanka, and Maldives have combined forces in a trilateral security effort led by their respective national security advisers, creating a regional mechanism for tackling nontraditional threats in South Asia. Despite limited success, the initiative has helped showcase India's security efforts in the regional commons, especially the Indian Navy's continuing efforts to assist the maritime agencies of Mauritius, Maldives, and Seychelles in building capacity as well as the provision of local surveillance and hydrographical services.

A key component of the Indian Navy's operational doctrine is the diplomatic dimension of regional maritime missions. Intent on improving the tenor of nautical outreach in the neighborhood, the navy's latest maritime strategy document supports nautical multilateralism. The document describes India's outreach in the IOR as a series of bridge-building initiatives that seek to combine security with development.

India is also refining the content of its bilateral maritime relationships. The Indian Navy recognizes that it must share responsibility for the region's littoral spaces with friendly maritime agencies to create the operational capacities needed to shoulder the regional security burden. The importance of sharing operational responsibility goes beyond considerations of preserving the balance of power to also include nontraditional security and developmental initiatives. To this end, Indian policymaking is ever more cognizant of the imperatives of maritime economics in South Asia: "blue economy" projects, sustainable growth, maritime infrastructure, and renewable energy feature prominently in the contemporary discourse on maritime security.

India's principal predicament in the Indian Ocean, however, is still finding the right balance in its maritime relationship with China. While the PLAN's growing presence and influence in the IOR is a source of abiding concern for the Indian Navy, New Delhi feels compelled to desist from publicly voicing its anxiety. This is in spite of deepening misgivings about the composition of PLAN antipiracy patrols in the region (now comprising submarines, amphibious ships, and guided missile frigates), as well as Beijing's maritime Silk Road proposal, which Indian observers allege is a pretext for a robust naval presence in the Indian Ocean.

There is also suspicion in New Delhi that China's IOR blueprint includes plans for the construction of multiple logistical facilities. Since February, when the Chinese government signed a ten-year agreement with Djibouti to set up a rest and replenishment facility in the northern Obock region, Indian strategic circles have been abuzz with speculation about an operational Chinese naval base in the IOR. Beijing officially described the new facility as "Djibouti's participation in developing the 21st-century Maritime Silk Road," but many in New Delhi are convinced that it is meant to provide cover for PLAN operations in the region.

These fears and suspicions explain why New Delhi recently chose to emphasize its stakes in the Indian Ocean. India realizes that it must stress its geopolitical interests in South Asia, while creating the capacity to play a security role in the wider Asian littoral. To achieve these strategic objectives, India must act in concert with friendly states—both in the Indian Ocean and beyond.

India's widening spectrum of maritime operations and partnerships should be viewed in the context of South Asia's evolving maritime politics. More frequent deployments in the regional commons and the improving maritime relations with the United States are all signs that New Delhi is willing to act creatively to protect its regional equities. In the near future, the Indian Navy can be expected to combine political outreach and economic engagement with a hard-power presence and traditional maritime operations in a bid to emphasize its strategic leverage in India's near neighborhood.

POVERTY REDUCTION IN CHINA AND INDIA

China and India are generally regarded as the two large countries in the developing world that are the "success stories" of globalisation. This success has been defined by the high and sustained rates of growth of aggregate and per capita national income; and the substantial reduction in income poverty. Further, both China and India are seen as heralding a major shift in the international division of labour through changes in their own output and employment patterns: thus, China is typically described as becoming the "work-shop" or "factory" of the world through the expansion of manufacturing production, and India as becoming the "office" of the world in particular because of its ability to take advantage of IT-enabled services off-shoring. These results, in turn, are viewed as the consequences of a combination of a "prudent" yet extensive programme of global economic integration and domestic deregulation, as well as sound macroeconomic management. Consequently, the presumed success of these two countries has been used to argue the case for globalization and to indicate the potential benefits that other developing countries can reap.

The importance of these two countries spills over into discussions of international inequality as well. This makes comparison of the extent of poverty reduction in India and China, and the possible causes of the revealed patterns, of particular current relevance.

It should be noted, however, that despite the similarity of the current international hype about their future economic prospects and also despite their obvious differences, both China and India face rather similar economic problems at present, especially with respect to the sustainability of growth and the emerging in-equalities.

These concerns actually predate the current global financial crisis and the associated slowdown in many economies, which have obviously also affected growth prospects in China and India. In both countries, the strategy of development had delivered relatively high income growth without commensurate increases in employment, especially in the organised sector; the bulk of new employment has been in lower productivity activities under uncertain and often oppressive conditions.

In both countries, the growth has been associated with sharp increases in spatial and vertical inequalities, greater fragility of incomes among marginalised groups and adverse shifts in certain human development indicators. In both countries, 2004 marked a shift in declared political priorities towards more inclusive growth, with varying effects.

The two economies are fundamentally dissimilar in some important ways. Although there are superficial attributes in common, such as large populations covering substantial geographical areas, regional diversity, relatively high rates of growth over the recent period and so on, the institutional conditions in the two economies remain very different. India was a traditional "mixed" developing economy with significant private sector participation (including a large private corporate sector) from Independence onwards, and even during the "dirigiste" period, the emphasis was predominantly on the regulation of private capital.

Indeed, one of the problems of the so-called "planned economy" in India was the inability of the state to make the private sector behave in ways that fit in with the plan allocations of the state, leading to mismatches between production and private demand as well as periodic macroeconomic imbalances. The neo-liberal reforms un-dertaken during the phase of globalization have further expanded the scope for private activity and reduced regulation. Essentially, in India, macroeconomic policies have occurred in contexts similar to those in other capitalist economies, where involuntary unemployment is rampant and fiscal and monetary measures have to be used to stimulate effective demand. The inability to undertake land reforms or other strategies that would have involved substantial redistribution of assets not only meant that wealth and income inequalities continued to be very high, but also affected the ability of the Indian state to undertake economic policies that would be perceived as going against the interests of the landed and other elites.

However, China, by contrast, has had a very different economic structure for most of this period, where the basic elements of a command economy have been much more in evidence. The most important difference to be noted here is that after the revolution of 1949, the Chinese state embarked on comprehensive and sweeping land reforms that dramatically altered asset distribution in the country and changed the political economic landscape that determined subsequent policies.

While land relations have undergone numerous changes since then, from collectivization to more dependence on independent small holder peasants, the dominance of landlordism was clearly eliminated and greater equality of access to land and other assets also affected the conditions of access to other forms of wealth and avenues for economic and social mobility. They also meant that economic policies had very different results than they would have had in a more economically unequal context.

Even after the quite sweeping economic reforms that have taken place since 1979, state control over macroeconomic balances remains substantial. Furthermore, because of the significance of state-owned enter-prises and the township and village enterprises (TVEs) in total production, the ability of the state to influence aggregate demand does not depend only on fiscal policy in terms of purely budgetary measures, since many "off-budget" expenditures can be increased or reduced. Further, monetary policy, as it is generally understood in capitalist economies, has very little meaning in China where private financial activity is limited and state-owned banks still overwhelmingly dominate the provision of credit.

Rather, macroeconomic adjustment has typically taken the form of "administrative measures", such as moving to slow down an overheating economy through a squeeze on credit provision to regional and provincial governments and public and private corporations ensured through administrative fiat, rather than the use of traditional macroeconomic measures. It is true that the Chinese economy is currently in a phase of transition to one where more traditional "capitalist macroeconomics" is applicable. But the Chinese government's continuing ability to quickly ensure macroeconomic correction when required is because that transition is still limited.

The control over the domestic economy in China has been most significant in the financial sector. In India, the financial sector was typical of the "mixed economy", and even bank nationalisation did not lead to comprehensive government control over the financial system; in any case, financial liberalisation over the 1990s has involved progressive deregulation and further loss of control over financial allocations by the state in India. But the financial system in China still remains heavily under the control of the state, despite recent liberalisation and the sale of some shares to foreign investors.

Four major public sector banks handle the bulk of transactions in the economy, and over the past several decades, the Chinese authorities have essentially used control over the consequent financial flows to regulate the volume of credit (and thus manage the economic cycle) as well as direct credit to priority sectors. Off-budget official finance (called "fund-raising" by firms) has accounted for more than half the capital formation in China even in recent years, and that, together with direct budgetary appropriations, has determined nearly two thirds of the level of aggregate investment.

Another difference has been becoming less evident in recent years—the dramatically high rate of GDP growth in China compared to the more moderate expansion in India. The Chinese economy has grown at an average annual rate of 9.8 per cent for two and a half decades, while India's economy has grown at around 5–6 per cent per year over the same period.

Chinese growth has been relatively volatile around this trend, reflecting stop-go cycles of state response to inflation through aggregate credit management. The Indian economy broke from its average post-Independence annual rate of around 3 per cent growth to achieve annual rates of more than 5 per cent from the early 1980s.

It is only in the four-year period before the global economic crisis starting late 2008 that the Indian economy grew at rates in excess of 8.5 per cent per annum, coming close to the Chinese average.

The higher growth in China has essentially occurred because of the much higher rate of investment in China. The investment rate in China (investment as a share of GDP) has fluctuated between 35 and 45 per cent over the past 25 years, compared to 20 to 26 per cent in India (very recently increasing to 35 per cent). Aggregate incremental capital-output ratios (ICORs) have been around the same in both economies. Within this, there is the critical role of infrastructure investment, which has averaged 19 per cent of GDP in China compared to 2 per cent in India from the early 1990s. It is sometimes argued that China can afford to have such a high investment rate because it has attracted so much foreign direct investment (FDI), and is the second largest recipient of FDI in the world at present. But FDI has accounted for only 3–5 per cent of GDP in China since 1990, and at its peak was still only 8 per cent. In the period 2000–07, FDI accounted for only 6 per cent of domestic investment. In fact, in recent times, the inflow of capital has not added to the domestic investment rate at all, macroeconomically speaking, but has essentially led to the further accumulation of international reserves, which have been increasing by more than $100 billion per year.

In terms of economic diversification and structural change, China has followed what could be described as the classic industrialisation pattern, moving from primary to manufacturing activities in the past 25 years. The manufacturing sector has doubled its share of the workforce and tripled its share of output, which, given the size of the Chinese economy and population, has increasingly made China "the workshop of the world". In India, by contrast, the move has been mainly from agriculture to services in terms of share of output, with no substantial increase in manufacturing, while the structure of employment has been stub-bornly resistant to change.

The share of the primary sector in national income has fallen from 60 per cent in the early 1950s to 25 per cent in 2001–03, but the share of the primary sector in employment continues to be more than 60 per cent, indicating a worrying persistence of low productivity employment for most of the labour force. The higher rates of investment in India over the past two decades have not generated more expansion of industry in terms of share of GDP, but have instead been associated with an apparent explosion in services, that catch-all sector of varying components. The recent expansion of some services employment in India has been at both the high and low value added ends of services sub-sectors, reflecting both some dynamism and some increase in "refugee" low productivity employment.

Another major difference relates to trade policy and trade patterns. Chinese export growth has been much more rapid, involving aggressive increases in world market shares. This export growth has largely been based on relocative capital which has been attracted not only by cheap labour, but also by excellent and heavily subsidised infrastructure, resulting from the high rate of infrastructure investment. In addition, since the Chinese state provision of basic goods in terms of housing, food and cheap transport facilities for registered urban dwellers has played an important role in reducing labour costs for employers. In India, cheap labour has been because of low absolute wages rather than public provision and underwriting of labour costs, and infrastructure development has been minimal. So it is not surprising that it has not really been an attractive location for export-oriented investment, its rate of export growth has been much lower, and exports were not an engine of growth until relatively recently. This difference was also reflected in employment patterns: in China until the late 1990s, the rapid export growth generated employment which constituted a net addition to domestic employment, since until its WTO accession, China had undertaken much less trade liberalisation than most other developing countries. This is why manufacturing employment grew so rapidly in China until the mid-1990s, because it was not counterbalanced by major losses of employment due to the effects of displacement of domestic industry because of import competition. This is unlike the case in India, where in-creases in export employment were outweighed by employment losses especially in small enterprises because of import competition.

In terms of inequality, the recent pattern of growth has been disequalizing in both economies. In China, the spatial inequalities—across regions—have been the sharpest. In India, vertical inequalities and the rural-urban divide have become much more marked. In China recently, as a response to this, there have been some top-down measures to reduce inequality, for example through changes in tax rates, greater public investment in western and interior regions and improved social security benefits. In India, it is political change, through electoral verdicts, that has forced greater attention to redressing inequalities, though the process is still very incipient.

In terms of future prospects, surprisingly both economies end up with very similar issues despite these major differences. There are clear questions of the sustainability of the current pattern of economic expansion in China, since it is based on a high export-high accumulation model which requires constantly increasing shares of world markets and very high investment rates. This model is obviously directly challenged by the global economic and financial crisis starting from mid-2008, which very quickly had adverse effects on manufacturing exports.

Similarly, the hope in some policy quarters in India—that IT-enabled services would become the engine of growth for the entire economy—raises questions of sustainability, quite apart from questions about whether it will be enough to transform India's huge labour force into higher productivity activities. The most important current problems in the two economies are also rather similar—the agrarian crisis and the need to generate more employment. These are in addition to the need to deal with the effects of the global financial crisis, which have been evident in the real economies of both countries and especially marked in India's financial sector. In both economies, public intervention in the social sectors has been neglected until recently. In both countries, therefore, despite the very different institutional conditions and other dissimilarities, even in the way that recent economic trends have played out, the crucial policy concern is still that of ensuring sustainable productive employment generation for the majority of the labour force.

CHINA'S ROAD & BELT INITIATIVE: INDIAN PERSPECTIVE

China's 'One Belt, One Road', which was initially proposed in September 2013 and consolidates the twin activities of the Silk Road Economic Belt and 21st Century Maritime Silk Road, is a stupendous idea that imagines China supporting the globe.

Conceivably covering 55 percent of the world GNP, 70 percent of the worldwide populace, and 75 percent of known vitality saves, it is basically an arrangement for a China-fabricated area and ocean transportation corridor to connection China's creation focuses with business sectors and common asset bases on the world. In the meantime it will saddle a lot of China's heretofore sit out of gear economy, labor and framework innovation stores to get truly necessary returns. It can possibly twist outskirts and modify existing conditions in China's neighborhood – as it as of now has done in South Asia – and antagonistically affects India straightforwardly. The activity mixes geopolitical and strategic destinations and has a solid household motivation.

The proposed "One Belt, One Road" (OBOR) is an approximately US$ 1.4 trillion project. China claims to be willing to make a huge financial commitment upwards of US$ 300 billion in infrastructure financing for the project in the coming years, though some multilateral and bilateral pledges may overlap. Underscoring China's commitment, the official China Daily reported on May 28, 2015 that Beijing plans to invest US$ 900 billion. The OBOR is planned to be completed over 35 years, in time for the 100th anniversary of the People's Republic of China in 2049!

The 'Belt Corridors' run along the major Eurasian Land Bridges, through China-Mongolia-Russia, China-Central and West Asia, China-Indochina Peninsula, China-Pakistan, Bangladesh-China-India-Myanmar. The Maritime Silk Route or "Road" is the maritime equivalent of the 'Belt Corridors' and comprises a network of planned ports and other coastal infrastructure projects that dot the map from South and Southeast Asia to East Africa and the northern Mediterranean Sea.

The most publicised recent bilateral commitment to OBOR was the investment pledged for the China-Pakistan Economic Corridor (CPEC) by Xi Jinping during his two-day visit to Pakistan in April 2015. Pakistani analysts have valued it at US$ 46 billion. Deals valued at a further US$ 15.7 billion were subsequently signed in Belarus that May. More might have been signed during Xi Jinping's visits to Kazakhstan and Russia on the same trip. Discussions are known to be underway with Russia on overland transport, energy, and cyber-connectivity. Concrete data in respect of OBOR-related agreements is, however, not easily available in published Chinese sources.

International financial institutions, some of them new, are getting involved with OBOR like the Asian Infrastructure Investment Bank (AIIB), BRICS' New Development Bank, Silk Road Fund, a CIC-backed fund (announced recently, during Li Keqiang's visit to Brazil), and, possibly, a SCO Development Bank. This has had an effect on private investors, lenders and countries in the region. Japan, for example, announced a $110 billion infrastructure fund for Asia and the Asian Development Bank (ADB) revised its disbursement rules to increase lending capacity. The AIIB is to serve as the financing arm of OBOR. An effort by China to use these banks, especially the AIIB, to extend fiscal assistance to Pakistan for projects in the CPEC in furtherance of its strategic objectives immediately puts India to the test. On May 9, 2016, the official English-language China Daily reported that the AIIB announced it would co-finance a US$ 300 million motorway project in Pakistan with the Asian Development Bank. Asserting that "Pakistan is a strong ally of China", the report indicated there would be more such projects. To advance its national interest, China had used its economic clout with the ADB to block developmental assistance for poverty alleviation projects in India's north-eastern state of Arunachal Pradesh on the ground that it was disputed. Identically, the CPEC goes through India-claimed and disputed territory.

While Chinese officials and academics emphasise the economic aspects and commercial advantages of OBOR, it is definitely a geopolitical and diplomatic offensive. Chinese President Xi Jinping's articulation of a "community of destiny" among Asians is relevant. Despite Chinese interlocutors insisting that China seeks to "supplement" the existing international order rather than revise it, the numerous statements by influential Chinese strategists asserting that the time is now opportune for China to alter the status quo, are strong in the background. Implementation of OBOR will also augment China's economic influence in the participating countries. The strategy of disbursing them large sums as loans and aid will enhance the financial power that China already exercises through its trading relationship.

Huang Yiping, a Professor of Economics at Peking University's National School of Development, assessed in February 2015, that OBOR represents a sea change in China's international profile. According to him, OBOR has ended the phase of low-profile diplomacy based on Deng Xiaoping's advice to "hide your capabilities and bide your time" and transformed China into "a new great power" which "is trying to supplement the international economic order". Huang Yiping sought to justify China's more active role as an attempt to redress the limited role given to developing countries in international institutions and in line with US President Barack Obama's demand that China take on more responsibility for providing international public goods. A Renmin University report similarly asserted the need to "supplement, not challenge" the existing order because of the "zero-sum thinking" which ensured that OBOR projects were greeted with scepticism including in China's immediate neighbourhood. Taking note of the challenges ahead, Huang Yiping conceded that: "One Belt, One Road is a good international economic strategy, but for now it is certainly not an easy one".

A report in 2014 from Renmin University, described by the official Xinhua news agency as the first think tank report on the projects, clearly outlined the scale of the project's ambition and limits of current planning. It revealed that China will commence strategic planning in 2016 and this would take five years. The report estimates that the Silk Road (OBOR) projects will be fully realised in about 35 years by 2049, the 100th anniversary of the foundation of the People's Republic of China! Chinese President Xi Jinping was quoted by Xinhua on December 6, 2014, as describing the OBOR at a Politburo session as a "new round of opening to the world." This was echoed by a Ministry of Commerce official who – implicitly underscored the domestic political agenda – by telling Caijing magazine that the "new 30 years" will put today's China on the threshold of a third era comparable to those begun by Mao Zedong and Deng Xiaoping!

While the basis for OBOR appears to be geopolitics and export of its huge infrastructure-building capacities, there are foreseeable difficulties. Geographical and geopolitical conditions differ widely outside China and the investment climates are uncertain in many of the countries which can be categorised as low-return and high-risk countries. This has triggered debate among government academics and strategists as to the advisability of making massive investments in such countries. There is additionally, concern about over-reliance on public financing and State-owned Enterprises. There is also concern about the reactions from China's neighbours. Acknowledging the "great potential" of OBOR, Jia Qingguo, a member of the Standing Committee of the Chinese People's Political Consultative Conference (CPPCC) and Dean of the University of International relations at Beijing University, highlighted the need for caution and said China should not succumb to "wishful thinking".

Confirming the differences between academics and government officials about the goal and scope of the project, he said for OBOR to succeed it will need a clear plan and solutions will have to be found to the problems of harsh terrain, political instability, and geopolitical threats. Stating that regional powers like Russia are wary of China's rise, he said China must avoid giving rise to the perception that it is challenging Russia's position in Central Asia. Interestingly, linking with Russia was an afterthought and not in the original OBOR plan. Russia was included only after Putin called Xi Jinping in the Spring of 2015 and Moscow dispatched an emissary to Moscow after which the Russian "loop" was included. Problems, however, remain regarding routing of the railway. Jia Qingguo pointed out that many of the target countries for the Maritime Silk Road project are currently involved in territorial disputes with China, which may make them reluctant to cooperate. To overcome their scepticism, China should use its growing strength to persuade its neighbours to "shelve disputes and pursue joint development."

In similar vein Chu Yin, an Associate Professor of International Relations at the prestigious Tsinghua University in Beijing, in an article in January 2015 focussed on political risk and warned China not to take smaller countries for granted. He said: "Although we are a righteous country, free of Western imperialism, colonialism, and racism, we and the OBOR countries are absolutely not equals". He pointed out that Chinese planners had frequently failed to consider local and regional politics, which exposed projects to political risk both from local opposition parties and from competing regional powers. He said recent events in Thailand and Myanmar showed that political instability is a major risk. In an interesting observation, he said the defeat of a Beijing-friendly government during the elections in Sri Lanka could disrupt the construction of a key port there since, in contrast to the US during the Marshall Plan, China does not have the luxury of militarily occupying the countries in which it invests. He said on a regional level, India, the US, Russia, and Japan are all important players in OBOR countries and could use their power to block China's plans.

Security is obviously a major challenge For example, protection of the 81,000 kilometers (about 50,000 miles) of high-speed railway that China proposes to build through 65 countries, will be a major task. Similar will be the case with the 51 planned projects in the CPEC, which passes through Baluchistan — among the world's most vulnerable and domestic insurgency-ridden territories.

As reflected by the ongoing military reforms, China has begun to address some of these issues. The Conference on Peripheral Diplomacy held in Beijing on October 24-25, 2013, prepared the ground for the OBOR. Identifying countries for the first time ever as "friend" and "enemy", it decided that 'friends' would receive "untold benefits", including those flowing from China's international standing and diplomatic clout. It promised that China could even offer "security alliances". The China-Pakistan Economic Corridor (CPEC), which is part of OBOR and envisages road links, pipelines, energy centres and ports, is a good example. It combines financial assistance with diplomatic support reinforced by military muscle.

By announcing the CPEC, Beijing dispelled the ambiguity maintained by China thus far on the issue of Kashmir. It is also preparing to protect the CPEC inside Pakistan. A secure fibre-optic link has been laid connecting Kashgar with Rawalpindi, highlighting the close military coordination between Pakistan and China. The establishment early this year of the People's Liberation Army (PLA)'s West Zone is intended to safeguard Chinese investments and projects in the CPEC in addition to protecting China's land frontiers. China has at the same time informed Islamabad that it is creating a Division-strength "private army" for deployment in the areas covered by the CPEC. The West Zone's operational jurisdiction is anticipated, in course of time, to include eastern Africa where China has considerable economic interests and where it has very recently signed an agreement for a base at Djibouti. China has already put in place a domestic legal basis for the deployment of Chinese troops and security personnel to protect Chinese investments and workers abroad. The operational tasks assigned to the PLA's West Zone represent the first of more such arrangements.

For India the Bangladesh-China-India-Myanmar (BCIM) corridor, which is part of OBOR and which Beijing is pressurising India to sign on to, is not feasible. Opening the BCIM would mean that Chinese goods — neither Myanmar nor Bangladesh produce goods in demand in India — will flood India's northeast where poor connectivity presently makes access difficult for Indian products and people. There is the additional risk of thousands of Chinese illegally settling in India's sparsely populated north-eastern states, as they have in other countries. A detailed posting on a PLA-maintained website had, in fact, a few years earlier enumerated the advantages of "recovering"

Arunachal Pradesh including to settle China's growing population.

The economic import of the OBOR has correctly been emphasised by Chinese academics and officials. Jia Qingguo observed that OBOR is an international strategy, but its success will be measured by its effects on China's domestic economic rebalancing. While China will send out its own capital, technology, and management experience and promote the development and prosperity of neighbouring countries, he was emphatic that the yardstick for gauging OBOR's success would be whether it encourages China's own economic transformation and makes it the centre of the regional economy. He recommended that to ensure that investment is allocated efficiently and state assets are protected, private capital should take the lead. Jia Qingguo recommended making private enterprises the 'backbone' of the project – to leverage their energy, flexibility, and sensitivity to investment efficiency, and avoid the "drainage" effect of SoEs.

Caution has been expressed also by Chen Gong, Chief Researcher at Anbound, a Chinese consulting firm and think-tank of the PRC State Council. He suggested that OBOR projects are a large-scale reproduction of China's unbalanced model of development over the last ten years: based on public actors and infrastructure spending, and excessively supply-based. He said this goes against the government's desire to put these stimulus-based growth levers aside – but agreed that perhaps using them outside China is more acceptable and less contentious. Chen Gong particularly questioned the advantage of the Maritime Silk Route, saying: "What China produces, ASEAN countries also produce, and what China thinks about developing, ASEAN also wants to develop". Therefore, the two regions are bound to compete more intensively, and China will face much greater difficulties along the Maritime Silk Road than it would have if it had focused only on the western route.

The main players in OBOR projects will, however, be China's State-owned Enterprises (SoEs). According to Xu Gao, Chief Economist at Guangda Securities and former economist for the

IMF and the World Bank, this implies that the opportunity cost would actually be negative for China. He has assessed that because China's economic structure is dominated by SoEs, further investment should actually reduce waste in the public sector and help to stabilise employment as well as the economy. It will offer a new investment opportunity for China's huge foreign exchange reserves, which have so far been heavily invested in low-return US bonds.

Meanwhile, data released at the end of 2014 by the State-owned Assets Supervision and Administration Commission of the State Council (SASAC) gives an overview of the preparedness of Chinese SoEs for participating in 'OBOR'. The report shows that 107 SoEs out of 110 had set up 8,515 braches overseas by the end of 2014, and among them over 80 Chinese SoEs had established branches in countries and regions along the "Belt and Road." Statistics show that the total overseas assets of Chinese SoEs had risen from 2.7 trillion yuan to 4.6 trillion yuan since the implementation of the 12th Five-Year Plan. Chinese SoEs have undertaken major projects like crude-oil pipelines of China-Russia, China-Kazakhstan, and China-Myanmar, natural gas pipelines of China-Russia, China-Central Asia, and China-Myanmar, and railway construction with Myanmar, Thailand, Laos etc. The SASAC report added that over 40 SoEs have set up International Business Management Departments and over 30 have drawn-up overseas legal risk prevention plans.

Separately, Xinhua quoted China's State Administration of Taxation as announcing on March 14, 2016, that Tax treaties with countries along the "Belt and Road" will save financial institutions in China 9.6 billion yuan (about US$ 1.5 billion) in taxes.

While for the present countries cannot ignore China's economic strength or track record in building massive infrastructure, serious doubts remain as to Beijing's real objectives. That Beijing is aware of these concerns is evident in Chinese Foreign Minister Wang Yi's annual address to the press on the sidelines of the CPPCC-NPC sessions in March

2015 and 2016. He asserted that the OBOR was not a "tool of geopolitics" and should not be viewed through an "out-dated Cold War mentality". This March, Wang Yi again emphasised that China is a responsible emerging country and promotes periphery diplomacy with reciprocal benefits. He said the "Belt and Road" initiative has made significant progress, including establishment of the Asia Infrastructure Investment Bank (AIIB) and launch of the New Silk Road Fund, and enhanced connectivity with participating countries in economic and trade cooperation, cultural and educational exchanges. China's Vice Foreign Minister, Zhang Yesui, echoed this message of reassurance at the China Development Forum in March 2015. Later the same month he described China as fully integrated into the international system and reiterated that OBOR is "not directed against any specific country or organisation" but intended to "complement" existing international and regional institutions.

Nevertheless, major difficulties confront the OBOR. The slowing domestic economy is one. Chinese economists have warned the Chinese government against taking on too much of the project, saying this would risk repeating the errors made in the development of China's west, but this time on an international scale. The problem is compounded by the desire of many local and provincial governments in more than 22 provinces to participate in OBOR. An article in February 2015 in the 'Guoji Jinrong Bao' cautioned that this could lead to wastage. It pointed out that many international railway projects are coming up on expensive and often underused routes and that a number of provinces have poured subsidies into projects that are not economically viable. Another future complication affecting social stability could stem from plans for cooperation with Central Asian countries developed by local officials and focused on narrow regional interests.

Though 20 European countries are engaged in talks with China on the OBOR and despite China's offers of economic assistance, the EU in May 2016 declined to give China market economy status (MES) based on the 2001 terms of China's accession to the World Trade Organization (WTO). Differences over interest rates, with Thailand complaining in March 2016 that they are too high, now threaten the Chinese-Thai Rail project.

Problems of harsh terrain, political instability, and geopolitical threats, are likely to get accentuated by the inherent political turbulence in many of the regions that the OBOR traverses. The rising tide of Islamic extremism in Pakistan, Afghanistan and potentially soon in the Central Asian Republics, will threaten stability in the Xinjiang Uyghur Autonomous Region and other Muslim areas in China. Safeguarding the CPEC's 51 projects in Baluchistan — among the world's most vulnerable and domestic insurgency-ridden territory – will also be difficult. Together, these cast serious doubts about the viability of the OBOR.

ENTER SECURITY ISSUES FROM A GROWTH PERSPECTIVE

Security is widely considered the Number One issue for Afghanistan's reconstruction and development agenda. Dealing with the legacy of nearly a quarter-century of protracted conflict, and with the difficult security issues currently facing the country, has been and will continue to be a major challenge. The main security issues in Afghanistan from a development perspective (not necessarily in order of importance) are outlined briefly below. Needless to say, many of them are closely interrelated with each other.

Continuing conflict/insurgency/terrorism and associated insecurity. Although outright insurgency and significant military conflict are concentrated in areas in the south and east of the country (where much terrorist activity is occurs as well), this conflict has been continuing on a significant scale albeit with seasonal and other fluctuations, and is adversely affecting security in these areas with important development implications. Elsewhere, sporadic acts of terrorism have occurred from time to time, but not on a widespread scale or in a sustained manner. These have a disproportionate impact on perceptions of the security situation particularly from outside the country, and hence deter foreign investment. Another adverse implication is movement restrictions on aid agencies and higher security costs for development activities, as well as for private business. For example, highway reconstruction projects reported that their direct spending on security added 3-15% to project costs, and a recent survey of private business firms found that their reported spending on security infrastructure accounted for close to 15% of sales revenue, and that an additional 3% of sales was reportedly spent on protection payments to commanders, government officials, or organized criminals (World Bank, 2006).

Lack of rule of law and poorly functioning judicial system. This is a fundamental problem, seriously affecting Afghans in their daily lives, which is both a manifestation of underlying insecurity and itself contributes to continuing insecurity. Rule of law and the judiciary were weak during most of the past quarter-century, and restoring let alone enhancing these critical components of the security system will be a major challenge. More specifically the police, weakened and largely captured by factional forces during the conflict, has often been more a source of insecurity than of security for most Afghans. Anecdotal evidence indicates that District officials are unable to reliably resolve local disputes in their official capacity, unless they have personal prestige through their traditional connections to do so. Few police officers in rural areas have professional training, and many are former mujahedin or militia members who became police officers when their commanders joined the Government after 2001. Police forces continue to operate largely independently from a centralized command structure under the Ministry of Interior, and many remain loyal to their former commanders. The police force is overwhelmingly male, and many districts lack detention facilities for women. The lack of women police officers to handle the arrest, detention, or transport of female detainees places any woman arrested at heightened risk of abuse.

The formal judicial system was devastated during the conflict, and its rebuilding since 2001 has been slow. In addition to the lack of recourse for Afghans and inability to effectively punish serious crimes (including those committed during the conflict), the weakness of the formal judicial system is a deterrent to business activity in the formal sector and to foreign investment. Although historically Afghanistan has relied much more on customary and traditional practices and adjudication mechanisms, these also were significantly eroded in many respects during the conflict, and/or "captured" by warlords and commanders, with adverse effects on local security as well as on business activities and livelihoods.

An important manifestation of these problems is the widespread uncertainties and disputes over land, leading to ambiguities and insecurity related to land tenure as well as theft and illegal appropriation of land. Confirming other information, recent fieldwork in Nangarhar and Laghman provinces found that conflict over agricultural land (and related water supplies) was the most common source of violence (Koehler and Zurcher, 2005). Access to land is the second most widely cited constraint on business activity in a recent survey of firms (World Bank, 2006).

Finally, there is a long tradition of the Judiciary being an exclusively male domain, and only around 3% of judges currently are women. With the exception of the heads of the juvenile and family courts in Kabul, women are not found in key positions within the judiciary. Where women do serve as judges, reports indicate that they do not perform the same functions as their male counterparts. Female judges tend to act in the capacity of judicial clerks and are rarely involved in the adjudication of cases, which severely limits the ability of Afghan women to approach the courts.

Dominant drug industry. The opium economy, which is estimated to comprise more than a third of total economic activity in Afghanistan, is a direct source of insecurity (drug-related conflict and violence, financing of armed groups and warlords and commanders who provide protection). But even more important, the drug industry is a major force working against state-building and good governance, and thereby has a major adverse effect on security indirectly as well. The drug industry can thrive in a situation where there is a weak, corruptible state and security forces, no or ineffective rule of law, and inadequate sanctions or negative incentives to discourage the whole range of actors - from farmers to drug traders to their sponsors inside and outside of government as well as regional drug industry actors. Therefore the drug industry comprises a powerful interest group diametrically opposed to the heart of Afghanistan's reconstruction agenda and thereby promoting insecurity.

Remaining factional forces. Although as noted earlier the DDR process has been completed, there are numerous "illegal armed combatants" not included in DDR. The new program for Disbandment of Illegal Armed Groups (DIAG) is intended to address this problem; however, this is expected to take several years.

Moreover, Afghanistan by tradition and even more during the conflict has had an armed population, and this is not expected to change very quickly. Widespread ownership of small arms can be a source of insecurity as long as there is not basic rule of law and a minimum adequate level of government functionality in the security sector. Popular revulsion against warlords and commanders and their armed groups potentially can be a very powerful force, but it has not yet been harnessed. The Government's MDG report makes strong reference to the urgent need for licensing of arms.

Violent and other crime, including corruption. Although it is difficult with available data to ascertain whether violent crime and other forms of ordinary crime are more pervasive than in other low-income countries, anecdotal evidence and surveys suggest that crime is an important issue for Afghans. Criminality can thrive in a conflict or post-conflict situation where legal, law enforcement, and social checks are weakened. The same is true of corruption; rough indicators compiled by the World Bank, which have substantial margins of error, suggest that Afghanistan is perceived to be among the countries most severely affected by corruption. The recent Transparency

International index of perceptions of corruption similarly indicates that Afghanistan has a serious corruption problem.

It should be noted that while corruption in government contracting, the tax regime, licenses and permits, etc. may be significant problems in Afghanistan, the enormous role of the drug industry in promoting corruption, as well as to a lesser extent the role of other parts of the informal/illicit economy, must be emphasized.

The huge sums of money involved - in 2004 gross value of opiate production in Afghanistan was roughly estimated at $2.8 billion, of which $2.2 billion went to traders and processors and only $600 million to farmers - virtually guarantee massive levels of corruption. Moreover, narcotics-related corruption most likely to a considerable extent takes the form of "grand corruption" and capture of parts of the state apparatus, which is profoundly damaging to the state-building agenda as compared with smaller "petty corruption". Corruption contributes to personal and business insecurity, as the "rules of the game" are not clear and can change depending on who is in particular government positions, and also can take coercive forms like extortion of payments.

Landmines. Afghanistan inherited from its long period of conflict one of the worst landmine problems in the world, as well as enormous amounts of unexploded ordnance. While progress has been made in clearing mines in urban areas and some other parts of the country, enormous numbers remain and continue to kill and maim people, harm livestock, and render many areas unusable.

Finally, from a developmental perspective the impact of insecurity on vulnerable groups like women continues to be very serious. In the absence of effective mechanisms to investigate gender related violence, the vast majority of such violations are not reported to the criminal justice system and almost none are subject to investigation or prosecution. The practice of detention and prosecution of women for *zina* crimes (adultery and consensual sex outside marriage) is common in major cities, while in more conservative rural areas the family might deal with such a case by killing the girl or woman involved. The predominance of customary law in traditional jirga/shura decisions by and large works to the disadvantage of women, as customary law tends to grant fewer rights to them than Islamic law or civil law in matters relating to inheritance, property, and marriage, as well as in relation to crimes like so-called "honor killings" for which the perpetrators are generally not punished.

Customary law's bias against women is also illustrated when for example murder cases are resolved by the jirga ordering that the alleged perpetrator provide the family of the alleged victim with a young girl or girls, usually below the legal marriage age, to compensate for the alleged crime. The girl is then forcibly married to a male member of the victim's family. Such arrangements are also sometimes used to settle large opium-related debts. A sign of the impact of conflict, violence, and lack of access to justice on women is the reported dramatic upsurge of female suicides, often to escape unwanted arranged or forced marriages.

3

The 21st Century Maritime Silk Road

The 21st Century Maritime Silk "Road" (MSR) will begin from China, moving on to the South China Sea and then Southeast Asia, the Indian Ocean, Africa, and Europe. The southern extension of the route offers access to the South Pacific. According to the National Development and Reform Commission of China (2015), the New Silk Road is based on five principles of the United Nations charter: *mutual respect, mutual non-aggression, mutual non-interference, equality and mutual benefit, and peaceful coexistence*. The MSR would play a vital role for development in the seas through regional cooperation based on infrastructure development, financial integration, free trade, and scientific and human exchanges. The same is supported by academic literature and government reports that how the MSR may evolve newer patterns of regional trade and diplomacy.

China's ambitions support a multilateral approach under international relations where cooperation is promoted on common interests. On similar lines, many experts have raised speculations towards ownership, governance, geo-politics, and prevailing conflicts in the South China Sea. Can initiatives such as the Asian Infrastructure Investment Bank (AIIB) indicate practical steps from China that defy perceptions limiting political constructs towards hegemony? What is important to understand in today's context is that development and harmony would fail through a bilateral or a unilateral approach. Collaboration between states through the MSR not only produces economic gains, but results in greater exchange between societies that will promote culture rooted in harmony and cooperation.

A comparative view of the Ancient and 21st Century Maritime Silk Road includes varying perspectives. However, common grounds are based on principles of economic exchanges through peace in a humanistic approach that strengthens regional integration through cooperation and cultural avenues. The significant difference for MSR today falls under freedom of navigation. International laws and regulations have defined boundaries, which was not the case in ancient times. Another prominent facet of ancient times was the draw of exploration of the seas. Civilizations wanted to get in contact for trade, prosperity, and learning. What remains a question with regard to today's geo-political dynamics is the following: can great powers co-exist, especially with today's complex political dynamics? The rhetorical debate over the 21st Century Maritime Silk Road has ambiguities, but participating nations from Europe, Africa and Asia must realize the need for an integrated network. Like ancient times, states need their economic expertise to be promoted, which not only manifests itself in monetary value, but also in mutually cooperative societies that may initiate a sustainable track towards global peace.

SILK ROAD

The Silk Road or Silk Route was an old system of exchange courses that for quite a long time were vital to social collaboration through locales of the Asian landmass interfacing the West and East from China to the Mediterranean Sea.

The Silk Road gets its name from the lucrative exchange Chinese silkcarried out along its length, starting amid the Han administration (207 BCE – 220 CE). The Han line extended Central Asian segments of the exchange courses around 114 BCE by the Han administration, to a great extent through the missions and investigations of the Chinese majestic emissary, Zhang Qian.

The Chinese appreciated the wellbeing of their exchange items and expanded the Great Wall of China to guarantee the assurance of the exchange course.

Exchange on the Silk Road assumed a noteworthy part in the improvement of the human advancements of China, the Indian subcontinent, Persia, Europe, the Horn of Africa and Arabia, opening long-separate, political and financial relations between the civic establishments. In spite of the fact that silk was positively the real exchange thing sent out from China, numerous different merchandise were exchanged, and religions,syncretic theories, and different advances, and additionally ailments, likewise spread along the Silk Routes. Notwithstanding monetary exchange, the Silk Road served as a method for doing social exchange among the human advancements along its system.

The main traders during antiquity included the Chinese, Arabs, Turks,Indians, Persians, Somalis, Greeks, Syrians, Romans, Armenians, Bactrians, and (from the 5th to the 8th century) the Sogdians. In June 2014 UNESCO designated the Chang'an-Tianshan corridor of the Silk Road as a World Heritage Site.

Name

The Silk Road derives its name from the lucrative Chinese silk trade, a major reason for the connection of trade routes into an extensive transcontinental network.The German terms *Seidenstraße* and *Seidenstraßen* ("the Silk Road/Route") were coined by Ferdinand von Richthofen, who made seven expeditions to China from 1868 to 1872. Some scholars prefer the term "Silk Routes" because the road included an extensive network of routes, though few were more than rough caravan tracks.

History

Precursors—Cross-continental Journeys

As the domestication of pack animals and the development of shipping technology highly increased the capacity for prehistoric people to carry heavier loads over greater distances, cultural exchanges and trade developed rapidly. In addition, the vast grassland steppes of Asia provided fertile grazing, water, and easy passage forcaravans, enabling merchants to travel immense distances, from the shores of the Pacific to Africa and deep into Europe, without trespassing on agricultural lands and arousing hostility.

Chinese and Central Asian contacts

From the 2nd millennium BCE, nephrite jade was being traded from mines in the region of Yarkand and Khotan to China. Significantly, these mines were not very far from the lapis lazuli and spinel ("Balas Ruby") mines in Badakhshan, and, although separated by the formidable Pamir Mountains, routes across them were apparently in use from very early times. Some remnants of what was probably Chinese silk have been found in Ancient Egyptfrom 1070 BCE. The Great Oasis cities of central Asia played a crucial role in the effective functioning of the silk road trades. The originating source seems sufficiently reliable, but silk unfortunately degrades very rapidly. It is therefore impossible to verify whether it was actually cultivated silk (which would almost certainly have come from China) or a type of "wild silk", which might have come from the Mediterranean region or the Middle East.

Following contacts between metropolitan China and nomadic western border territories in the 8th century BCE, gold was introduced from Central Asia, and Chinese jade carvers began to make imitation designs of the steppes, adopting theScythian-style animal art of the steppes (depictions of animals locked in combat). This style is particularly reflected in the rectangular belt plaques made of gold and bronze with alternate versions in jade and steatite.

The expansion of Scythian cultures, stretching from the Hungarian plain and theCarpathians to the Chinese Kansu Corridor, and linking the Middle East with Northern India and the Punjab, undoubtedly played an important role in the development of the Silk Road. Scythians accompanied the

Assyrian Esarhaddon on his invasion of Egypt, and their distinctive triangular arrowheads have been found as far south as Aswan. These nomadic peoples were dependent upon neighbouring settled populations for a number of important technologies, and in addition to raiding vulnerable settlements for these commodities, they also encouraged long-distance merchants as a source of income through the enforced payment of tariffs. Soghdian Scythian merchants played a vital role in later periods in the development of the Silk Road.

Persian Royal Road

By the time of Herodotus (c. 475 BCE), the Royal Road of the Persian Empireran some 2,857 km (1,775 mi) from the city of Susa on the Karun (250 km (155 mi) east of the Tigris) to the port of Smyrna (modern Ýzmir in Turkey) on the Aegean Sea. It was maintained and protected by the Achaemenid Empire(c. 500–330 BCE) and had postal stations and relays at regular intervals. By having fresh horses and riders ready at each relay, royal couriers could carry messages the entire distance in nine days, while normal travellers took about three months.

Hellenistic era

The next major step in the development of the Silk Road was the expansion of the Greekempire of Alexander the Great into Central Asia. In August 329 BCE, at the mouth of theFergana Valley in Tajikistan across the mountain pass from the modern Chinese province ofXinjiang, Alexander founded the city of Alexandria Eschate or "Alexandria The Furthest".This later became a major staging point on the northern Silk Route.

The Greeks remained in Central Asia for the next three centuries, first through the administration of the Seleucid Empire, and then with the establishment of the Greco-Bactrian Kingdom (250 BCE-125 BCE) in Bactria (modern Afghanistan, Tajikistan, and Pakistan) and the later Indo-Greek Kingdom (180 BCE - 10 CE) in modern northern Pakistan and Afghanistan. They continued to expand eastward, especially during the reign of Euthydemus(230–200 BCE), who extended his control beyond Alexandria Eschate to Sogdiana. There are indications that he may have led expeditions as far as Kashgar in Chinese Turkestan, leading to the first known contacts between China and the West around 200 BCE. The Greek historian Strabo writes, *"they extended their empire even as far as the Seres (China) and the Phryni."*

The Hellenistic world and Classical Greek philosophy mixed with Eastern philosophies,leading to syncretisms such as Greco-Buddhism.

Chinese exploration of Central Asia

With the Mediterranean linked to the Fergana Valley, the next step was to open a route across the Tarim Basin and the Hexi Corridor to China Proper. This extension came around 130 BCE, with the embassies of the Han dynasty to Central Asia following the reports of the ambassadorZhang Qian (who was originally sent to obtain an alliance with theYuezhi against the Xiongnu).Zhang Qian visited directly the kingdom ofDayuan in Ferghana, the territories of the Yuezhi in Transoxiana, theBactrian country of Daxia with its remnants of Greco-Bactrian rule, andKangju.

He also made reports on neighbouring countries that he did not visit, such as Anxi (Parthia), Tiaozhi (Mesopotamia), Shendu (Pakistan) and the Wusun. Zhang Qian's report suggested the economic reason for Chinese expansion and wall-building westward, and trailblazed the silk road which is one of the most famous trade routes. After the defeat of the Xiongnu, however, Chinese armies established themselves in Central Asia, initiating the Silk Route as a major avenue of international trade. Some say that the Chinese Emperor Wu became interested in developing commercial relationships with the sophisticated urban civilizations of Ferghana, Bactria, and the Parthian Empire: "The Son of Heaven on hearing all this reasoned thus: Ferghana (Dayuan *"Great Ionians"*) and the possessions of Bactria (Ta-Hsia) and Parthian Empire (Anxi) are large countries, full of rare things, with a population living in fixed abodes and given to occupations somewhat identical with those of the Chinese people, but with weak armies, and placing great value on the rich produce of China" (*Hou Hanshu*, Later Han History). Others say that Emperor Wu was mainly interested infighting the Xiongnu and that major trade began only after the Chinese pacified the Hexi Corridor.

"China snatched control of the Silk Road from the Hsiung-nu", when the Chinese general Cheng Ki "installed himself as protector of the Tarim at Wu-lei, situated between Kara Shahr and Kucha." "China's control of the Silk Road at the time of the later Han, by ensuring the freedom of transcontinental trade along the double chain of oases north and south of theTarim, favoured the dissemination of Buddhism in the river basin, and with it Indian literature and Hellenistic art."

The Chinese were also strongly attracted by the tall and powerful horses (named "Heavenly horses") in the possession of the Dayuan (literally the "Great Ionians", theGreek kingdoms of Central Asia), which were of capital importance in fighting the nomadic Xiongnu. The Chinese subsequently sent numerous embassies, around ten every year, to these countries and as far as Seleucid Syria. "Thus more embassies were dispatched to Anxi [Parthia], Yancai [who later joined the Alans], Lijian [Syria under the Greek Seleucids], Tiaozhi (Mesopotamia), and Tianzhu [northwestern India]... As a rule, rather more than ten such missions went forward in the course of a year, and at the least five or six." (*Hou Hanshu*, Later Han History).These connections marked the beginning of the Silk Road trade network that extended to the Roman Empire. The Chinese campaigned in Central Asia on several occasions, and direct encounters between Han troops and Roman legionaries (probably captured or recruited as mercenaries by the Xiong Nu) are recorded, particularly in the 36 BCE battle of Sogdiana (Joseph Needham, Sidney Shapiro). It has been suggested that the Chinese crossbow was transmitted to the Roman world on such occasions, although the Greekgastraphetes provides an alternative origin. R. Ernest Dupuy and Trevor N. Dupuy suggest that in 36 BCE, a "Han expedition into central Asia, west of Jaxartes River, apparently encountered and defeated a contingent of Roman legionaries. The Romans may have been part of Antony's army invading Parthia. Sogdiana (modern Bukhara), east of the Oxus River, on the Polytimetus River, was apparently the most easterly penetration ever made by Roman forces in Asia. The margin of Chinese victory appears to have been their crossbows, whose bolts and darts seem easily to have penetrated Roman shields and armour." The Roman historian Florus also describes the visit of numerous envoys, which included*Seres*(China), to the first Roman Emperor Augustus, who reigned between 27 BCE and 14 CE:

Even the rest of the nations of the world which were not subject to the imperial sway were sensible of its grandeur, and looked with reverence to the Roman people, the great conqueror of nations. Thus even Scythians and Sarmatians sent envoys to seek the friendship of Rome. Nay, the Seres came likewise, and the Indians who dwelt beneath the vertical sun, bringing presents of precious stones and pearls and elephants, but thinking all of less moment than the vastness of the journey which they had undertaken, and which they said had occupied four years. In truth it needed but to look at their complexion to see that they were people of another world than ours. — *Henry Yule, Cathay and the way thither*

The Han army regularly policed the trade route against nomadic bandit forces generally identified as Xiongnu. Han generalBan Chao led an army of 70,000 mounted infantry and light cavalry troops in the 1st century CE to secure the trade routes, reaching far west to the Tarim basin. Ban Chao expanded his conquests across the Pamirs to the shores of the Caspian Sea and the borders of Parthia. It was from here that the Han general dispatched envoy Gan Ying to Daqin (Rome).The Silk Road essentially came into being from the 1st century BCE, following these efforts by China to consolidate a road to the Western world and India, both through direct settlements in the area of the Tarim Basin and diplomatic relations with the countries of the Dayuan, Parthians and Bactrians further west. The Silk Roads were a "complex network of trade routes" that gave people the chance to exchange goods and culture. A maritime Silk Route opened up between Chinese-controlled Giao ChÉ (centred in modern Vietnam, near Hanoi), probably by the 1st century. It extended, via ports on the coasts of India and Sri Lanka, all the way to Roman-controlled ports in Egyptand the Nabataean territories on the northeastern coast of the Red Sea.

THE MARITIME SILK ROAD

The situation of the overland Silk Road is mirrored in the 21st Century Maritime Silk Road. The 2015 Visions and Action plan calls for two transboundary maritime economic routes, linking deep water ports across the South China Sea, Indian Ocean and beyond. It has been extensively documented that both China and India are competing to build networks of maritime infrastructure across these regions, amongst growing anxieties over freedom of navigation rights and the need for strategic locations for seaborne trade.6 In response to the Chinese financing of deep water ports and Strategic Maritime Distribution Centers in littoral regions across Africa and South America, India has increased funding to its navy and maritime defence capacities. Against this backdrop sits heritage diplomacy, with China and India assembling countries in the region for maritime themed world heritage nominations, namely the 'Maritime Silk Road' and the Indian Ocean 'Project Mausam' respectively.

As Erickson and Bond have noted, maritime archaeology has formed part of China's strategy for claiming territory in the disputed South China Sea.7 Various maritime archaeology institutes including the National Center for Conservation of Underwater Cultural Heritage, together with ships and submersibles equipped for deep water shipwreck hunting, have endeavoured to find material evidence in support of claims for territorial jurisdiction over the East and South China seas based on historical right. In contrast to many Western expert commentaries that point to twentieth century laws and treaties, within China discoveries of porcelain and other artefacts dating as far back as the ninth century Tang dynasty substantiate the country's position over the disputed waters.8 Crucially, however, the notion of a Maritime Silk Road flips this excavation of shipwrecks from mere evidence of historical presence towards a much larger, and more diplomatically expedient language of region-wide trade, encounter and exchange. Belt and Road's emphasis on maritime connections also sustains claims that China ranks alongside its European counterparts as one of the great naval powers in world history.

One figure in particular, Admiral Zheng He, embodies this grand narrative. A Muslim eunuch who led seven fleets across to South Asia, the Arabian peninsula and West Africa between 1405 and 1433 during the Ming dynasty, Zheng He is widely celebrated as a peaceful envoy in both China and by the overseas Chinese living in Malaysia, Indonesia and elsewhere. In addition to the museums, mosques, and artefacts now appearing around the region celebrating his voyages, China has given millions of dollars to Sri Lanka and Kenya to support the search for remains of Zheng He's fleet. Both countries are key nodes in the Belt and Road infrastructure network, with China financing the construction of deep water ports in Colombo and Hambantota in Sri Lanka, and Lamu in Kenya. In 2005 Singapore also celebrated the 600th anniversary of Zheng He's voyages, hosting multiple events over the course of the year.9 These helped raise public awareness about Singapore's maritime history and connections to China; an historical narrative political leaders now explicitly invoke to garner domestic support for Singapore's strategic engagement in Belt and Road. Given the networked nature of the initiative, over the coming years we will see other states in the Persian Gulf, East Africa, and South-Southeast Asia excavate – both physically and discursively – their own maritime pasts and build heritage industries and museums around stories of trade, connection and exchange.

The connections of silk

By speaking to the construct of the Silk Road, One Belt One Road sits on a deep history of cultural entanglements and flows, which countries across Eurasia and beyond can buy into and appropriate for their own ends. As a bridge, this complex trans-boundary cultural history is reduced to a series of heritage narratives that directly align with the foreign policy and trade ambitions of governments today. The Silk Road is a story of connectivity, one that enables countries and cities to strategically respond to the shifting geopolitics of the region and use the past as a means for building competitive advantage in an increasingly networked Sinocentric economy. Culture forms part of the international diplomatic arena now, and with routes, hubs and corridors serving as the mantra of Belt and Road, countries will continue to find points of cultural connection through the language of shared heritage in order to gain regional influence and loyalty. But this also raises important questions concerning new forms of cultural erasure and coloniality and the political violence they deliver. The lives of vulnerable communities, particularly those located in borderland regions, will be deeply affected by the developments outlined here. In both its land and sea forms, Belt and Road gives impetus to a network of heritage diplomacy that fosters institutional and interpersonal connections. This in turn provides the foundation for the more informal people-to-people connections that will lie at the heart of Silk Road tourism. Indeed, framed by the political and economic imperatives of One Belt One Road, there is a distinct possibility that the heritage diplomacy of silk will have lasting consequences that far outlive the tensions of twentieth century conflict and occupation.

THE 21ST CENTURY MARITIME SILK ROAD INITIATIVE

Historically the maritime silk road refers to the ancient maritime trade and cultural route between China and other parts of Asia, Europe, East Africa and the Middle East. Xi's MSR is an initiative to restore the historical maritime prestige and influence that China once wielded as a maritime power. It is the counterpart of the Silk Road Economic Belt initiative that Xi announced in September 2013, which focuses on overland connectivity between China and Central Asia into Europe. The Chinese refer to this pair of initiatives as "One Belt and One

Road". At the Central Conference on Work Relating to Foreign Affairs in late November 2014, Xi announced his foreign relations objectives, which included the agenda to "turn China's neighborhood areas into a community of common destiny ... and boost win-win cooperation and connectivity with our neighbors."

In the context of this plan, these two Silk Road initiatives are aimed at promoting bilateral and multilateral partnerships across Asia to consolidate China's leadership status in the region and are linked to China's continued efforts at national rejuvenation as a Comprehensive National Power. However, the exact plans for the two initiatives are still being drafted by the National Development and Reform Commission. As a result, the MSR, while focused on developing maritime connectivity and infrastructure access across Asia, remains a vague agenda thin on details.

The MSR is in part an investment-driven regional engagement strategy promoted by China against the backdrop of US re-balancing in Asia. Economically, it is meant to create more economic opportunities between China and the littoral states in Asia. Diplomatically, China is hoping to repair its image, which has been damaged by the South China Sea disputes. Strategically, it is to enhance China's access to the SLOCs through the development of a network of maritime facilities in the Indian and West Pacific Oceans. Such infrastructure investments are in part intended to enable China to secure better access to natural resources from abroad. For example, in Southeast Asia, the China-financed US$2.5 billion deep-water port and pipeline project in Kyaukphyuon Myanmar's west coast opened recently in January 2015. Through this energy corridor, China will be able to transport some of its Middle Eastern oil imports (up to 440,000 barrels a day) via a 771 km pipeline from the Bay of Bengal into Yunnan Province, China, bypassing the Strait of Malacca. In South Asia, China is also interested in developing Gwadar, Pakistan as a maritime hub. The deep-sea port of Gwadar is situated on the Arabian Sea at the mouth of the Persian Gulf, about 400 km from the critical oil supply chokepoint, the Strait of Hormuz. This port lies in the volatile Baluchistan Province but if it can be successfully developed, it would enable western China access to the Middle East and could potentially serve as the shortest route for overland oil imports into China if a pipeline connection can be built and secured.

To support the two silk road initiatives, China initiated the creation of the Asian Infrastructure Investment Bank (AIIB) to provide infrastructure loans and invited other Asian countries to join as founding members. On October 24, 2014, the representatives of 21 countries signed the intergovernmental Memorandum of Understanding (MOU) on Establishing the AIIB in Beijing. As of January 2015, 26 countries have signed up as prospective founding members, including the 10 ASEAN members. Negotiations on the AIIB Articles of Agreement (AOA) are underway, and this process is expected to be completed by the end of 2015. Countries that subsequently sign and ratify the AOA will officially become founding members of the AIIB.

The AIIB has an authorized capital of US$100 billion, of which China has pledged half the amount – US$50 billion – as initial subscribed capital. In November 2014, China further pledged another US$40 billion to a new Silk Road Fund to develop the infrastructure and resources along the land and sea trade routes. Earlier in 2009, China had established a US $10 billion China–ASEAN Fund on Investment Cooperation and a US $15 billion credit line for infrastructure projects in ASEAN. Two years later, it pledged RMB 3 billion (US$490 million) to the China–ASEAN Maritime Cooperation Fund. What makes the AIIB and Silk Road Fund significant compared to these earlier initiatives is that it is framed as part of a China-centric regional vision to "turn China's neighborhood areas into a community of common destiny."

CHINA'S NEW SILK ROAD: TACTICS, OVERSTRETCH OR GRAND STRATEGY?

Outside arrangement has generally been a bit of hindsight for China's pioneers for a great part of the nation's present day history. With the attention on the usage of socialism and communism involving the Mao period, resulting rulers have concentrated on the nation's monetary opening and what has been esteemed its "quiet ascent". Since accepting force in 2013, Xi Jinping has started to lead a more emphatic remote strategy, while seeking after a "purging" of the socialist party in what might be history's biggest against debasement battle and as yet concentrating on advancing, yet gradually, financial changes. As of late however, China seems to have made the jump to planning what seems, by all accounts, to be an amazing system, of sorts: the making of the "Silk Road Economic Belt" and the "21st-Century Maritime Silk Road", named the "One Belt, One Road" methodology. This activity apparently means to support availability and business amongst China and 65 nations in Eurasia and Northern Africa, which has an aggregate populace of 4.4bn. The arrangement is tobuild systems of streets, railroads, pipelines, ports and other foundation crosswise over Asia associating China to Europe, the Middle East, South-and Southeast Asia. Along the way China would like to work out vital, monetary and exchanging associations with the nations on the course, while securing genuinely necessary characteristic assets.

This yearning venture has been relevantly named: The New Silk Road. The verifiable Silk Road, which existed in different structures from ancient history through the start of the current age, was a noteworthy element in the improvement of China, India, Persia, the Levant and Europe, making political and financial linkages between these far flung civic establishments. All the more vitally maybe, the Silk Road was the methods by which China's Han administration broadened power and impact from the 3.4m sq km of domain acquired from the Qin to more than 6m sq km 2000 years back. In a nation, for example, China, with 5,000 years of constant civilisation, recollections are long and these names matter.

China's Marshall Plan or the British Empire's Railways Project?

The scope and scale of China's New Silk Road initiative is perhaps unrivalled in history and has been called China's

Marshall Plan by Western commentators. Indeed, there are a number of similarities with the $120bn (in current terms) post WW II program that sought to rebuild Europe through kick-starting infrastructure and heavy industry as the basis for growth. But while the U.S. Marshall Plan sought to rebuild and stabilise Europe in the context of the imminent Cold War, the New Silk Road strategy is interesting since it comes in peace time and crosses continents. Its scale also poses the question as to whether it is more akin to the railways that the British Empire built across the colonies. Railways were the infrastructure used to cement its control over its own colonies. This was particularly the case not just in India, where a huge network of lines was created partly for military purposes, but also in Egypt where rail lines allowed the British to reclaim control over Sudan.

The evident primary purpose of The New Silk Road from public statements appears to be the generation of economic benefits to China itself. The initial focus of the strategy is on the financing and build-out of hard infrastructure, and most of the projects initiated or envisaged to date include a major role for Chinese companies, either as suppliers of equipment and materials or in construction and execution. The building of transport and trade linkages benefits China but also its neighbours for the trade they will facilitate. Further, Central Asia, in particular, is rich in resources that China needs for its continued development, including oil, gas, coal, gold, copper and uranium, and the build-out of sea links to the Middle East and the Mediterranean is critical to securing China's sea lines of communication on a route through which 80% of it is oil imports pass. Economically speaking, China's increased westward focus clearly makes sense: the region the strategy covers contains 65% of the world's population but accounts for only 26% of China's foreign trade, representing a significant growth opportunity.

The primary focus of the New Silk Road initiative, at least initially, appears to be infrastructure build-out, and the majority of commitments announced to date have been on scaled cross-border transportation linkages focusing on six geographic segments, or corridors, creating trade routes along which further economic activity is expected to develop. The map highlights the key corridors and routes of the New Silk Road. Projects initiated or currently under consideration include new highways and rail-lines connecting China to Central Asia, high-speed railway networks in Europe, including a Hungary-Serbia link, the build-out of a network of port facilities stretching from Athens to Malaysia and a canal through the Isthmus of Kraa in Thailand that would dwarf the Panama Canal.

China's play to build-out regional infrastructure is highly ambitious, the annual "gap" between the supply and demand for infrastructure spending in Asia being estimated at \$800bn. With existing international institutions such as the World Bank, the Asian Development Bank and the IMF currently not positioned to adequately address this gap, China has emerged as a welcome financier to countries requiring infrastructure investment, particularly given its traditional policy of granting loans without imposing the reform and governance requirements set by other lending institutions. Given the massive geographic scale of the New Silk Road initiative, the scope of China's required financing activities is equally large. The countries defined as being part of the strategy are already capturing over 75% of the overseas loan commitments made by Beijing's largest policy lenders, the China Development Bank and the China Export-Import Bank, making obvious the need for significant additional financing to execute the strategy. Estimates of the total investment vary, but China has committed to finance the build-out through multiple pools of capital, including the US\$100bn Asian Infrastructure Investment Bank (AIIB), a dedicated US\$40bn Silk Road Fund, and the injection of US\$62bn of fresh capital into the state-owned policy banks, as well as a number of funding commitments at the bilateral level, such as the \$45bn funding of the China-Pakistan Economic Corridor. China's total investment (and its partners' in the AIIB) in its master plan could exceed US\$1.4 trillion by some estimates, making it 12 times larger than the Marshall Plan, or approximately 15% of China's GDP

The scale of its funding requirement aside, China's New Silk Road is ambitious in that it touches on virtually every important issue facing the country today, although in certain cases it appears to be set to exacerbate rather than resolve many of these issues.

The relationships with key powers appears to be one of the most significant shortfalls of the New Silk Road initiative or at the least it is a factor for which China's aims and strategy have not been declared. For all of its focus on immediate economic benefits for China, very little is said about the New Silk Road's long-term political implications, particularly with regards to the countries that are not, or are only marginal beneficiaries of the initiative, but are impacted by its implications nonetheless. The list of these includes some of the world's most important countries and the initiative could easily lead to uniting them in opposition to China on a far wider front.

There are four significant potential geopolitical implications of a successful implementation of the initiative.

- The United States: Outpivoting the Pivot. The US, China's largest trading partner by a significant margin, is wholly outside of the scope and spirit of the New Silk Road strategy, which is a geographic counterpoint to America's own pivot westward into the Pacific. In parallel to building links westward, China appears to be drawing increasingly hard borders eastward, both in terms of defence and economics, with increasing territorial tensions with its Eastern and South-eastern neighbours, the extension of China's own air defence identification zone into those of Korea and Japan and a build-up of naval power, while progress on the proposed China–Japan-South Korea Free Trade Agreement appears to have stalled China has refused to take part in the 12 country, US led, Tran-Pacific Partnership (while the US, conversely, is not supporting the 51 country, China led, AIIB). With the US seeking to set the next generation of trade and investment rules for the Asian Pacific, China is increasingly looking to the Eurasian continent for economic growth and presumably long-term influence.

- Japan: Out in the Cold. The US's closest regional ally Japan, China's second largest sovereign trading partner, is similarly shut out of the New Silk Road initiative. With Sino-Japanese foreign policy relations already a casualty of both country's increasing nationalism, Japan stands to be one of the key losers of the New Silk Road strategy, with trade and investment shifting away from it. While Japan certainly does not require further infrastructure build-out, the Abe government has called for foreign direct investment into the country to double by 2020 to $280bn, with China currently investing less than US$500m in Japan annually, representing a significant lost opportunity for both Japanese and Chinese companies. More importantly, given Japan has historically been one of top three providers of FDI to China, this initiative potentially puts at risk a key source of foreign capital for the country.
- India: Encirclement Risk. Although technically, India is part of the New Silk Road strategy by virtue of the Bangladesh-China-India-Myanmar Economic Corridor, this is not at all how India views this part of the initiative. India very clearly sees encirclement by China. The Maritime Road passes through the Indian Ocean to the country's south, establishing ports and potentially naval bases in places that India considers within its sphere of influence, such Sri Lanka, or strategically sensitive, such as Pakistan. Similarly, the overland silk route bypasses the country's northern border to India's exclusion and to the benefit of its regional rival Pakistan.
- Russia: Security Encroachment. A full [5 000] km of the New Silk Road skirt Russia's southern borders, running through countries that until recently were part of or satellites of the Soviet Union. China has already eclipsed Russia as the largest trading partner of the five post-Soviet central Asian states, all of which the latter

considers security buffer states. For the time being it appears that Russia and China have come to an agreement with regards to sharing regional power, with Russia recognising China's de facto economic dominance while remaining the sole military powerbase when it comes to hard security in the region. It remains to be seen, however, how stress-resistant this arrangement turns out to be, with both countries continuing to nurturing competing economic and security institutions as a potential back-up.

Clearly, it is hard to imagine that a country that plans as thoroughly as China would develop a mega-scaled project with a highly complex cross-border strategic thrust unfolding over decades without having planned out its political dimensions, too. However, if the New Silk Road truly lacks the political dimension, it highlights a key difference between it and the Marshall Plan and the British Empire's railways programme, both of which were part of a grand strategy driven by a set of long-term geopolitical foreign policy or military goals; the New Silk Road would be exclusively focused on economic issues and seemingly tactical ones at that. Supporting that idea, China's foreign affairs institutions do not appear to be directly involved with the initiative, it being under the remit of Zhang Gaoli, a ranking member of the standing committee of the politburo and the second-in-charge of China's government and economic sector. The key question this prompts is whether the lack of an evident political dimension is an oversight or a carefully weighed and determined geo-political move? The supplementary question is whether this is an economic initiative or a political one? If it is an economic one, then is it a tactical one or a strategic one? This in turn raises the question for others to determine what it means for them. In the absence of clarity on China's aims, they will need to form strategies under various scenarios. There are three distinct possibilities regarding the underlying nature of China's engagement on the New Silk Road.things. However, while China's current level of planning is unclear, a political strategic New Silk Road is certainly within its capabilities, and even a purely economic initiative today provides it with options to develop complementary political strategies.

Political Strategic Initiative. The New Silk Road, under this scenario, would be the play out of a long and patient game around the country's political position and the build-out of its power, under the cover of an initiative ostensibly run by the country's economic leaders. In support of this view, is the evidence that China in other areas has proven to be both highly strategic, willing to play long-term games patiently and has been shifting to a more muscular foreign policy in recent years. In this scenario, China's political non-engagement to date is a strategic tool that helps to obscure the country's end game. Having made a conscious decision to obscure, it make sense to de-politicise the initial stages of the strategy and thereby build credibility and trust as well as economic momentum while setting the pieces for later political moves. For example, the protection of economic interests in foreign countries have historically provided justifications for subsequent strategic and even military interventions, as Britain's expansion in India through the East India Company demonstrates. The key argument against this view is that such a strategy would represent a premature shift in the country's priorities: Chinese leaders since Deng Xiaoping have focused on economic development and the creation of a "moderately well off" society, a transformation process that remains difficult and is on-going. In this interpretation, China's more active foreign policy is a natural consequence of its growing importance and increasing global integration, rather than a necessary active choice. If it were indeed a political strategic initiative, the New Silk Road, given its scope, would be a major play in "great power" politics, which is something that countries can only afford when they are otherwise highly stable or desperate. China today is neither of these things. However, while China's current level of planning is unclear, a political strategic New Silk Road is certainly within its capabilities, and even a purely economic initiative today provides it with options to develop complementary political strategies.

Economic Strategic Initiative. Alternatively, the New Silk Road's primary objective might be economic and strategic because it has the potential to own the trade corridor linking the Middle East to East Asia, one of the world's most energy dependent regions. China currently imports 60% of its oil from overseas. Although oil contributes less than 20% of its primary energy consumption, China's demand makes it the largest net importer of petroleum globally. While China has sought to diversify its sources of oil by purchasing from places such as South America and Africa, two-thirds of its oil imports today come from the Middle East and the former Soviet Union. Locking in supply and controlling transportation infrastructure in the region is clearly highly strategic for China, given energy security is crucial for further economic development and stability. Per capita energy consumption in China today is only a quarter of that of advanced industrial economies such as a Japan and Germany, pointing a massive increase in China's medium to long-term energy requirements. Additionally, securing petroleum access is also highly strategic for many of its neighbours, who are even more dependent on foreign oil than China is, with imported oil representing approximately 25% of India's and 40% of Japan and Korea's total primary energy consumption. Owning key access routes for is neighbour's essential resources would provide China with significant future strategic leverage in trade negotiations. Executing the New Silk Road as an economic strategic initiative that ties into China's long-term development is significantly more complex than executing one focused on boosting trade and investment but the strategic value to China is commensurately greater, too.

Economic Tactical Initiative. While at first glance unlikely, it does remain possible that the New Silk Road, at least initially, is tactical, in that it is predominantly about utilising excess capacity in construction and related finance. Under this view, it would be argued that the New Silk Road is not a strategy at all, but a convenient label to group together a series of initiatives China has already been pursuing for over a decade, kicked off when former President Jiang Zemin told Chinese businesses to "go out". The various funding mechanisms and the vagueness of official language, which for examples waivers between calling the China-Pakistan corridor a part of the strategy or a closely related initiative, points to a lack of top level coordination. The "vision" of the New Silk Road espoused by Xi Jinping has been back-solved, adding the illusion of grand strategy to an ongoing series of tactical moves. However, the lack of an upfront long-term strategy does not preclude its development over time to something more strategic.

From the perspective of foreign policy makers, one of the lessons of history is how trade and infrastructure lead to ownership and control. So, whatever might be the initial objectives of The New Silk Road, policy makers would need to focus on the natural development of a political dimension over time: building out trade links provides influence over the movement of people, trade and information between two or more points and therefore virtually guarantees the accrual of political clout over time. History is full examples of infrastructure both enabling and requiring the use of political power. Egypt for example became a de-facto Anglo-French protectorate following the establishment of the Suez Canal and US intervention triggered by its interests in the Panama Canal drove the separation of Panama from Colombia.Especially poignant for the East is the story of the East India Company and how its trade linked sowed the seeds of the British Empire in India. From China's perspective, the issues being addressed by the New Silk Road are well understood and have been areas of focus of its leadership for some time. If there is a indeed a masterplan that was drawn up in Zhongnanhai it will have drawn upon the inputs from diverse sources and will have been drafted in a way that makes it acceptable to the various factions in China's leadership today, which means supporting multiple and differing views and providing flexibility in terms of future execution and focus. Regardless of China's current level of thinking on the New Silk Road, it is clear that unless thwarted, this initiative has long-term potential of a strategic and political nature.

Executing a Long-Term Strategy: The Long Road

Looking ahead, a successful New Silk Road will need to encompass a number of additional policy areas, both economic and political, which still appear to be missing today, including credibility, sustainability accountability and the parallel execution of domestic reform.

- Strategic Partnership. In terms of building credibility, China today has failed to build a base of soft power in the world today commensurate with its economic power and growing political clout. The New Silk Road in some ways represents a major soft power push, promising Chinese capital, expertise, good and services to countries along the route, along with closer relationships with Beijing, with its success depending on China being accepted as a credible partner. As currently envisaged though, the New Silk Road also represents a liability to China's credibility, in that it comes at the expense of the countries outside of the routes, many of which have been its long standing economic partners. By turning its back on the countries that played an important part in its development until today, such as Japan and to a lesser degree South Korea and Vietnam, China risks sending signals that it is not a long-term strategic and economic partner. More importantly, China's increasing focus on the New Silk Road is allowing it to leave a growing number of issues with these countries unresolved. If China wants to be credible as a partner to the countries on the New Silk Road it will need to demonstrate both the long-term nature of the partnerships it is seeking to establish as well as its ability to constructively resolve the differences that surely will arise over time. If and once the New Silk Road is successful, China is very capable of using it of course to bring others to participate in it and thereby further enhance its power and influence.
- Sustainable Financing. Equally as important as credibility in winning acceptance as a strategic partner

is sustainability and financial viability. China's policy in the past has often focused on providing soft loans with little or no financial accountability. The scaled infrastructure projects of the New Silk Road will need to pay for themselves however, at least over the long term. If the New Silk Road projects do not generate sustainable benefits to local economies however, China risks suffering political backlash from local electorates, as it has done in parts of Africa. This financial sustainability requirement creates a potentially high bar for projects on the route: China's own infrastructure investments in its sparsely populated western regions have seen much lower returns than its earlier coastal investments. China and its partners will need to build solid business cases for scaled projects even further afield for these to succeed over the long term.

- Security and Military Exposure. The New Silk Road passes through a number of global hotspots suffering from political instability that threaten the safety of traffic on the route and China's investments. Afghanistan, Iran, Sudan and Syria are all along or next to major proposed arteries of the road, and China's policy of non-intervention in other countries' affairs is not attuned to the needs of the New Silk Road strategy. As the architect and financier of the road, China will need to assume security accountability for its infrastructure and traffic. Once the precedent is set, it, one can envisage China playing a more active role in international affairs, contributing to international peacekeeping and disaster relief efforts generally as well as a as a proactive mediator helping to solve specific regional issues. This would initially be seen as China becoming a broader responsible stakeholder. It is also one of the first step in China learning how the international conflict system works as a participant rather than an observer and as the world has seen in the sphere of trade, what begins as a participant ends with China becoming a force to reckon with.

- Domestic Reform. Most importantly, perhaps, China will also need to execute comprehensive domestic reforms. As currently formulated, the New Silk Road is a rear-guard action protecting China's investment led economic model, allowing it export overcapacity in sectors whose productive contribution to the Chinese economy is declining. Given that the country's economic restructuring is progressing only slowly, the New Silk Road initiative is one way of sustaining otherwise declining industries and making up for their contribution shortfalls to domestic growth. China's key long-term strategic objective needs to be the reshaping of its economy, and the New Silk Road initiative must clearly be recognised for what it is: one tool that affords China the opportunity to do so.

Ensuring the success of the New Silk Road, even if defined in a narrow economic fashion will therefore require expanding its scope significantly, from trade and investment today to foreign and security policy as well as governance and development, while also expanding its geographic scale to integrate or at least accommodate important constituents currently left outside the initiative. This suggests that it is irrelevant where the initiative began, even if that were tactical and economic, it has to end up as strategic and to some extent political in the end if it is to be successful.

For the New Silk Road to deliver its true potential to China, it will need to simultaneously execute a wide range of ambitious initiatives covering development, security, engagement in multilateral institutions and foreign policy that unpin its strategic nature.

Foreign policy implications and actions aside, it is also important for its leaders to consider the potential socio-political consequences of the New Silk Road at home. If China is able to achieve only a fraction of the potential vision for the New Silk Road, the domestic impact will be significant, and not just from an economic development perspective. The past 30 years of China's rise have created a mind-set in its leadership that is focused on hard assets: hard currency, hard trade, and hard power. Much like the original, the New Silk Road will also be a cultural transmission route for the exchange of ideas, and one runs in both directions. The original Silk Road, in addition to exporting China's goods to the world, also imported Buddhism, which became the state religion for centuries, and later Islam, which also had a major impact on Chinese history and culture. This transmission will certainly happen again and China's ability to absorb and successfully integrate new ideas will be a function of its openness. In the absence of openness and flexibility, new ideas can disrupt society rather than providing stimulus for further growth and development, and China's leadership's current categorical dismissal of Western "cultures and values" calls in question its receptiveness to the powerful new influences that that New Silk Road will bring.

Conclusion: Foreign Policy Considerations for the Rest of the World

Given the long-term strategic execution requirements of such a far-reaching initiative, the New Silk Road has the potential to be one of the defining economic and political constructs of the first half of the 21st Century, driving development, integrating and promoting trade and providing stability across the world's largest landmass and beyond as well as cementing China's position as a regional and global superpower. Foreign countries, whether in or outside of the scope of the New Silk Road, will need to formulate a response to China's moves, based on both their own strategic priorities and their views on the plan, its risks and benefits and its chances of success. These views and priorities can give rise to three distinct responses:

Accommodate and Influence. Countries seeking to benefit from the New Silk Road are the most likely candidates to be accommodating, welcoming engagement with China and with its trade and investment. This list includes both countries with pressing needs and limited alternatives to China's plans, such as the Central Asian countries, and mature developed countries that believe engagement creates win-win situations, such as the UK. PM David Cameron's red carpet roll-out to President Xi Jinping in London last month and its willingness to sign up to the AIIB speaks loudly to the UK government's conviction that an early submission to China's plans will reap greater benefits than a later one. Whether this will be the case remains to be seen.

Counterbalance and Contain. Countries potentially threatened by China's New Silk Road or by its rise to superpower status will more likely seek to counterbalance its actions and policies, containing China's expansion and influence. Japan and the US may well adopt this position; most of the US's presidential candidates appear to be adopting a more hawkish stance on China. The actions of these countries will be built on the view that constructive engagement with China is not and is unlikely to bear fruit and so measures are required to counteract the growth of China's power and influence. The US alone today has the experience to galvanise the array of chess pieces required to execute such a strategy in East Asia. This will also require the US to undertake a series of initiatives in Central and South Asia, the Middle East and Southeast Europe too that have the scope to counterbalance the New Silk Road. This will require the US to leapfrog the initiative through its ingenuity and resources while undermining it directly. This is by no means an easy task.

Wait and See. A standing option is of course to do nothing for the time being and wait and see. The challenges facing China today, whether domestically or internationally are significant and the country has recently proven itself to be unable to address these effectively. The scope and scale of the New Silk Road would require China to solve all of these problems as well as a number of additional issues simultaneously and in a coordinated fashion, a scenario which many believe is highly unlikely. If the New Silk Road represents a classic example of overextension, a studied policy of limited engagement is an effective option for China's rivals on both sides of the road's fence. In this view, China will likely muddle through a series of economic reforms that keep the country creeping forward but not leaping ahead, while a carefully chosen mix of accommodating and counterbalancing responses to the New Silk Road will result in a patchwork of initiatives and investments that are never fully integrated. Countries that adopt this position can respond to events flexibly, accommodating China in areas where it needs them and counterbalancing it in those where China's interests run up against its own, getting the benefits of both strategies in areas where they are most effective and relevant.

Of course some countries may effectively default to the third option simply by lacking a coherent strategy for engaging with China. India today could fall into this category, having alternated between viewing China as a competitor for resources and as a partner for development. Whatever the view of world leaders, the New Silk Road is clearly a move with serious geo-political consequence and one only to be ignored at their own, if not the international order's, peril.

THE DEVELOPMENT OF THE ROUTE

The development of these Central Asian trade routes caused some problems for the Han rulers in China. Bandits soon learnt of the precious goods travelling up the Gansu Corridor and skirting the Taklimakan, and took advantage of the terrain to plunder these caravans. Caravans of goods needed their own defence forces, and this was an added cost for the merchants making the trip. The route took the caravans to the farthest extent of the Han Empire, and policing this route became a big problem. This was partially overcome by building forts and defensive walls along part of the route. Sections of 'Great Wall' were built along the northern side of the Gansu Corridor, to try to prevent the Xiongnu from harming the trade; Tibetan bandits from the Qilian mountains to the south were also a problem. Sections of Han dynasty wall can still be seen as far as Yumen Guan, well beyond the recognised beginning of the Great Wall at Jiayuguan. However, these fortifications were not all as effective as intended, as the Chinese lost control of sections of the route at regular intervals.

The Han dynasty set up the local government at Wulei, not far from Kuqa on the northern border of the Taklimakan, in order to 'protect' the states in this area, which numbered about 50 at the time. At about the same period the city of Gaochang was constructed in the Turfan basin. This developed into the centre of the Huihe kingdom; these peoples later became the Uygur minority who now make up a large proportion of the local population. Many settlements were set up along the way, mostly in the oasis areas, and profited from the passing trade. They also absorbed a lot of the local culture, and the cultures that passed them by along the route. Very few merchants traversed the full length of the road; most simply covered part of the journey, selling their wares a little further from home, and then returning with the proceeds. Goods therefore tended to moved slowly across Asia, changing hands many times. Local people no doubt acted as guides for the caravans over the most dangerous sections of the journey.

After the Western Han dynasty, successive dynasties brought more states under Chinese control. Settlements came and went, as they changed hands or lost importance due to a change in the routes. The chinese garrison town of Loulan, for example, on the edge of the Lop Nor lake, was important in the third century A.D., but was abandoned when the Chinese lost control of the route for a period. Many settlements were buried during times of abandonment by the sands of the Taklimakan, and could not be repopulated.

The settlements reflected the nature of the trade passing through the region. Silk, on its way to the west, often got no further than this region of Central Asia. The Astana tombs, where the nobles of Gaochang were buried, have turned up examples of silk cloth from China, as well as objects from as far afield as Persia and India. Much can be learned about the customs of the time from the objects found in these graves, and from the art work of the time, which has been excellently preserved on the tomb walls, due to the extremely dry conditions. The bodies themselves have also been well preserved, and may allow scientific studies to ascertain their origins.

The most significant commodity carried along this route was not silk, but religion. Buddhism came to China from India this way, along the northern branch of the route. The first influences came as the passes over the Karakorum were first explored. The Eastern Han emperor Mingdi is thought to have sent a representative to India to discover more about this strange faith, and further missions returned bearing scriptures, and bringing with them India priests. With this came influences from the Indian sub-continent, including Buddhist art work, examples of which have been found in several early second century tombs in present-day Sichuan province. This was considerably influenced by the Himalayan Massif, an effective barrier between China and India, and hence the Buddhism in China is effectively derived from the Gandhara culture by the bend in the Indus river, rather than directly from India. Buddhism reached the pastures of Tibet at a rather later period, not developing fully until the seventh century. Along the way it developed under many different influences, before reaching central China. This is displayed very cleared in the artwork, where many of the cave paintings show people with clearly different ethnic backgrounds, rather than the expected Cental and East Asian peoples.

The greatest flux of Buddhism into China occurred during the Northern Wei dynasty, in the fourth and fifth centuries A.D. This was at a time when China was divided into several different kingdoms, and the Northern Wei dynasty had its capital in Datong in present day Shanxi province. The rulers encouraged the development of Buddhism, and more missions were sent towards India. The new religion spread slowly eastwards, through the oases surrounding the Taklimakan, encouraged by an increasing number of merchants, missionaries and pilgrims. Many of the local peoples, the Huihe included, adopted Buddhism as their own religion. Faxian, a pilgrim from China, records the religious life in the Kingdoms of Khotan and Kashgar in 399 A.D. in great detail. He describes the large number of monasteries that had been built, and a large Buddhist festival that was held while he was there.

Some devotees were sufficiently inspired by the new ideas that they headed off in search of the source, towards Gandhara and India; others started to build monasteries, grottos and stupas. The development of the grotto is particularly interesting; the edges of the Taklimakan hide some of the best examples in the world. The hills surrounding the desert are mostly of sandstone, with any streams or rivers carving cliffs that can be relatively easily dug into; there was also no shortage of funds for the work, particularly from wealthy merchants, anxious to invoke protection or give thanks for a safe desert crossing. Gifts and donations of this kind were seen as an act of merit, which might enable the donor to escape rebirth into this world. In many of the murals, the donors themselves are depicted, often in pious attitude. This explains why the Mogao grottos contain some of the best examples of Buddhist artwork; Dunhuang is the starting point for the most difficult section of the Taklimakan crossing.

The grottos were mostly started at about the same period, and coincided with the beginning of the Northern Wei Dynasty. There are a large cluster in the Kuqa region, the best examples being the Kyzil grottos; similarly there are clusters close to Gaochang, the largest being the Bezeklik grottos. Probably the best known ones are the Mogao grottos at Dunhuang, at the eastern end of the Taklimakan. It is here that the greatest number, and some of the best examples, are to be found. More is known about the origins of these, too, as large quantities of ancient documents have been found. These are on a wide range of subjects, and include a large number of Buddhist scriptures in Chinese, Sanskrit, Tibetan, Uygur and other languages, some still unknown. There are documents from the other faiths that developed in the area, and also some official documents and letters that reveal a lot about the system of government at the time. The grotto building was not confined to the Taklimakan; there is a large cluster at Bamiyan in the Hindu Kush, in present-day Afghanistan. It is here that the second largest sculpture of Buddha in the world can be found, at 55 metres high.

For the archaeologist these grottos are particularly valuable sources of information about the Silk Road. Along with the images of Buddhas and Boddhisatvas, there are scenes of the everyday life of the people at the time. Scenes of celebration and dancing give an insight into local customs and costume. The influences of the Silk Road traffic are therefore quite clear in the mix of cultures that appears on these murals at different dates. In particular, the development of Buddhism from the Indian/Gandharan style to a more individual faith is evident on studying the murals from different eras in any of the grotto clusters. Those from the Gandharan school have more classical features, with wavy hair and a sharper brow; they tend to be dressed in toga-like robes rather than a loin cloth. Those of the Northern Wei have a more Indian appearance, with narrower faces, stretched ear-lobes, and a more serene aura. By the Tang dynasty, when Buddhism was well developed in China, many of the statues and murals show much plumper, more rounded and amiable looking figures. By the Tang dynasty, the Apsara (flying deity, similar to an angel in Christianity) was a popular subject for the artists.

It is also interesting to trace the changes in styles along the length of the route, from Kuqa in the west, via the Turfan area and Dunhuang, to the Maijishan grottos about 350 kilometres from Xian, and then as far into China as Datong. The Northern Wei dynasty, that is perhaps the most responsible for the spread of Buddhism in China, started the construction of the Yungang grottos in northern Shanxi province. When the capital of the Northern Wei was transfered to Luoyang, the artists and masons started again from scratch, building the Longmen grottos. These two more 'Chinese' grottos emphasised carving and statuary rather than the delicate murals of the Taklimakan regions, and the figures are quite impressive in their size; the largest figure at Yungang measures more than 17 metres in height, second only in China to the great Leshan Buddha in Sichuan, which was constructed in the early 8th Century. The figures are mostly depicted in the 'reassurance' pose, with right hand raised, as an apology to the adherents of the Buddhist faith for the period of persecution that had occurred during the early Northern Wei Dynasty before construction was started.

The Buddhist faith gave birth to a number of different sects in Central Asia. Of these, the 'Pure Land' and 'Chan' (Zen) sects were particularly strong, and were even taken beyond China; they are both still flourishing in Japan.

Christianity also made an early appearance on the scene. The Nestorian sect was outlawed in Europe by the Roman church in 432 A.D., and its followers were driven eastwards. From their foothold in Northern Iran, merchants brought the faith along the Silk Road, and the first Nestorian church was consecrated at Changan in 638 A.D. This sect took root on the Silk Road, and survived many later attempts to wipe them out, lasting into the fourteenth century. Many Nestorian writings have been found with other documents at Dunhuang and Turfan. Manichaeism, a third century Persian religion, also influenced the area, and had become quite well developed by the beginning of the Tang Dynasty.

The Greatest Years

The height of the importance of the Silk Road was during the Tang dynasty, with relative internal stability in China after the divisions of the earlier dynasties since the Han. The individual states has mostly been assimilated, and the threats from marauding peoples was rather less.

During this period, in the seventh century, the Chinese traveller Xuan Zhuang crossed the region on his way to obtain Buddhist scriptures from India. He followed the northern branch round the Taklimakan on his outward journey, and the southern route on his return; he carefully recorded the cultures and styles of Buddhism along the way. On his return to the Tang capital at Changan, he was permitted to build the 'Great Goose Pagoda' in the southern half of the city, to house the more than 600 scriptures that he had brought back from India. He is still seen by the Chinese as an important influence in the development of Buddhism in China, and his travels were dramatised by in the popular classic 'Tales of a Journey to the West'.

The art and civilisation of the Silk Road achieved its highest point in the Tang Dynasty. Changan, as the starting point of the route, as well as the capital of the dynasty, developed into one of the largest and most cosmopolitan cities of the time. By 742 A.D., the population had reached almost two million, and the city itself covered almost the same area as present-day Xian, considerably more than within the present walls of the city. The 754 A.D. census showed that five thousand foreigners lived in the city; Turks, Iranians, Indians and others from along the Road, as well as Japanese, Koreans and Malays from the east. Many were missionaries, merchants or pilgrims, but every other occupation was also represented. Rare plants, medicines, spices and other goods from the west were to be found in the bazaars of the city. It is quite clear, however, despite the exotic imports, that the Chinese regarded all foreigners as barbarians; the gifts provided for the Emperors by foreign rulers were simply considered as tribute from vassal states.

After the Tang, however, the traffic along the road subsided, along with the grotto building and art of the period. The Five Dynasties period did not maintain the internal stability of the Tang dynasty, and again neighbouring states started to plunder the caravans. China was partially unified again in the Song dynasty, but the Silk Road was not as important as it had been in the Tang.

From the point of view of those in the far west, China was still an unknown territory, and silk production was not understood. Since the days of Alexander the Great, there had been some knowledge of India, but there was no real knowledge of, or contact with, the 'Seres' until about the 7th century, when information started to filter along the Road. It was at this time that the rise of Islam started to affect Asia, and a curtain came down between the east and west. Trade relations soon resumed, however, with the Moslems playing the part of middlemen. The sea route to China was explored at this time, and the 'Sea Silk

Route' was opened, eventually holding a more important place than the land route itself, as the land route became less profitable.

But the final shake-up that occurred was to come from a different direction; the hoards from the grasslands of Mongolia.

The Mongols

Trade along the route was adversely affected by the strife which built up between the Christian and Moslem worlds. The Crusades brought the Christian world a little nearer to Central Asia, but the unified Moslem armies under Saladin drove them back again. In the Fourth Crusade, the forces of Latin Christianity scored a triumph over their Greek rivals, with the capture of Constantinople (Istanbul). However, it was not the Christians who finally split the Moslem world, but the Mongols from the east. Whilst Europe and Western Asia were torn by religious differences, the Mongols had only the vaguest of religious beliefs. Several of the tribes of Turkestan which had launched offensives westwards towards Persia and Arabia, came to adopt Islam, and Islam had spread far across Central Asia, but had not reached as far as the tribes which wandered the vast grasslands of Mongolia.

These nomadic peoples had perfected the arts of archery and horsemanship. With an eye to expanding their sphere of influence, they met in 1206 and elected a leader for their unified forces; he took the title Great Khan. Under the leadership of Genghis Khan, they rapidly proceeded to conquer a huge region of Asia.

The former Han city of Jiaohe, to the west of Turfan, was decimated by the Mongols as they passed through on their way westwards. The Empire they carved out enveloped the whole of Central Asia from China to Persia, and stretched as far west as the Mediterranean. This Mongol empire was maintained after Genghis' death, with the western section of the empire divided into three main lordships, falling to various of his descendents as lesser Khans, and with the eastern part remaining under the rule of the Great Khan, a title which was inherited from by Kublai Khan. Kubilai completed the conquest of China, subduing the Song in the South of the country, and established the Yuan dynasty.

The partial unification of so many states under the Mongol Empire allowed a significant interaction between cultures of different regions. The route of the Silk Road became important as a path for communication between different parts of the Empire, and trading was continued. Although less 'civilised' than people in the west, the Mongols were more open to ideas. Kubilai Khan, in particular, is reported to have been quite sympathetic to most religions, and a large number of people of different nationalities and creeds took part in the trade across Asia, and settled in China. The most popular religion in China at the time was Daoism, which at first the Mongols favoured. However, from the middle of the thirteenth century onwards, buddhist influence increased, and the early lamaist Buddhism from Tibet was particularly favoured. The two religions existed side by side for a long period during the Yuan dynasty. This religious liberalism was extended to all; Christianity first made headway in China in this period, with the first Roman Catholic arch-bishopric set up in Beijing in 1307. The Nestorian church was quite widespread in China; Jews and Moslems also populated several of the major cities, though they do not seem to have made many converts.

It was at this time that Europeans first ventured towards the lands of the 'Seres'. The earliest were probably Fransiscan friars who are reported to have visited the Mongolian city of Karakorum. The first Europeans to arrive at Kubilai's court were Northern European traders, who arrived in 1261. However, the most well known and best documented visitor was the Italian Marco Polo. As a member of a merchant family from Venice, he was a good businessman and a keen observer. Starting in 1271, at the age of only seventeen, his travels with his father and uncle took him across Persia, and then along the southern branch of the Silk Road, via Khotan, finally ending at the court of Kubilai Khan at Khanbalik, the site of present-day Beijing, and the summer palace, better known as Xanadu. He travelled quite extensively in China, before returning to Italy by ship, via Sumatra and India to Hormuz and Constantinople.

He describes the way of life in the cities and small kingdoms through which his party passed, with particular interest on the trade and marriage customs. His classification of other races centre mainly on their religion, and he looks at things with the eyes of one brought up under the auspices of the Catholic Church; it is therefore not surprising that he has a great mistrust of the Moslems, but he seems to have viewed the 'Idolaters' (Buddhists and Hindus) with more tolerance. He judges towns and countryside in terms of productivity; he appears to be have been quick to observe available sources of food and water along the way, and to size up the products and manufacture techniques of the places they passed through. His description of exotic plants and beasts are sufficiently accurate to be quite easily recognizable, and better than most of the textbooks of the period. He seems to have shown little interest in the history of the regions he was passing through, however, and his reports of military campaigns are full of inaccuracies, though this might be due to other additions or misinformation.

The 'Travels' were not actually written by Marco Polo himself. After his return to the West in 1295, he was captured as a prisoner of war in Genoa, when serving in the Venetian forces. Whilst detained in prison for a year, he met Rustichello of Pisa, a relatively well-known romance writer and a fellow prisoner of war. Rustichello was obviously attracted to the possibilities of writing a romantic tale of adventure about Polo's travels; it should be remembered that the book was written for entertainment rather than as a historic document. However, the collaboration between them, assuming that the story has not been embroidered excessively by Rustichello, gives an interesting picture of life along the Silk Road in the time of the Khans. Some of the tales are no doubt due to the romance-writing instincts of Rustichello, and some of those due to Polo are at best third-hand reports from people he met; however, much of the material can be verified against Chinese and Persian records. As a whole, the book captured public notice at the time, and added much to what was known of Asian geography, customs and natural history.

'NEW SILK ROAD' AND CHINA'S HEGEMONIC AMBITIONS

Analyst Siegfried Wolf tells DW that China's "One Belt, One Road" initiative is not only economically burdensome for Asian countries, it would also trigger serious domestic and geopolitical conflicts in the region.DW: How would you gauge the success of the "One Belt, One Road" (OBOR) summit in China? Siegfried O Wolf: Only less than a half of the countries officially involved with the OBOR initiative, which is also known as the "New Silk Road," sent their delegations to the "Building the Belt and Road: Concept, Practice and China's Contribution" summit in Beijing. A number of countries crucial to OBOR's success - India for instance - are still undecided regarding their involvement in the project. The United States sent a team led by Matt Pottinger, special assistant to President Donald Trump and senior director for East Asia at the National Security Council, a relatively low-profile delegation. The European Union, meanwhile, sent out a "common message" outlining its main interests and concerns about OBOR. It is obvious that apart from China's official rhetoric about the initiative, and the enthusiasm shown by Pakistan, Russia, Iran, and Turkey, the two-day summit that started on Sunday highlighted unease and concerns about China's ambitious New Silk Road project.

The summit failed to allay concerns about Beijing's bilateralism, a lack of transparency, and the corruption issues related to OBOR. Also China is unwilling to address the EU's objections regarding the protection of market rules, norms, technical standards, and economic interaction. The summit's policy document confirms the increasing criticism of the project, especially the one leveled by the EU, which was represented in the China summit by the EU Commission's Vice President, Jyrki Katainen. Is OBOR really an economic game changer for the participating countries as claimed by Beijing?

The OBOR comes not only with a huge financial burden for the future generations, it will also create severe socio-economic and political problems for the participating countries. For example, in Pakistan, which is home to OBOR's flagship project, the China-Pakistan Economic Corridor (CPEC), the initiative is accompanied by economic, political, and social problems such as an exclusion of the regions in decision-making processes; exploitation of regional resources without adequate remuneration; land grabbing; forced displacement of the local communities; internal migration, and massive distortions of fair and free economic competition. In this context, one should emphasize that Beijing clearly underestimates the resilience of local conflict dynamics and geopolitical rivalries. It is also interesting to note that many of the OBOR projects have actually nothing to do with OBOR and have long been in planning or in discussion.

For the sake of OBOR's promotion, all old and new development projects have been merged with this initiative. What are the European Union's major concerns regarding OBOR? Do you think that Brussels and Beijing can overcome their issues in the coming months? Despite OBOR's positive aspects, potential cooperation partners like the EU remain skeptical.

There are several reasons behind this mistrust. Firstly, there is the problem that OBOR has no formal institutional structure. Secondly, China prefers to negotiate the OBOR projects in bilateral arrangements, which was also confirmed in the summit. This does not favor the establishment of a multilateral dialogue which the EU espouses.

Also, there is a lack of transparency in decision-making combined with an insufficient level of communication by Chinese authorities regarding OBOR. Consequently, it seems that China cooperates with EU institutions when it finds suitable for its objectives, otherwise it deals with individual states. An effective OBOR dialogue platform between the EU and China is still missing. This would ensure that the EU economic actors have a fair chance to compete for business through open, transparent and non-discriminatory procurement procedures with Chinese competitors.

As long as China doesn't make any effort to bridge the gap between OBOR and different EU approaches, move toward multilateralism, and address the EU values based on good governance, the rule of law, human rights and democracy, skepticism regarding OBOR will persist. Some analysts say China's aiming to increase its global hegemony through OBOR. Do you agree? The OBOR project is the most ambitious economic activity undertaken by China since the founding of the People's Republic in 1949.

It should be seen as Beijing's effort to extend its economic success of the last decades to a geopolitical sphere. China claims that OBOR is based on principles of mutual benefit and that it is not interested in interfering in the participating countries' internal affairs. Beijing also claims that it does not seek to increase its sphere of influence or exercise hegemony. But the current developments linked with the OBOR implementation show that Beijing will be - or already has been - drawn into existing inter- and intra-state conflicts, for instance the Indian-Pakistani rivalry.

Therefore, OBOR must be identified as a Chinese attempt to win over new strategic partners and build a multi-polar world order conducive for China's national interests. Should the participating countries with weaker economies be careful about their level of involvement in OBOR? OBOR could intensify existing governance problems, especially economic accountability and corruption. It could also help empower governments that have a poor track record on democracy, human rights, security and development.

The initiative also has long-term geopolitical implications; it increases political and economic dependencies. In this context, one must not forget that China's financial support in the OBOR framework is primarily based on loans. As such, participation in OBOR can produce a tremendous, unsustainable debt burden with disastrous consequences for the weaker economies. How's the Trump administration in Washington viewing OBOR and

China's global ambitions? Despite the fact that the US sent a low-level delegation to the summit in Beijing, and that it "recognizes the importance" of OBOR, Washington has kept its distance from the project. The Trump administration has not formulated a clear-cut policy on it. Washington is concerned that OBOR is creating "fault-lines" that will have negative implications for US interests in Asia. It is emboldening countries that have a clear anti-US stance like Iran and Russia or that are interested in reducing the US leverage in the region, such as Pakistan.

We see that China is getting increasingly involved in regional security and defense initiatives, for example the multilateral talks on Afghanistan organized by Russia. Furthermore, Washington also perceives OBOR as a threat to its interests in the Asia-Pacific region. Despite these concerns, the US does not consider OBOR as an economic threat, especially in terms of its trade relations with Europe that are based on a decades-old economic and political alignment. Siegfried O.

SILK ROAD INITIATIVE CONNECTS COUNTRIES ON PATH OF PROSPERITY

It was a dream with world-evolving suggestions, an unfurling arrangement that would weave quite a bit of Asia, Europe, Africa, Oceania and the Middle East considerably more firmly together through an interwoven of discretion, new framework and facilitated commerce zones. In China, where it has been enormous news, the plan's modelers call it the Belt and Road Initiative, to be specific the Silk Road Economic Belt and the 21st Century Maritime Silk Road.

However for some individuals in Europe, this fabulous configuration, for all its undoubted significance and intense, broad desire that are driving it, has remained generally obscure. In any case, a few weeks back it took solid shape. On a visit to Pakistan on April 20, Chinese President Xi Jinping divulged the principal real venture to be subsidized by the $40 billion Silk Road Fund that China set up to make the Belt and Road Initiative a reality.

The project was a £1 billion hydropower plant on the Jhelum River in north eastern Pakistan. The Karot Hydropower Project, which is being built by a subsidiary of China Three Gorges Corp, is to begin construction by the end of this year, and was the subject of just one of 51 agreements worth a total of $46 billion (£30 billion) signed by China and Pakistan during the president's visit.

Kamel Mellahi, a professor of strategic management at Warwick Business School, said the investment would shorten China's energy import route from the Middle East and transform Pakistan into a regional economic hub.

"This is China's Silk Road strategy in action," he said. "Regional connectivity is the main objective of the strategy, and there is little doubt that we are going to see similar — albeit not this large — Chinese investment projects in other parts of Asia. It's a win-win project for all involved." In April, a government official working on the Belt and Road Initiative, Ou Xiaoli, said China's leadership had already approved a list of big-ticket infrastructure projects.

Although details about the location and nature of those other projects were yet to be made public, the news came after official documents issued in March confirmed the scope of the plan China hopes to forge in consultation with more than 60 countries and regions. The "vision and proposed action plan" issued by China's State Council called for stakeholders to "jointly push forward the construction of international trunk passageways and form an infrastructure network connecting all sub-regions in Asia, and between Asia, Europe and Africa, step by step".

It also revealed that China has been advocating a network of free trade and bonded zones, and massive cross-border financial reform, potentially across three continents.

'Flexibility of mind'

The initiative has dominated discussion in political, business and media circles in China, and has begun to gain more attention in Central and Southeast Asia. But in Europe, the Belt and

Road Initiative has continued to be accompanied by a question mark. So what exactly is it?

The idea, first floated by President Xi in late 2013, was to create contemporary equivalents of the ancient Silk Road trade route that linked Asia and the Mediterranean. However, the modern belt and road would attempt to go well beyond bales of Chinese silk on swaying camel backs or crates of spices crossing oceans on trade winds. Professor Kerry Brown, director of the Sydney University China Studies Center, said the initiative would seek to create a "massive free trade zone", a "belt of prosperity" and "an area of common economic interest" that in part leveraged the shared cultural and historical narrative of the Silk Road. "It's a relatively easy way of China demonstrating more regional importance without people leaping up and down and saying, 'This is China being too domineering.' It stresses reciprocity," he said.

"Presumably, it's going to involve things that all the countries (involved) want to embrace. "So far, the idea has been embraced. There are a lot of other countries keen on it. People haven't been getting too uneasy." While the scope and scale of China's initiative remained hazy, Prof Rana Mitter, director of the University of Oxford China Centre, said what could be interpreted as a lack of detail may be planning flexibility on the part of China.

"I suspect there's been a great deal of planning behind the scenes in various think tanks and institutions in China to put flesh on the bones of the idea, but I suspect there's also a certain amount of flexibility of mind," he said. Ever since the era of opening-up and reform, there's been a willingness to be flexible on economic thinking in China. "It will be likely that, in this particular case, there will be a certain amount of understanding that one will have to adapt to circumstances as the policies are put forward and things actually change."

Sheng Shiliang, a researcher at the State Council's Development Research Center, one of the think tanks that has helped to shape the Belt and Road Initiative, described it as a means for countries to "connect development strategies with each other and make their respective advantages complementary to each other". The connections would be literal, Mr Sheng said, creating physical trade routes and integrated zones of economic collaboration that stretch north, west and south of China. "The belt emphasises creating passages (from China's) west and south," he said. "It includes a road that will connect to Europe through Central Asia and Russia, a road that connects (China) with the Persian Gulf and the Mediterranean Sea through Central Asia and West Asia, and a route through Southeast Asia, South Asia and the Indian Ocean.

"The road will head southwards. It will include two routes, one from coastal ports in China to the Indian Ocean through the South China Sea that eventually goes to Europe, and another from coastal ports in China to the South Pacific Ocean through the South China Sea." Arterial roads suitable for freight and heavy traffic, new airports and deep-water ports, and international, conventional and high-speed rail lines have all been options either predicted by experts or mooted by the Chinese government. In the Pakistan deal, almost all of these options have been employed.

Prof Brown said a high-speed railway linking China to places such as Europe and Russia was a "perfectly doable deal". "The idea of having fast trains to get from Beijing to Moscow in a couple of days, or even into Europe, would be revolutionary," he said. "It has actually been talked about. It's not an issue of technology. The capital probably is there. It's kind of a question of all parties agreeing and feeling like they get something, and (then working out) who pays what."

Bu Shaohua, a research assistant with the Ministry of Foreign Affairs' Research Institute, said participating countries would be connected by a patchwork of old and new infrastructure. "It's a mixture of both (old and new)," he said. "In some areas we need to improve the railways that exist, but in other areas we need to build new ones, like those connecting Kazakhstan, Turkmenistan and Iran, and the south Caucasus."

Beyond physically connecting participating countries, the initiative would also seek to create trade and financial compatibility. This, experts said, is the wild card in the deck that could prove to be either the easiest or most difficult to play. "At present, the level of economic collaboration between China and other countries along the road is not good enough to set up free trade zones, but there is no doubt that free trade zones will eventually become a reality," Mr Sheng said.

Asia has lacked a common economic framework for a long time, according to Prof Brown, who said Asian economies do not easily work together because they were at different levels of development.

"In one fell swoop, this Belt and Road Initiative kind of creates a world in which, economically, everyone's path ends at the door of China," he said. "But it's not a path that people are unwilling to walk. It's not a political domination; it's more like a stressing of mutual benefits."

Investment partners

For all the mystery that has enshrouded the initiative for some people, the biggest question that hangs in the air may be over who is going to pay for what. Fifty-seven countries have signed on as founding members of the new China-initiated Asian Infrastructure Investment Bank, the establishment of which Brown said was a sign China is "willing to offer some capital support".

In addition to the $100 billion for the bank's coffers, China has also pumped $40 billion into the Silk Road Fund, and in March private investors created the Green Silk Road Fund with 30 billion yuan (£3.2 million). While Prof Brown said it was possible China would provide some countries along the road with low-interest, long-term loans, similar to those given in Africa for large infrastructure projects, he believed that for the most part Beijing would be seeking investment partners.

"They will probably look for reciprocal deals where part of the money comes from China and part of the money comes from elsewhere," he said. "They would want a pretty big benefit, or it would have to be a pretty important sector for them to go ahead solo. "I don't think China at the moment is in a position where it is going to be a big giver of charity. It wants reciprocity and shared risk, and I think that's more sustainable."

The other big question international commentators have been grappling with is China's motives for the Belt and Road Initiative. Some pundits have seen it primarily as a push for more diplomatic clout. Prof Mitter said the initiative was a new vision of geopolitical order in which China is seen as a co-operative, responsible power that brings something to the table in terms of a recasting of order. "The idea of the Silk Road strategy, I think, is very much to try to go to the next stage in terms of this idea or a new offer in international order. I think the only way that such an order can be successful is if there are advantages to be found on all sides " he said.

"Clearly other actors, whether it is countries or international institutions, are not going to sign up to a new vision of order where they are going to be disadvantaged compared with the present scenario. Therefore, if China is taking a leadership role in this, it has to think very carefully and very strategically about how it can bring that about." Prof Yang Cheng at East China Normal University said that beyond politics, China's economy needed the plan to work, particularly because making landlocked western China a trade gateway to Europe and Asia and the Middle East would provide the long-sought-after springboard for the region to develop.

"We need it in both political and economic terms," he said. "As China is undergoing economic transformation, economic growth is slowing down. Against the background of this new normal (lower GDP growth as a result of economic restructuring), we should find a new engine for development. So we need to seek new markets to export our products. "Another domestic problem is that the level of development in the eastern, central and western regions of China is not balanced. The central and western regions lag behind the eastern region (in turns of development and) in going global. This problem is urgent because it affects our sustainable development."

Prof Brown said it was possible that, like in Africa, Chinese companies would most likely benefit from any infrastructure boom in Asia driven by the initiative. In the case of the recent Pakistan deal, Chinese companies have won contracts to build and operate a number of facilities, including the new hydropower dam. However, he said just because the Belt and Road Initiative was good for China does not mean it was not good for other countries. Inherent in the need to get countries on board was the opportunity for other players to get what they want, he said.

"They (participating countries) can probably get a lot from this engagement if they are very clear about what they want," he said. Prof Mitter agreed: "One would imagine that there would be a whole variety of people coming out of Beijing going and saying to a variety of potential partners, 'What is it that will help you to buy into this vision?'"

Beyond Asia, he said he saw clear opportunities for Europe, and added that one thing that would be advantageous for Britain and Europe as a whole was access to a much more integrated trading area in Eurasia.

"What seem key here are free trade agreements," he said. "If free trade agreements are actually signed up and genuinely offer a reduction of the current investment barriers that exist in large parts of the region, that will be a huge advantage." Experts said the benefits of the initiative could go two ways, with participating countries able to get more access to sell their goods and services in China's growing consumer market.

That may still be far off. As Prof Mitter put it, China's challenge of juggling a changing domestic economy at home while pushing forward with the Belt and Road Initiative outside its borders could not be understated. However, when it came to the kind of financial reform, new infrastructure and free trade agreements called for in the initiative, Prof Brown said China had a big incentive "to do it, and do it quickly".

"I think they'll want to see some kind of specific returns soon, even in the next seven or eight years," he said. "They will want to see action and joint projects and some increases in trade volumes... They are thinking 10, 20 and 30 years down the line. Its both a short- and long-term strategy."

21ST CENTURY MARITIME SILK ROAD FROM A GLOBAL PERSPECTIVE

In the twenty-first century, countries have become more inter-connected by the ocean in conducting market, technological and information exchanges. The world is now in an era that values maritime cooperation and development. China's proposal to build a Maritime Silk Road conforms with larger developments in economic globalization and taps into common interests that China shares with countries along the route. The goal is to forge a community of interest with political mutual trust, integrated economies, inclusive culture and inter-connectivity. The construction of a 21st Century Maritime Silk Road is a global ini-tiative that pursues win-win results through cross-border cooperation. It is thus of great importance to view it from the perspective of multi-polarization, economic globalization and the co-existence and ba-lancing of cooperation and competition.

Building a 21st Century Maritime Silk Road will help stimulate all-round maritime opening-up and benefit ASEAN and relevant countries. Oceans contain a treasure trove of resources for sustainable development. China is currently at a critical stage in its economic reform process and must pay more attention to the ocean. As mentioned in the resolution of the Third Plenum, "[China] needs to enhance opening-up in coastal regions and boost the connectivity construction with neighboring countries and regions to spur all-round opening-up."

The Maritime Silk Road of the 21st century will further unite and expand common interests between China and other countries situated along the route, activate potential growth and achieve mutual benefits in wider areas. The Maritime Silk Road will extend southward from China's ports, through the South China Sea, the Straits of Malacca, Lombok and Sunda and then along the north Indian Ocean to the Persian Gulf, Red Sea and Gulf of Aden. In other words, the Road will extend from Asia to the Middle East, East Africa and Europe, and it will mainly rely on ASEAN countries. Building the Maritime

Silk Road will connect China's ports with other countries through maritime connectivity, intercity cooperation and economic cooperation. On the one hand, the Road will strengthen the economic basis for China to cooperate with countries along the route and better connect Europe and Asia. On the other hand, the Road will facilitate the development of the Regional Comprehensive Economic Partnership (RCEP), bringing benefits to China, ASEAN and other countries along the road.

The Maritime Silk Road will increase trust and regional peace and stability

As the world's economic and political center shifts towards the Asia Pacific, the region has stepped into a stage of geopolitics characterized by intersecting, overlapping and conflicting interests. By facilitating communication between countries along the road, the Maritime Silk Road will help build a community that represents the common concerns, interests and expectations of all countries. The community is expected to guide and support a peaceful and stable Asia Pacific landscape.

Moreover, the Maritime Silk Road will further bring together the "Silk Road Economic Belt," the "Bangladesh-China-India-Myanmar Economic Corridor" and the "China-Pakistan Economic Corridor" that together connect Europe and Asia. Such connections will greatly enhance China and other countries' abilities to develop economically while limiting external risks. The Maritime Silk Road will also enhance cooperation in non-traditional security areas while maintaining maritime security.

MARITIME SECURITY: CHINA, INDIA AND THE IMPACT OF THE UNITED STATES

In this context, the traditional land powers of India and China have recognized the importance of naval power, and are subsequently in the process of modernizing their navies. In addition to this regional buildup, the United States fundamentally impacts maritime security in the region due to its hegemonic dominance, both in terms of naval capabilities and technological superiority. The collision of interests between these three nations defines the geopolitical environment within the Asia Pacific.

In the past two decades China has rapidly attempted to modernize its navy, with military expenditures increasing by over 140 percent since 1997. Recent military modernization within China has been focused towards upgrading its naval capabilities, and developing a blue-water navy capable of power-projection throughout the Asia Pacific.

An analysis of Chinese naval modernization can best be explored through their drive for a modern aircraft-carrier. In 2009, Defence Minister Ling Guanglie announced that the Chinese navy will be equipped with two aircraft carriers by as early as 2015. China then launched its first aircraft carrier in August 2011, which was a refitted version of a Soviet carrier. While the carrier is currently only fit of training purposes, and will not be a fully operational combat vessel for years to come, it represents China's growing naval power. The attainment of an aircraft carrier provides China with the traditional symbol of a world power while also providing the capability to secure the SLOCs through which its oil and resource exports have to travel through.

India has similarly been modernizing its military capabilities. India doubled its defence budget between 1994 and 2004, and currently has plans to spend US$40 billion on military expansion over the next four years. India's naval modernization, however, has been arguably more efficient and effective than China's, as the former has focused on quality over quantity, and invested in state-of-the-art weapons systems.

Within India, there is recognition that a strong naval power is not only vital to upholding its security interests, but also for its continued prosperity. India already has possession of one aircraft carrier, and importantly, is planning to increase this number to a total of three carriers by 2020. India's drive for maritime dominance has recently intensified with its 2012-2013 defence budget increasing by 13 percent, and with the navy receiving the largest share in comparison to the other arms of its military.

Already, Indian naval modernization efforts have seen commendable results. As recently as last month, India launched two new classes of submarines, including a nuclear powered submarine, and conducted the first flight of the naval version of its light combat aircraft.

A main source of competition between China and India is in the field of energy security. Access to and transportation of valuable resources has increasingly meant that geopolitical processes define strategic policy in the region.

India does not want to see a Chinese naval build-up in the region, yet it is clear that China has pressed its maritime agenda into the region. In response to this, we see India trying to counter-balance China. As the Chinese navy modernizes, India has become increasingly wary of being encircled in the Indian Ocean.

For example, China's "string of pearls" strategy, which refers to the negotiation of basing rights along the sea route which connects China to the Middle East, does not include interaction with India. Indian policy-makers increasingly are worried about the future control of SLOCs and the security of India's energy. Due to this "string of pearls," for example, China is able to check India's rise, and monitor their maritime exercises due to the leverage they gain with having basing rights in Pakistan. Furthermore, China's strategy allows access to routes that bypass the Malacca Strait. This impacts India's geoeconomic stability and regional standing, as any blockade to the strait would heavily damage India, while China would have an alternative route it can rely on.

It is India's relationship with the United States, however, that is the most important tool for India's counter-balancing of China. Both China and India have been suspicious about the other's relationship with the United States, yet both have been trying to foster a strategic relationship with Washington. India currently has the more strategically advantageous relationship, which is a great worry for China. It is perceived that China is being countered while India is being bolstered as the regional power. The United States is relying upon India to secure the crucial sea lanes, and has increasingly been conceding leadership of the Indian Ocean to India. Former Secretary of State Colin Powell has publicly stated that "India has the potential to keep the peace in the vast Indian Ocean and its periphery."

China's ability to uphold its maritime security in the region largely rests on its ability to operate under the naval dominance of the United States. Even though there have been friendly military exchanges between the two countries, their strategic trust remains very low.

For example, China's reaction to the U.S. proposal for a Global Maritime Partnership was met with negativity and distrust. It was at first suggested that such a partnership would make great breakthroughs in Sino-U.S. relations, but analysts from within China claimed that such a proposal only furthered U.S. domination of maritime affairs at the global level.

A defining feature of the geopolitical environment within the Asia Pacific in the years to come will be whether or not China and India will be able to uphold their maritime interests without unnecessary escalation or confrontation. The United States is central to this scenario, due to its role as regional hegemon and its capacity to provide India a strategic advantage by countering Chinese naval ambitions.

INDIAN OCEAN MARINE AFFAIRS CO-OPERATION (IOMAC)

The IOMAC programme of co-operation was developed on the basis of the identification of national priorities at the Preparatory Meeting in June 1985, and deliberations thereon at the Consultative and Final Phases of the First Conference (IOMAC-I) in July 1985 and January 1987.

In view of the considerable range of varying national requirements and the wide scope of activities envisaged, it was found necessary to draw from the programme salient items of common interest which were brought together in a more focussed plan of action. For purposes of practical implementation, the

Secretariat undertook to prepare and implement a work programme under the guidance of the Standing Committee. The programme of

co-operation was based on the deliberations of the Consultative Phase of the First Conference and provided an identification of areas for co-operation in respect of each of the principal sectors of IOMAC activity: marine science, technology and ocean services; living resources; non-living resources; ocean law, policy and management; marine transport and communications; and the marine environment.

The Second Conference (IOMAC-II) reviewed the programme of co-operation and provided an appraisal and supplementary guidelines for future activities. In the plan of action, specific areas of co-operation were identified for implementation on an immediate, medium- or long-term basis. The First Conference noted that certain items for immediate implementation could of necessity also have a medium- and/ or long-term character. The rapid implementation of a wide-ranging work programme was a major achievement of IOMAC.

Initiation of a number of new activities in areas not fully addressed by earlier and existing programmes, as well as organisational mandates, served to demonstrate the usefulness and effectiveness of a collective regional undertaking committed to serving national needs. IOMAC organised comprehensive programmes of activity in each of the principle sectors through expert meetings followed by practical measures. Up to the mid-1990s, the following were the salient aspects of IOMAC activities:

Marine Science, Technology and Ocean Services

On a proposal made by Tanzania, the Conference adopted the Resolution on a New Era of Indian Ocean Exploration which called for a systematic, co-ordinated long-term collective international effort to explore the Indian Ocean along the lines of the International Indian Ocean Expedition (1962-1965). This new effort, however, was required to concentrate on near-shore areas and to give emphasis to the needs of developing states, as well as to secure their participation.

Taken in the light of the seaward extension of national jurisdiction and the new framework for the conduct of marine scientific research under the Law of the Sea Convention of 1982, the IOMAC Declaration of a New Era of Indian Ocean Exploration was expected to go some way in providing reassurance to developed nations conducting marine scientific research, as much as to strengthen the capabilities of developing Indian Ocean states in this field.

A major IOMAC international marine science symposium was held in 1992. This provided an opportunity to review existing programmes, national priorities and new avenues for co-operative activities in the region. In addition to the important IOMAC-UN Technical Workshops held in Colombo (1986) and Karachi (1989) on space technology applications, IOMAC prepared a manual on Remote Sensing Applications for the Indian Ocean region, began initiating a number of pilot projects, and held a training workshop in the region in 1992.

Living Resources

The IOMAC- I Preparatory Meeting, as well as the First Conference at its Consultative Phase in 1985, and the Final Phase in 1987, for the first time took cognisance at intergovernmental level of the rapid development of a major industrial-scale distant-water tuna fishery in the Indian Ocean in the early 1980s, and called for the early establishment of an appropriate regulatory body for the management of Indian Ocean tuna.

Subsequent IOMAC meetings, especially at the Standing Committee, kept relevant developments under review, and acted as a catalyst for deliberations on the establishment of such a body, which eventually emerged under the auspices of the Food and Agriculture Organisation (FAO) in the form of the Indian Ocean Tuna Commission (IOTC).

In January 1989, a group of IOMAC fisheries and legal experts met in Jakarta to prepare common positions for intergovernmental deliberations on the subject. In this context, IOMAC had consistently maintained the importance of the participation of distant water fishing nations (DWFNs) in a future management regime that would ensure its effectiveness, as well as emphasising the importance of the increased participation of developing Indian Ocean states in harnessing the resource.

Furthermore, the Seventh Meeting of the IOMAC Standing Committee adopted a Declaration banning the use of large-scale drift nets in the Indian Ocean.

Non-Living Resources

In July 1988, the IOMAC Meeting on Offshore Prospecting for Mineral Resources in the Indian Ocean, hosted by the Government of Pakistan in Karachi, generated a strong intergovernmental mandate for initiating a programme of co-operation in this field, with the collaboration and assistance of states with technologically advanced capabilities in this field.

Ocean Law, Policy and Management

IOMAC regularly conducted marine affairs management training in collaboration with the International Ocean Institute (IOI). The annual IOMAC-IOI Marine Affairs Training Programmes were held in Arusha, Kuala Lumpur, Cairo, and Mauritius. Each 10-week course accommodated 25 participants from developing Indian Ocean states and provided training in integrated ocean/marine affairs management to mid-level career officers responsible for managing marine activities in their countries.

Maritime Transport and Communications

The Second Conference endorsed a number of proposals made by the IOMAC Meeting of Experts in Shipping and Port Development hosted by the Government of Kenya and held in Mombasa in August 1990. In July 1991, the Seventh Meeting of the Standing Committee adopted, and recommended for governmental approval, terms of reference for the IOMAC Association of Shipping and Port Authorities. It was envisaged that some of the co-operative measures identified would be taken up for implementation by the Association.

Marine Environment

Dumping of hazardous waste and toxic materials, pollution of the sea by oil, and potential adverse impacts on the marine environment of proposed deep seabed mining were the relevant issues here. In 1988, the Third Meeting of the IOMAC Standing Committee reviewed these specific aspects of concern to Indian Ocean countries and recommended that the Secretary-General identify an effective mechanism to monitor and develop regional capabilities of coastal states for prevention of such environmental hazards with assistance from the competent international agencies.

Following consultations between the International Maritime Organisation (IMO) and the IOMAC Secretariat, the Seventh Meeting of the Standing Committee requested the Secretariat to take necessary steps in consultation with the IMO, United Nations Environment Programme and other interested entities for the early establishment of an Indian Ocean network. In the mid-1990s preparatory work was under way for the convening of an Indian Ocean Environment Conference which was expected to review the health of the Indian Ocean, identify environmental problems, and determine a common programme for co-operation in this field.

The Interests and Needs of Land-Locked States

Accommodation of the interests of land-locked nations in the context of marine affairs was recognised very early by IOMAC as a logical corollary to the rights of land-locked countries in respect of access to living resources, and access to and from the sea. Although a technical meeting on the subject was planned under the joint co-ordination of Uganda and Nepal, this was deferred in favour of an expert study on key issues and trends.

Training, Information and Other Fields Relevant to Co-operation in Marine Affairs

Work on the establishment of an Indian Ocean Marine Affairs and Aquatic Resources Information System (IO-

MAARIS) commenced in 1987, at the Second Meeting of the Standing Committee. The Committee reviewed and endorsed the IOMAC/United Nations Conference on Trade and Development/United Nations Development Programme sponsored Mission Report, which detailed three major components of the proposed system: the institutional element involving the creation of three nodes in the region as a first step; a training and educational element; and an outputs element. The IOMAC Information Workshop held in Jakarta in February 1990 reviewed and identified a number of practical measures for putting into operation the proposed information system. The Secretariat also published an Indian Ocean Newsletter which provided an update on IOMAC activities and other related developments.

By 1998, however, only six states (Indonesia, Kenya, Mauritius, Mozambique, Pakistan and Sri Lanka) had ratified the 1990 Arusha Agreement (IOMAC II), even though a further three (Iran, Nepal and Tanzania) had signed it. In accordance with Article 16 of that agreement, it required ratification by a minimum of eight states to enter into force. Moreover, major Indian Ocean states such as India, Australia and South Africa had not become members of IOMAC for a variety of political reasons.

MARITIME PARTNERSHIPS ARE THE KEY TO BUILDING THE MARITIME SILK ROAD

At a speech before the Indonesian parliament in 2013, President Xi Jinping stated that Southeast Asia has become an important hub for the maritime silk road and that China is willing to enhance maritime cooperation with ASEAN countries, boost maritime partnerships and build a 21st Century Maritime Silk Road. President Xi's speech set forth a clear path for developing road. Enhancing maritime cooperation will be a priority task in building the Maritime Silk Road. The first step will involve China and countries along the route promoting pragmatic maritime cooperation. Connecting multiple regions and uniting wide areas of co-operation, the tasks put forth in the 21st Century Maritime Silk Road will not be achieved in the immediate future. Instead, these tasks call for China and relevant countries to work in a step-by-step and practical manner. Building the Maritime Silk road will require diverse forms of cooperation. With a focus on economic cooperation, the Road will give consideration to all parties involved. It will be based on the existing cooperation mechanisms and platforms and be promoted by China and other countries along the route.

The 21st Century Maritime Silk Road will cover more than 20 countries and regions that share a broad consensus on enhancing exchanges, friendship, promoting development, safety and stability within the region and beyond. The Silk Road has already received positive responses and support from many relevant countries. Greek Prime Minister Antonidis Samaras, for example, made it clear that Greece will "support and actively participate in building the 21st Century Maritime Silk Road proposed by China." The Road runs through a region that is sensitive to international strategy and has complex geopolitics. The countries in the region differ in size, development, history, religion, language and culture. Therefore, the 21st Century Maritime Silk Road will accommodate various countries' demands and apply suitable policies to each country. Meanwhile, the Road must change and consolidate new patterns of cooperation.

China has been building friendships and partnerships with nei-ghboring countries and developing maritime partnerships with its ocean neighbors, providing a solid foundation for cooperation with ASEAN and countries in the region. The 21st Century Maritime Silk Road requires the following efforts: First, consensus must be reached between major countries along the route to enhance maritime cooperation. During high-level dialogues in recent years, the Chinese leadership made maritime cooperation an important topic of bilateral discussions and established the China-ASEAN and China-Indonesia Maritime Cooperation Fund. At the same time, China has actively promoted maritime cooperation between Southeast Asia, South Asia and African countries and established high-level mechanisms between various national maritime departments.

Second, countries must engage in pragmatic cooperation along the route in the areas of trade, the economy, culture and infrastructure. In 2012, the trade volume of countries along the route accounted for 17.9 percent of China's total trade. The contracted turnover in countries along the route accounted for 37.9 percent of China's overseas contracted turnover. People-to-people exchanges between China and ASEAN recently topped 15 million, while two-way students reached more than 170,000.

Third, countries along the route must engage in effective cooperation on ocean and climate change, marine disaster prevention and mitigation, biodiversity preservation and other areas of maritime policy. In 2010, the Indonesia-China Center for Ocean & Climate (ICCOC) was established. In 2013, the China-Thailand Climate and Marine Ecosystem Joint Lab were both launched. In 2012, the Chinese government set up a Marine Scholarship, and from that year onward, the scholarship will sponsor young people from developing countries in Southeast Asia, Africa and Latin America to obtain a master's degree or doctorate in China to enhance the marine capabilities of their own countries.

4

The China's Economics of the Silk Road Economic Belt

On 20 October 2015, RUSI held a day-long workshop in Almaty, Kazakhstan, in collaboration with KIMEP University and the Friedrich Ebert Stiftung (FES). The focus of the workshop was the economics behind the Chinese Silk Road Economic Belt (SREB) and its impact in Central Asia. The key areas of discussion examined the potential benefits that the SREB could bring to participating countries, the integration of the SREB with other economic projects and the various funding mechanisms through which the SREB will be financed. The workshop brought together participants from Almaty, Astana, London, Beijing, Shanghai, New Delhi and Russia, including representatives from academia, the private sector and think tanks.

The first session discussed the real benefits of the SREB to both China and participating countries along the road. There is a risk that the SREB will simply turn Eurasia into a set of transport routes emanating from China, aimed at increasing the volume of Chinese goods going to Europe.

Other than transit fees, China has not made it explicitly clear as to what other value participating in the SREB can add to economic development. Special economic and free-trade zones are one opportunity, such as that of Khorgos on the border of Kazakhstan and China, or those planned for Pakistan.

However, the extent to which these are benefitting Central Asia is still unclear, and those for Pakistan are still under discussion. Kazakhstan's side of this free-trade zone is noticeably less developed than that of China's, highlighting that not all of these projects are implemented to meet maximum potential.

Furthermore, China's emphasis on connectivity as a key goal of the SREB runs the risk of over-emphasising railway development as an end goal, since not all goods are cost-effective to transport by rail.

High-value goods are the ideal product: one participant from Kazakhstan noted that Kazakhstan Temir Zholy, the national railway operator, had begun transporting Apple products from China, cutting down delivery time from sixty days (by sea) to eighteen days (by rail). For the SREB project to be successful, therefore, both Xinjiang, the northwestern Chinese province, and the countries along the Silk Road route need to increase their high-tech manufacturing capacity to produce these high-value goods for transport, neither of which are currently visible.

Understanding of the project has been limited by Beijing's vagueness on practical implementation. The Chinese government's 'Visions and Actions on Jointly Building Silk Road Economic Belt and 21st Century Maritime Silk Road' strategy paper, published by the National Development and Reform Commission (NDRC), emphasises the objectives of the SREB, such as connectivity and greater financial integration. However, it does not give practical detail on how this will be achieved. This approach of laying out a grand vision without detail is typical of the Chinese government. So far there is not even a formally government-endorsed map of the exact routes of the SREB.

The workshop discussion highlighted a potential explanation for this. China's goal may not be to unpack the details itself but instead to seek ideas and engagement from SREB countries to determine where participation can provide most benefit to them. China does not want to limit its options or jeopardise the project's 'inclusivity' by over-defining its approach.

There is an opportunity, therefore, for countries along the SREB to provide proposals back to China. However, there are some practical questions that China will need to address. Although its openended encouragement of connectivity is central to the SREB, certain political and geographical difficulties in implementing this are so far unresolved. Anyone who has travelled within Central Asia knows the difficulty of flying direct between most regional capitals, while land travel between the countries in the region is hindered by longstanding border disputes.

Although the SREB has broadly been received with enthusiasm by Central and South Asia, the lack of clarity around its planned implementation has led to some suspicion.

India stands out as the country in the region most apprehensive of China's plans. As one workshop participant said, 'there is no Indian perspective at the moment', in part due to a perceived lack of information from Beijing. The suspicions relate to whether there is a broader Chinese geopolitical strategy behind the SREB and whether political strings will become attached to China's infrastructure investment.

India's concerns over a geopolitical strategy are mainly due to the maritime element of the '21st Century Maritime Silk Road', which runs through the Indian Ocean. It covers ports in countries located around India, such as Sri Lanka, Maldives and Pakistan, but not India itself. This has raised alarm bells in New Delhi, who perceive China as encroaching on India's waterways. China's investment into the China–Pakistan Economic Corridor (CPEC), which cuts through the disputed areas of Kashmir as well as highlighting China's strong connection with Pakistan, is also a challenge for India. There are areas where India and China can co-operate on this SREB project, such as the Bangladesh–China–India–Burma corridor or areas where both have interests, like Iran. However, India requires more detail and reassurances regarding China's intentions.

A large part of the day's discussion focused on the issue of integrating the SREB with other economic projects. Russia has recently voiced its desire to integrate the SREB with the Eurasian Economic Union (EEU) and Kazakhstan has proposed something similar with its 'Bright Road' (Nurly Zhol) policy.

Although the Bright Road policy, which focuses on infrastructure development, is consistent with the aims of the Chinese project, SREB integration with the EEU is somewhat more complex. As one workshop participant pointed out, the EEU is an organisation with an institutional and regulatory framework, whereas the SREB is more of a 'vision' covering a variety of concrete projects. 'Integrating' these in practice may be difficult. A special economic zone may once again be an answer to this, and the EEU and China are currently exploring this idea. The EEU's external tariffs may present an immediate barrier to increased trade with China, although one benefit is that once this barrier is overcome countries gain access to a significant economic space consisting of five countries. However, to facilitate trade, China and Russia will need to address a number of bilateral trade issues. For example, the Russian–Chinese border currently suffers from excessive bureaucracy that, in particular, prevents cross-border travel and trade.

The third key aspect of the discussions examined the means by which the SREB will be funded. A major tool will be multilateral and national institutions driven by Beijing. China has allocated $29.8 billion to the Asian Infrastructure Investment Bank's (AIIB) overall $100 billion capitalisation and $40 billion to the national Silk Road Fund.

Furthermore, the China Development Bank (CDB) is the lead financial body for the SREB, investing $890 billion into over 900 projects. There are also bilateral funding relations between SREB countries and Chinese provinces.

For example, the recent Tbilisi Silk Road Forum held in Georgia was the first event on the SREB co-sponsored by the Chinese state held outside of China. The principals on the Chinese side were the provincial governments of Xinjiang and Shaanxi. On top of this, China is seeking to stimulate public–private partnerships to help progress the project finance, as well as exploring opportunities of collaboration with other international financial institutions like the Asian Development Bank (ADB), the European Bank for Reconstruction and Development (EBRD) and the European Investment Bank (EIB).

Most participants agreed, however, that the predominant mechanism for SREB co-operation will continue to be bilateral agreements. As one workshop participant mentioned, China recently pledged $46 billion for the China–Pakistan Economic Corridor alone, a number that puts China's commitment into context when it is compared to the total $100 billion capitalisation of the AIIB. This highlights the degree to which China is likely to continue to prioritise bilateral agreements over its multilateral financial vehicles. A note of caution was made regarding the enormity of some of the SREB deals announced. As one participant pointed out, it seems in reality that the CPEC deal included a repackaging – or at least a reinvigoration – of some historical agreements between China and Pakistan, such as the development of Gwadar port and the Karakorum Highway, projects that have been underway for years. This demonstrates a lack of clarity in the detail behind some of these enormous declarations of financial support.

A repeated theme that came up during this discussion related to the broader transparency and governance of the SREB, particularly in participating countries outside of China. One workshop participant highlighted the need for SREB countries to ensure necessary reforms are conducted in the domestic markets to provide a degree of security and flexibility and to avoid an over-reliance on Chinese investment. The slow-down in the Chinese economy may produce constraints on China's ability to meet its ambitious investment programme. A lack of transparency as regards the relevant information has led to questions over China's asset quality. One workshop participant stated that a 'sudden large injection of external cash could exacerbate existing problems [in the domestic economy] rather than help'. Thus, SREB participants should ensure they protect and reform their own markets in preparation for any large investments from China to maximise returns and protect against a lack of transparency in the deals.

Another question mark surrounding China's funding of the SREB projects is the value this produces for China itself. The divestment opportunities or returns China makes on its infrastructure development projects in, for example, Central Asia, remain unclear. Much of the historical bilateral projects have been funded through linked loans, where China provides the funding through loans that have stipulations attached to them, such as the requirement that Chinese companies implement the projects on the ground. In other cases where China's Eximbank or CDB has provided loans to fund projects, it is unclear whether there are any short- or medium-term returns or even security on the investment. One workshop participant pointed out that given the dominance of the state in China's economic policy and the government's long-term vision of investments, China can afford more time to sit on these investments without requiring immediate returns. Moreover, another participant noted that some projects, such as when Eximbank loaned the money for the high-voltage power line recently unveiled in Kyrgyzstan, provide the Chinese government with foreign investment legitimacy and thus material return is not necessarily the priority.

It is clear that no one wants to be left out of China's SREB initiative. However, questions remain over the implementation plan of the project. For some SREB countries, there are significant concerns over the project's ultimate geostrategic goal as well as the detail of the various routes, both of which need more clarification from Beijing. However, it is clear that while China has ideas for how the SREB should develop, it is also seeking proposals from other countries about its development. This presents an opportunity for SREB countries to take ownership over the direction of their participation and to determine how best to maximise the benefits nationally.

TRAVELLING THE SILK ROADS

The process of travelling the Silk Roads developed along with the roads themselves. In the Middle Ages, caravans consisting of horses or camels were the standard means of transporting goods across land. Caravanserais, large guest houses or inns designed to welcome travelling merchants, played a vital role in facilitating the passage of people and goods along these routes.

Found along the Silk Roads from Turkey to China, they provided not only a regular opportunity for merchants to eat well, rest and prepare themselves in safety for their onward journey, and also to exchange goods, trade with local markets and buy local products, and to meet other merchant travellers, and in doing so, to exchange cultures, languages and ideas.

As trade routes developed and became more lucrative, caravanserais became more of a necessity, and their construction intensified across Central Asia from the 10th century onwards, and continued until as late as the 19th century. This resulted in a network of caravanserais that stretched from China to the Indian subcontinent, Iran, the Caucasus, Turkey, and as far as North Africa, Russia and Eastern Europe, many of which still stand today.

Caravanserais were ideally positioned within a day's journey of each other, so as to prevent merchants (and more particularly, their precious cargos) from spending days or nights exposed to the dangers of the road. On average, this resulted in a caravanserai every 30 to 40 kilometres in well-maintained areas.

Maritime traders had different challenges to face on their lengthy journeys. The development of sailing technology, and in particular of ship-building knowledge, increased the safety of sea travel throughout the Middle Ages. Ports grew up on coasts along these maritime trading routes, providing vital opportunities for merchants not only to trade and disembark, but also to take on fresh water supplies, with one of the greatest threats to sailors in the Middle Ages being a lack of drinking water. Pirates were another risk faced by all merchant ships along the maritime Silk Roads, as their lucrative cargos made them attractive targets.

The legacy of the Silk Roads

In the nineteenth century, a new type of traveller ventured onto the Silk Roads: archaeologists and geographers, enthusiastic explorers looking for adventure. Coming from France, England, Germany, Russia and Japan, these researchers traversed the Taklamakan desert in western China, in what is now Xinjiang, to explore ancient sites along the Silk Roads, leading to many archaeological discoveries, numerous academic studies, and most of all, a renewed interest in the history of these routes.

Today, many historic buildings and monuments still stand, marking the passage of the Silk Roads through caravanserais, ports and cities. However, the long-standing and ongoing legacy of this remarkable network is reflected in the many distinct but interconnected cultures, languages, customs and religions that have developed over millennia along these routes. The passage of merchants and travellers of many different nationalities resulted not only in commercial exchange but in a continuous and widespread process of cultural interaction. As such, from their early, exploratory origins, the Silk Roads developed to become a driving force in the formation of diverse societies across Eurasia and far beyond.

RENEWAL OF THE SILK ROAD

Trade and economic relations between the two countries is an area which has seen a dramatic increase in activity during this period and in particular since the 1990s. One of the cornerstones of this increased economic relationship was the signing in October 1982 of the China-Pakistan Joint Committee on Economic, Trade, Scientific and Technology Cooperation.

Accordingly, bilateral trade grew rapidly from a low of about $50 million annual bilateral trade in the mid-1970s to one where China is now Pakistan s second largest trading partner.

In early 2006 the two countries signed the five-year Development Program on Economic and Trade Cooperation which set down the major fields and programs for bilateral economic and trade cooperation. This trade link was further deepened in November of that year during an official visit of Chinese President Hu Jintao to Pakistan when the two countries signed a free trade agreement which came into effect on 1 July 2007. That year the leaders agreed to aim to increase bilateral trade from US$5.2 billion to US. billion by 2010. And while bilateral trade had indeed grown significantly over the last ten years (US$964 million in 1996, i.e., 444 percent), their target was over-ambitious, reaching only around US$9 billion by 2010. Accordingly, during Chinese Premier Wen Jiabao s visit to Pakistan in 2010, the two countries revised their target date and agreed to aim to reach US$15-18 billion by 2015 instead. Finally, it is important to note that the bilateral trade is very much in China s favour, with Beijing enjoying a surplus of over US$8 billion in 2011.

Complementing bilateral trade are several big infrastructure and investment projects which have been finished or are in the process of being completed. For example, the two governments signed a US$300 million agreement in December 2010 to reconstruct the approximately 25 kilometres of the Karakoram Highway (KKH) which was submerged by a major landslide in January 2010. This important and complex project, which will take approximately two years to complete, will allow the resumption of normal traffic between the two countries. The rehabilitation of the KKH will also enable Pakistan to more easily tap into the economic development of Xinjiang province. There are plans to build a 600 kilometre railroad between Havelian in Pakistan and Kashgar, the westernmost city in Xinjiang province. Complementing the road link is a direct 90 minute air link between Islamabad and Kashgar. In 2006 Pakistani President General Pervez Musharraf had a grand bilateral plan which would entail multiple trade, transport and energy corridors between the two countries that would stretch from the deep sea port of Gwadar—whose construction (2002-2007) was 80 percent financed by the Chinese—to the border with Xinjiang in the north. This ambitious plan would neatly fit with the 2006 Framework Agreement on Energy Cooperation which would cover the construction of oil refineries, gas terminals, oil and gas storage and transit facilities.

However, this grand vision plan has run into problems and may quite possibly only remain a pipe dream. In 2009 the Chinese Government decided to shelve its multi-million dollar costal oil refinery project at Gwadar which was launched in 2006. Publicly, the principal reason for China s decision to cancel the Gwadar project was the economic fall out of the 2008 Global Financial Crisis. However, another more important factor in the pull-out—and one which should not be underestimated—were concerns with the security situation in Baluchistan, the large province where Gwadar is located. Baluchistan has been in the throes of a low-level insurgency since the early part of the twenty-first century. Non-Baluch residents, including Chinese workers, have increasingly been the targets of the Baluch insurgents who are opposed to large developmental projects which they feel do not benefit the Baluch. Since the decision not to proceed with the oil refinery in Gwadar, there has been no suggestion of reviving this massive project in any of the joint statements emanating from the high-level meetings between the political leaders of the two countries. Nevertheless, there are still ambitions in China and Pakistan that a pipeline from western China to Baluchistan would be laid to link up with much-talked about oil and gas pipelines that would originate from Iran or Turkmenistan and terminate in Pakistan. Needless to say such a project, if it came to be realised, would have very significant geo-strategic implications for the region. However, despite the fact that importing gas from Iran would be more efficient, cheaper, assured and safer than importing gas from Turkmenistan, and transiting through Afghanistan, Washington has made it very clear that it opposes the Iran-Pakistan gas pipeline.

The Gwadar oil refinery project setback has not deterred the two countries, however, from cooperating in other areas of the energy sector. Given that Pakistan s energy deficit is increasing—it already has to import two-thirds of its oil needs—

it is no surprise that the two countries have been putting a lot of effort into addressing this major weakness in Pakistan's economy. At each high-level bilateral meeting and in joint statement the issue of cooperation in the energy field is always discussed.

According to then Pakistani Prime Minister Yousaf Gilani, the annual energy requirements of Pakistan will increase from the present 20,000 megawatts (MW) to more than 160,000 MW by 2030.[38] Moreover, not only will energy requirements grow exponentially over the next two decades but, according to the Pakistani Government, the present chronic power shortage reduces economic growth by between two and two and half percent of gross domestic product every year. In order to assist Pakistan with its increasing energy needs, China has offered financial and technical assistance to develop hydro and wind power and upgrade the existing transmission system. For example, in 2010 the two countries signed a memorandum of understanding on building twelve small- to medium-sized dams.

But much more controversial in the bilateral relationship—at least as far as the international community is concerned—is the nuclear energy cooperation between the two countries. China has helped Pakistan build a nuclear plant in Chasma, which began operation in 2001, and a second nuclear plant, Chasma II, which is scheduled to be completed very soon. Under a 2003 agreement, China has agreed to supply Pakistan with an additional two nuclear reactors which should provide Pakistan with an additional 680 MW of energy. However, that China may be considering supplying a much larger reactor, perhaps as big as one gigawatt, rather than the 300 MW reactors in the initial agreement. Regardless of the final size of the reactors, the latest deal has concerned the 46-country Nuclear Suppliers Group (NSG) which bars nuclear commerce between Nuclear Non-Proliferation Treaty (NPT) members, including China, and non-members like Pakistan. However, China has dismissed those concerns by pointing out—quite correctly—that Washington had signed a civil nuclear deal of its own with India, also a non-member of the NPT club, in 2008. There is an important difference between the two deals, however. The Americans sought (and were granted) an exemption by the NSG for the India deal to go ahead. China, on the other hand, is not seeking a similar exemption for Pakistan; it is going ahead regardless of the NSG s position. Moreover, Beijing has pointed out that the nuclear agreement with Pakistan was signed before China had joined the NSG in 2004 and that in any case it is only for peaceful purposes. But in a reassuring move, the International Atomic Energy Agency has agreed to the Pakistani Government s request to safeguard these two reactors to ensure that the nuclear material from the reactors is not diverted to make nuclear weapons. However, while the deal will probably be ultimately approved by the NSG, one of the big worries about the plan to build these two nuclear plants is the outdated technology that will be used in this project. According to Mark Hibbs, an atomic energy expert at the Carnegie Endowment for International Peace, the technology the Chinese are using is some thirty years old. 44 And given the recent nuclear incident in Japan, there is heightened concern about older nuclear plants around the world.

PAKISTAN'S STRATEGIES

Geo-Political

After the emergence of the CARs, Pakistan moved actively into Central Asia, but policy makers were clearly divided as to what Pakistan would gain out of Central Asia. While some wanted an Islamic revolution in Central Asia, others wanted open trade links through Afghanistan. The dichotomy of views revealed the limits of Pakistan's Central Asia Policy. Moreover, during this period, the Central Asian leaders were extremely wary of Pakistan because of its involvement in the Afghan war and its support to the mujahideen. During the Pakistan-backed Taliban era in Afghanistan, bilateral relations between Pakistan and the Central Asian states touched rock bottom.

After Pakistan joined the global war against terrorism as a frontline state, bilateral relations began to be revisited. During the past few years, frequent visits by Central Asian and Pakistani officials to each other's states reflect the changing nature of their bilateral relations. A number of agreements have been signed covering such areas as trade and tourism, cultural and economic cooperation during these visits. Pakistan has developed institutionalised arrangements for this purpose. Joint Economic Commissions (JECs) have been established with all the Central Asian states. Under a Special Technical Assistance Programme (STAP) initiated in 1992-93, Pakistan provides training facilities, which are fully funded by Islamabad. The programme includes courses ranging from English language, banking and accountancy to diplomacy.

In this context President General Pervez Musharraf's visit to Uzbekistan and Kyrgyzstan in March 2005 was significant. Earlier, the two-day official visit of President Nursultan Nazarbayev of Kazakhstan in December 2003 to Islamabad was a step towards strengthening bilateral ties between the two countries. During this visit, both the leaders decided to hold annual foreign ministerial consultations. While speaking at the Pakistan-Kazakhstan Business Forum, President Nazarbayev identified three zones of technological parks of information and biotechnology where Pakistani companies could invest significantly.

It is important to note that during the Tajik Foreign Minister's visit to Islamabad in January 2004, he assured President Musharraf that Tajikistan would not allow Indian military bases on its soil. This was followed by the visit of Tajik President Emomali Rahmanov to Islamabad in May 2004. During this visit, eight agreements were inked covering abolition of visas for holders of diplomatic passports, avoidance of double taxation, cooperation between the education ministers and justice ministers, combating drug trafficking, and cooperation between official news agencies and promotion and protection of investment.

Pakistan-Uzbekistan relations have also been improving over the past few years given the changed security paradigm. During Uzbek President Karimov's recent visit to Islamabad in May 2006, both sides agreed to expand trade and economic ties and coordinate anti-terrorism activities. It was also planned to extend road and rail links that would enable the CARs, particularly Uzbekistan, to make use of Pakistan's seaports to develop commerce with other regions. A joint fight against extremism and terrorism has, of late, been on top of the list for both the countries.

During his March 2005 visit President Musharraf assured the Uzbek leader of his determination to wipe out terrorists, including a substantial number of Uzbek nationals, from the tribal areas. How far these promises will be fulfilled is yet to be seen.

In an attempt to build strong ties with Central Asia, Pakistan has sought to use its cultural links with this region. It is perceived that Pakistan is the cultural extension of the Central Asian region that in turn is seen to be in fusion with the South Asian social milieu.

In this context, a Pakistani scholar opined, "Pakistan's political existence and emergence on the world map would not have materialised but for the primordial relationship that glues us together. The roots of our faith, undoubtedly, lie in the Arabian soil but our cultural linkages are with Central Asian civilisation, which in itself is an amalgam of diverse influence and cross-cultural fertilisation"

Cooperation in the fields of education and culture is an important aspect of Pakistan-Central Asia relations. There are number of Central Asian students studying in Pakistan and similarly Pakistani students in the CARs. The lack of information makes it difficult to provide the total number of Pakistani students studying in all CARs. However, the example of Kyrgyzstan can be cited. Kyrgyz students have been pursuing studies in Pakistani educational institutions in various fields such as engineering, business administration, information technology and the English language. Kyrgyz civil servants also attend training programmes in Pakistan. Conversely, over 350 Pakistani students are currently pursuing studies, mainly in medical colleges, in Kyrgyzstan.

Quest for "Strategic Depth"

The emergence of Central Asia was viewed as an opportunity for Pakistan to spread its sphere of influence beyond Afghanistan thus providing "strategic depth" against India. As mentioned earlier, Pakistan's desire to expand its influence in Afghanistan has been very central to Islamabad's strategic thinking. In the view of Gen. Mirza Aslam Beg, "...Afghanistan will be a great source of strength to Pakistan to face any crisis and danger that it may encounter. In fact, the security of Pakistan, Iran and Afghanistan is interlinked and is indivisible..."

While examining Pakistan's Afghan policy, it has been argued that its defence planning has been handicapped by the lack of territorial depth to absorb an attack by India and then to retaliate. This elusive quest for strategic depth has guided Pakistan in its ambitious involvement in Afghanistan in spite of the multiple implications for its social fabric and political culture. Thus, Pakistan's Afghan policy was constructed with an objective to create a subservient government in Afghanistan that would be friendly to Pakistan, militarily too weak to question the Durand line and unstable to raise the Pushtunistan issue. In addition to this, the military strategists argued that a friendly Afghanistan would give Kashmiri militants a base from where they could be trained, funded and armed. The Central Asian region was seen as an extension of Pakistan's strategic space.

The end of the Taliban regime in Afghanistan has not brought any fundamental change in Pakistan's Afghan policy. Afghanistan is still very central to Pakistan's strategic thinking, and is akin to being Pakistan's backwaters. Wary about how the current situation would unfold in Afghanistan, Islamabad is trying to cement its ties with the current regime in Kabul while supporting Taliban elements and has not given up its grand strategy of establishing a friendly government in Kabul. It is believed that Pakistan's new proxy war in Afghanistan is slowly unravelling itself. There is the resurgence of Taliban in Afghanistan. The Taliban are supported by the Pakistani establishment itself – from low-level military officers and some ministers to religious parties and their jihadi infrastructure. The ISI too has been proactively working to bring the Taliban back to its life. There has been constant accusation by Afghanistan of Pakistan's interference and its support to the Taliban and Al Qaida elements to create trouble for Kabul. Afghan President Hamid Karzai during his visit in February 2006 provided evidence to President Musharraf implicating Pakistan in the recruitment, training and equipping of Islamic radical suicide bombers. The senior Afghan official who accompanied President Karzai said, "In places like Karachi, Pakistani extremist groups working on behalf of the Taliban for a fee, carry out the recruitment and then bring them to safe houses in Balochistan for training and equipping with vests." In a recent visit to Islamabad, Gen. Johan Abizaid, the head of the US Central Command reportedly showed the Pakistanis, intelligence photographs of Taliban training camps at an undisclosed location and asked for them to be shut down.

Three years ago, Dr. Timothy D. Hoyt, Associate Professor of Strategy and policy at the US Naval War College, in a hearing before the House Committee on International relations in October 2003 accused Pakistan of providing sanctuary to terrorist groups, that enjoy strong support among active and retired Army officers and intelligence officials. He said: "So long as Pakistan relies on terrorism to achieve its political objectives, it will be impossible to eliminate terrorism and the Al Qaeda presence in the region."

Islam as a Tool

Religion is seen as an important factor in developing relations between Pakistan and the Central Asian states. It is felt that since the majority of the Muslim people living in most of the CARs were Sunnis, they would naturally gravitate towards Pakistan. Sardar Assef Ali, Minister of State for Economic Affairs, who led the Pakistani delegation to Central Asia in December 1991 said: "They (Central Asians) have problems with Iran. Besides bitter legacies of the past, a majority of people living in Central Asia are Turks. Also 95 per cent of them are Sunni Muslim of Naqashbandi order. So they are uneasy with Iran because of these factors". Leaders of the Jamaat-e-Islami expressed similar views. In a press statement on September 2, 1991, Jamaate-Islami Chief Senator Qazi Hussain Ahmed stated: "Independence of the three Muslim states of the Soviet Union–Azerbaijan, Uzbekistan and Kyrgyzstan–is the realisation of the dream of the Muslim Ummah at a critical juncture of history". He also said that the CARs were "looking up to Pakistan as their ideal owing to its ideological foundations. Besides, due to its role in Jehad-e-Afghanistan, these states also regard Pakistan as their benefactor and have pinned many hopes on it."

The Jamaat-e-Islami supported the Tajik fundamentalists in 1992 and 1993. According to Gen Liaskhovskii, one attempt to intervene in the civil war in Tajikistan was undertaken at the end of January 1993. In Peshawar, a conference of representatives of Muslim countries reviewed the measures to provide assistance to "Tajik brothers" in the "holy war" and resolved to place, at the head of the Tajik armed units, Afghans who had acquired combat experience in the war against the Soviet army. In addition, substantial material funds were allocated for Tajik Islamists. Pakistan supplied assistance to 60,000-80,000 Tajik refugees stranded in northern Afghanistan. When Tajik opposition leader Himatzadeh visited Pakistan in 1993, not only were his associates given access to the Foreign Office but also his criticism of the Tajik government was ignored. Meanwhile, the ex-Director General of the ISI, General Hameed Gul, even issued a statement in favour of the Tajik opposition.

The Uzbek government has referred to the activities of the Jamaat-e-Islami as a part of the grand Islamic alliance against the Tajik government and its support to the Islamic Movement of Uzbekistan (IMU) at various intervals. It is believed that the ISI's discreet support to IMU has remained fairly consistent. It also reportedly gave refuge to IMU leader Yuldeshev in 1990s and arranged Namangani's frequent clandestine visits to Pakistan. It is also believed that unlike the Taliban, ISI does not trust the IMU but at the same time it wants to keep the

IMU on its payroll for tactical reasons. It wishes to use the IMU as leverage within Central Asia. The post-Taliban period has not seen any major reversal in Pakistan's support to these jihadi elements. As mentioned earlier, there are still strong elements within the Pakistani establishment wanting to install a weak and friendly government in Afghanistan. Such a government will also provide Islamabad easy access and influence in the CARs.

After 9/11, Pakistan followed a dual policy towards the Central Asian states. On the one hand, it adhered to a state policy of friendly relations with the CARs but on the other, it continued to back dissident groups to get more leverage over the régimes. In March 2004, Uzbek President Islam Karimov asked Pakistan to extradite a number of Al Qaida fighters of Uzbek origin captured during operations in Wana.

In addition to ISI's support, one also sees the involvement of other non-state actors such as extremist Islamic parties; Al Qaida; the truck and transport smuggling mafias; and drug traffickers who have close links with IMU and Taliban. This has resulted in an explosion of self-interest groups in Pakistan who have benefited from the Afghan civil war and the Islamic insurgency in the CARs. Therefore, these groups are interested in weakening the state authority, which in turn enables their business interests and Islamic agenda to flourish.

Pakistan's desire to use Islam as a tool to win over these states however received a major setback because of its support to extremist groups in the Tajik civil war. After this, a wave of extremist activities engulfed the region especially Tajikistan, Uzbekistan and Kyrgyzstan and these states began to view Pakistan with great suspicion.

Therefore, the much desired goal of the Pakistani policy makers to have a security belt stretching from Turkey to Pakistan with Central Asia as the 'Islamic heartland', providing it "strategic depth" and much-needed allies, in its policy struggle over Afghanistan and Kashmir, did not materialise. On the contrary, the secular Central Asian regimes looked towards Russia, China and the West for their security cooperation rather than Pakistan. The CARs signed the Commonwealth of Independent States (CIS) Security Treaty in May 1992 and in 1996 joined Shanghai Five Forum, which later became the Shanghai Cooperation Organisation (SCO) in 2001. They also joined NATO's partnership of peace programme.

Regional Organisations

Apart from using its Islamic card to tie the CARs in its strategic fold against India, Islamabad also sought to use multilateral bodies in the region. Its desire to balance India through regional organisations got manifested in their wooing neighbouring Iran, Turkey, Afghanistan, and the CARs into the Economic Co-operation Organisation (ECO). Under this forum, states are expected to develop closer economic interaction.

In November 1992, Pakistan, Iran, Turkey, Afghanistan and the five former Soviet republics of Kazakhstan, Azerbaijan, Kyrgyzstan, Turkmenistan, and Uzbekistan created an extended Muslim economic bloc linking Asia and Europe. Former Prime Minister Nawaz Sharif noted in a speech marking the occasion that the ECO "now corresponds to the boundaries of the ancient area, which brought prosperity and civilisation through fruitful exchanges along the historic silk route. The people of these lands have a shared history and common spiritual and cultural values." Nawaz Sharif added his belief that extensive investment in infrastructure and encouragement of the private sector were the most important immediate objectives. He noted that Pakistan was building a major highway network to link Central Asia to the Arabian Sea and that its railroads were "poised to link not only member-states but also ECO with Europe, Russia, and South Asia." He added: "peace in Afghanistan is essential for political harmony and fruitful cooperation in our entire region."

Speaking about the achievements of ECO, Pakistani foreign minister Khursheed Mahmood Kasuri stated that it had made considerable progress in the trade, transport and energy sectors. The second ECO Commerce Ministers' Meeting held in Islamabad in July 2003 approved the ECO Trade Agreement

(ECOTA). The agreement envisages reduction of tariffs up to 15 per cent over a period of eight years (15 years in case of Afghanistan) on at least 80 per cent of goods on tariff lines. Para-tariff and non-tariff barriers would be eliminated within a period of two years. He further stated that the implementation of ECOTA would pave the way for economic integration of the region. New strategies and plans are expected to be adopted to make the organisation more effective.

Despite claims made by Pakistan's ministers about ECO's progress, it has so far been a non-starter. The establishment of a free trade zone is difficult when basic infrastructure necessary in this regard is lacking. Moreover, the competing interests of Iran, Pakistan and Turkey limit the role ECO can play in the region. Instability in Afghanistan remains a major obstruction for expanding the area of cooperation.

Islamabad also sponsored the membership of the newly independent Central Asian countries in the Organisation of Islamic Countries (OIC). This was yet another drive to bring the CARs into the Ummah. Pakistan has also been keen to join the SCO. In early 2001, Pakistan applied for observer status but the Central Asian members of the organisation blocked its entry. A major stumbling block was Pakistan's support for the Taliban government in Afghanistan. Though China supported Pakistan's membership, Russia wanted India to simultaneously join SCO. It was only in June 2005 that the applications of Pakistan, Iran and India were simultaneously considered and approved with consensus for granting observer status in the SCO at the Council of Heads of States Meeting in Astana on July 5, 2005. Pakistan is also a member of Conference on Interaction and Confidence-Building Measures in Asia (CICA). Much to the chagrin of Pakistan, India is included in both these organisations.

Geo-Economic

Transport Corridors and Access to Warm Waters: Many Pakistani leaders refer to their country as the gateway to Central Asia and strongly believe that good relations with the region would not only enhance its security but also provide enormous economic opportunities. In the post-Cold War period, Islamabad tried to revive its fortunes with the West by selling its new geo-strategic importance. This brings us to the question, is Pakistan the gateway to Central Asia? Geographically, Pakistan provides a gateway to Central Asia from south/ southeast; but it is not the only gateway to the seas of the south. This is the impression that Pakistani leaders have tried to create in an attempt to identify themselves with Central Asia, further their co-operation with the region and make Pakistan more relevant not only to the CARs and its neighbouring states but also to the West. In fact, Iran provides another gateway to Central Asia and has done a great deal to develop good communication systems with the region. Yet another gateway is via Turkey in the southwest.

Pakistan has been trying to make itself more relevant to Central Asia by offering the states several proposals for creating trade and transport corridors and access to ports. President General Pervez Musharraf has emphasised this time and again. He said, "...our geo-strategic significance can't be reduced. We need to realise that we have understood that and therefore we have constructed a new port at Gwadar which is at the mouth of the Gulf almost." In March 2005, he stated again: "we are fully focused on making use of our central location and constructing ports and putting in place a network of infrastructure." Recently, he has approved a railways reconstruction programme, which would link Gwadar with the other countries via rail. It is believed that this could make Pakistan the economic and trade hub for the CARs, Gulf, Western China and South Asia.

Pakistan's geo-strategic location admittedly makes it difficult for Central Asia to ignore it. For Turkmenistan and southern Uzbekistan, the shortest route to the sea lies through Iran, but for all other states, the shortest route is through Afghanistan and Pakistan. Karachi is the nearest port city for Central Asia and by air Islamabad is closer to Tashkent than it is to Karachi. Dushanbe is only an hour's flight from

Islamabad, and by road through Afghanistan the distance from Dushanbe to Karachi is 2,720 km. In contrast, the port of Bandar Abbas is 3,400 km, Vladivostok 9,500 km and Rostov on the Don 4,200 km away. This makes Pakistan important for the CARs. Despite little success so far, Pakistan is trying to improve its connectivity to the CARs through Afghanistan and China.

In this respect, the ADB has offered $2 billion to the Pakistan railway network, which will enable Pakistan to become one of the most attractive international trade routes to the CARs, Iran and China. Pakistan and Afghanistan have already agreed to lay a 103-km railway track between Chaman and Kandahar, which would be extended to Turkmenistan and other CARs. The feasibility study of the Quetta-Kandahar railway track has been completed and Pakistan would construct the 10-12 km railway track to the Afghan border. The track from the Afghan border to Kandahar would be the responsibility of the Afghan government. The World Bank has agreed to provide $1.8 billion to Pakistan for its $6 billion National Trade Corridor (NTC) improvement programme to meet domestic transportation requirements and provide transit facilities to Central Asia, Western China, Afghanistan and Iran.

Pakistan has also proposed to construct a $90-million road through the Boroghil Pass in the Yarkhun valley to link it with the CARs. Of the 13 passes, which lead to Afghanistan from Chitral district, the Boroghil Pass is the easiest and lowest in altitude. This pass remains closed for a very short period late in winter. The road will extend to Wakhan, 13-65 km wide strategic strip in northeast Afghanistan. The area links Afghanistan with Pakistan in the south, Tajikistan in the north and China in the east. The Wakhan-Boroghil route has been preferred against the one passing through the central parts of Afghanistan due to the security situation. This road will connect the 12,484-foot-high Boroghil pass at the northwest of the Yarkhum valley in Chitral with Sarhad-i-Langar in Wakhan at a distance of about 95 km and move on to Iskashim in Tajikistan leading to the Tajik capital Dushanbe via the Korung-

Kalai Chumb and Kulob areas. From the Boroghil Pass, the road will traverse over 300 km long valley and reach Peshawar. The distance from Tajikistan to Peshawar via the Wakhan-Chitral route is estimated to be 700 km. This road will also branch off to the northern areas via the 10,500-foot-high Shandur Pass and merge into the Karakoram Highway. The Pakistan government has already sanctioned a number of road projects to interlink the northern areas and Chitral.

The quadrilateral agreement signed by Pakistan, China, Kyrgyzstan, and Kazakhstan is expected to give a boost to trading activities among member-nations through the Karakoram Highway. On October 10, 2006 a road connection along the Karakorum route, Islamabad-Kashgar-Bishkek-Almaty, was opened by Pakistan. Pakistan has also offered use of the Gwadar deep-sea port to the CARs. This port would serve as a mother port at the strategic location opposite to the Strait of Hormuz and at the mouth of the Persian Gulf. The first phase of this project is already over. The completion of the Gwadar Port would be a milestone for Pakistan in this context. When it comes online alongside Karachi, it will provide the shortest access to the Arabian Sea for large parts of Central Asia. On December 31, 2005, a meeting of Pakistan-Uzbekistan Joint Ministerial Commission was held in Tashkent, where the two sides agreed to enter into a trilateral transit trade agreement with Afghanistan to benefit from land routes and the Gwadar port facility.

During Kyrgyz President Askar Akaev's two-day visit to Pakistan on January 17-18, 2005, it was agreed that Pakistan would import electricity from Kyrgyzstan and both countries would build roads to improve trade. It was decided to strengthen links through Kashgar in China and on to Bishkek and also through the Karakoram Highway.

The road being constructed on the Karakoram Highway to link the two countries completed by 2006, promoting Pak-Kyrgzy trade. Establishment of a railway link from Gwadar to Taftan in Iran via Saindak is also being planned. A road from Gwadar to Sandak, running parallel to the Iran-Pakistan border, will make it the shortest route to reach Central Asia from the warm waters of the Arabian Sea. Another 515-km long highway connecting Gwadar via Pangur, Khaan, Chaghi and Rabat up to the heart of Western Afghanistan is being planned. This would link Pakistan by road directly with the CARs.

Pakistan is also giving priority to road and rail links and related facilities for more effective and mutually beneficial access to Central Asia. Air services to Tashkent and Almaty have already been resumed. Similar services to other parts of the region are under active consideration. The laying of railway tracks from Turkmenistan to Pakistan via Afghanistan is an important part of this programme. Pakistan's Ministry of Railways has completed a feasibility study for a Chaman-Kandahar rail project.

The quadrilateral agreement is also gradually being implemented. The completion of the Murghab-Kulma road from Tajikistan to China linking the Karakoram Highway to Pakistan is also a significant development. Once operational, it will boost transit trade between Pakistan and Central Asia.

Energy and Pipeline Politics: Pakistan is also looking at the huge energy resources of Central Asia. It wants to make Pakistan the energy-transit corridor in South Asia and the Asia-Pacific region, which will bring huge economic gains for the country. Pakistan is most likely to face a energy crisis in natural gas, power and oil in the next 3-4 that could choke its economic growth for many years to come. It is estimated that Pakistan's total energy requirement would increase by about 48 per cent to 80 million tonnes of oil equivalent (MTOE) in 2010 from about 54 MTOE currently.

According to official energy demand forecast, the demand for natural gas, having about 50 per cent share in the country's energy consumption would increase by 44 per cent to the 39 MTOE currently. The power shortage is expected to be little over 5,250 MW by 2010. Oil demand would also increase by over 23 per cent to about 21 million tonnes in 2010 from the current demand of 16.8 million tonnes. Therefore, Central Asia could be a future source of energy for Pakistan.

Pakistan's importance for Central Asian countries needs to be viewed in the context of the entire pipeline politics in the region. As a transit country, Pakistan provides these states with an outlet of their energy resources. In view of the instability in Afghanistan and Balochistan, the success of these pipelines from Central Asia however remains a big question mark. Despite these uncertainties Pakistan wants to keep the Central Asian states engaged with the hope of providing a transit route for their energy resources. In pursuit of its strategy to control the pipelines and gain greater influence, it is trying to sign various agreements with these Republics. Pakistan has signed 21 agreements and MoUs in oil, gas, energy, trade, science and culture with Turkmenistan. In the energy sector, Turkmenistan, Afghanistan and Pakistan (TAP) signed an agreement in December 2002 for a gas pipeline from Turkmenistan via Afghanistan to Pakistan, whose estimated cost is $2.5 billion.

The ADB is the lead coordinating partner. It has, in addition to financial and technical assistance, played an important role in integrating efforts to realise the project. Several sessions of the Steering Committee on the TAP Gas Pipeline Project have been held so far. During a ministerial level TAP meeting on February 16, 2006, in Ashkabad, Turkmenistan agreed to provide sovereign guarantees to Pakistan to supply 3.2 billion cubic feet gas per day for 30 years. This assurance was restated during Pakistan Foreign Minister Khursheed Kasuri's visit to Turkmenistan in May 2006. However, a major hurdle to the project remains the volatile situation in Afghanistan.

While Turkmenistan can provide gas to Pakistan, Tajikistan and Kyrgyzstan have the potential to be substantial producers of hydroelectric power. Being geographically closest to Tajikistan, Pakistan stands to benefit from its hydroelectric potential. An inter-governmental agreement to that effect has already been signed.

Pakistan's Water and Power Minister Liaquat Ali Jatoi has recently said, "the government is considering importing electricity from CARs via Afghanistan as an option to meet its demand and has signed an MoU with Tajikstan to import 1000

MW as well as initiated transmission routing assessment to bring such power to Pakistan." An advisor to Kyrgyz Prime Minister Omarov said that his government was also considering a transmission line from China to Pakistan with an estimated cost of $1.4 billion. Pakistan has also signed an agreement to import electricity from Kyrgyzstan through Tajikistan and Afghanistan. Indubitably, terrain and weather conditions are clear impediments to this project, yet both states appear determined to pursue it.

Trade

With the emergence of the newly independent Central Asian States, the business elite group in Pakistan viewed this region as offering immense economic opportunities. Central Asia was seen not only as a source of needed raw materials but also as a potential export market. Some estimates even suggested that the region had a potential market of $80 billion and if Pakistan secures even 5 per cent of this market, it could earn up to $4 billion a year. In December 1991, a 23-member delegation was send to Central Asia headed by the then Minister of Commerce Sardar Asif Ahmed Ali. A $30-million credit facility was given to Uzbekistan and $10 million to all other Central Asian Republics. These credit lines were not utilised by the Central Asian countries and Pakistan was unable to keep its commitment to provide the credit lines in future. The effort to open a fullfledged National Bank of Pakistan (NBP) met with complete failure. The NBP representative office was set up in 1995 in Tashkent but it could not facilitate the opening of a branch till 2002.

Despite high hopes, the trade between Pakistan and Central Asia remains limited. During 1992-93 Pakistani exports to the region amounted to $5.6 m and imports were $0.51 m. The figures for 1993-1995 indicate an increase as compared to 1992-93. During 1997-98 Pakistan's total trade with Kazakhstan accounted for $19.9 m.; for Kyrgyzstan 07.91m; Tajikistan $10.29m; Turkmenistan $07.75m; and Uzbekistan $35.34m. However, in subsequent years the trade figures do not indicate any major increase.

Pakistan's recent initiatives in Central Asia involve strengthening economic ties with the CARs. As mentioned earlier, Pakistan has established JECs with all the CARs. In its trade policy for 2006-07, Pakistan seeked to focus on export growth in regional Muslim countries, particularly Iran, Afghanistan and the CARs. It has been decided to establish export centres and warehouses at Peshawar and Quetta and an export centre in Islamabad. In this context the visit of Kyrgyzstan President Askar Akaev on January 17, 2005 is of significance. Both countries signed a MoU on cooperation between the foreign ministries of the two countries on different regional and international issues. Two agreements were signed on cooperation and mutual assistance in customs related matters and avoidance of double taxation. President Akaev also offered to provide electricity to Pakistan. This was his third visit, earlier ones being in 1994 and 1995. Kyrgyzstan and Pakistan are signatories to the Quadrilateral Agreement along with China and Kazakhstan, effective since May 2004, which aims at promoting regional trade through Pakistan's Karakoram Highway. During the first meeting of the Pakistan-Kyrgyz Joint Ministerial Commission (JMC) in Islamabad, both sides negotiated on issues of taxation, culture, and visa restrictions for enhancing the volume of bilateral ties. Pakistan is also exploring the possibility of investing in the pharmaceutical sector in Turkmenistan.

As mentioned earlier the ECO provides another common platform to generate economic activity in the region. Within the framework of the ECO the volume of trade has not increased significantly. In fact, the ECO has failed to bring about great economic or commercial results. Competition among the member-states has been the major limitation for the success of this organisation. As Pakistan's Prime Minister Shaukat Aziz recently emphasised, the organisation needs to be used for making result-oriented policies instead of offering mere lip service. ECO can be an effective organisation if the ECO Trade Agreement, Transit Transport Agreement and the Trade and Development Bank become operational. So far, Pakistan has not been able to achieve much in terms of building economic and trade ties with the CARs. Their efforts to set up banks and hotels have received severe setbacks in Central Asia.

RUSSIA

According to *Vision and Actions on Jointly Building Silk Road Economic Belt and 21st-Century Maritime Silk Road* (hereafter referred to as *Vision and Actions*), the official guiding document of OBOR, one of the three routes of the "Belt" passes Russia and two passes Central Asia, whereby Russia considers it to be a part of its historical economic and regional interests. Hence, Russia can be viewed as a key to the success of OBOR. In a sense, the construction of the "Belt" will face more challenges if it lacks Russia's cooperation, or at least consent.

A recent official remark in respect to bilateral relations between Russia and China seems quite optimistic. On Jan 17 and 18, 2017, Russian Foreign Minister Sergey Lavrov and a Chinese spokesperson for the Ministry of Foreign Affairs respectively stated that Sino-Russian relations were "at their best level ever in the two countries' history". Both of them also mentioned OBOR as a part of Sino-Russian cooperation. Though China has consistently been seeking support and cooperation with Russia (and all the other countries along OBOR as well), it is important to note, however, that Russia's position was not consistent and underwent an obvious shift.

Initially the Kremlin didn't give the OBOR initiative positive feedback and it didn't show enthusiasm for Asian Infrastructure Investment Bank (AIIB) in the first place, either, which reflected a dominant view of Russian elites that these would lead to a mutual distrust between the two countries.

Russia's concern about losing freight traffic was one reason for its unwillingness because the original route based on Chinese planning was to bypass Russia. More importantly, it worried that the closer economic ties between China and the Central Asian countries would compete with Russia's own integration plans for this region, which may further make the Central Asian countries drift away from Russia and embrace China.

But President Putin soon changed his position when China acknowledged Russia's concerns and agreed to make some concessions to accommodate Russia's needs, followed by the Russia's endorsement of OBOR and its joint declaration with China on coordinating and linking OBOR to Eurasian Economic Union (EEU) in the middle of 2015.

In fact, China did show considerable willingness and flexibility to cooperating and this was exemplified by China's "creation" of an economic corridor with Russia and Mongolia, which would connect the "Belt" to Russia's transcontinental railroad plan which was not in the initial plan of the OBOR. Besides, China's "Three Nos" principle in Central Asia, i.e. no interference with Central Asian countries' internal affairs; no attempt to seek a dominant role in regional affairs; and no desire to create a sphere of influence, being a policy for dealing with its relations with Central Asian countries, to some extent eased Russia's concern about China's involvement in this region, because such showed that China had no intention of changing the status quo (Russia's dominant influence) even though China didn't formally acknowledge Central Asia as Russia's backyard. So far the concessions China made with regards to Russia are probably the most significant ones made during the promotion of OBOR because no other country alone constituted a reason for China to change the route.

Russia's consideration is also based on the fact that some benefits, including infrastructure construction and cooperation on industrial capacity with China are not a priority and the only significant and substantial benefit to be incurred may be the receipt of funding from China. Rather, apart from the competing interest in Central Asia, some cooperation models as used in other countries such as contracting a construction project and dispatching thousands of Chinese workers there would hardly be acceptable for Russia due to its vigilance on the issue of Chinese migrants, especially in Far East region.

However, there are some reasons that Russia eventually decided to support this initiative. First, there is some tangible benefit that Russia can expect, though it doesn't seem so imperative for Russia to seek out for the time being. In addition to being another channel for funding of infrastructure, OBOR, after an adjustment to its route as per Russia's requirements, both in the plan and in practice, has brought some benefits to Russia.

Since Russia's transcontinental rail was connected to OBOR and China-Mongolia-Russia economic corridor started to build, freight volume rocketed up in the railway routes from China to Russia, and to Europe via Russia, both of which used Russia's transcontinental railroad, such as Chongqing-Inner Mongolia-Russia (Yu-Meng-E) and Hunan-Inner Mongolia-Europe (Xiang-Meng-Ou), which had positive effects for both China and Russia.

Second, EEU is currently Russia's priority. Though initially OBOR was viewed more as a rival, China's clarification and commitment on connecting the two projects eased Russia's concerns to a large extent. As a concrete step, a document was signed in the middle of 2016 in which the two governments decided to formally start negotiations on an economic partnership, mainly focusing on trade facilitation, merging different standards on intellectual property, customs, and other areas. Third, it might not be wise nor feasible for Russia to contain China's influence in Central Asia, or larger scope by boycotting this initiative.

For one thing, though the influence of Russia, the "elder brother" in Eurasia is still dominant, which is determined by its close political, economic, cultural, language and even people-to-people ties with the five republics in this region, the latter have long been seeking reducing their overdependence on Russia and striking a balance among big powers. Of course, Russia and China are the most important two in the region. In the past decade, China's influence in the field of economics in this region grew very quickly and as such China has been able to compete with Russia, if not surpass it.

In 2015, all Central Asian countries have a larger share of their two-way trade with China than with Russia except for China's exports to Kazakhstan and Turkmenistan and imports from Kyrgyzstan and Tajikistan. Besides, the build-up of mutual trust and cooperation in other areas such as that of anti-terrorism also increased China's influence and say in this region. These facts make it very difficult for Russia to sway these countries by one-sided action. It is even interesting that Kazakhstan, where Xi Jinping first announced the "One Belt" initiative, is exactly the country which has the closest relations with Russia in Central Asia. For the other, OBOR is basically based on the actual needs of both China and many other countries. Also, China has enough political will and financial resources to push forward with. These factors mean that it can still proceed even if the support from some of the local big powers is absent.

Data showed that Russia entered into a recession, with GDP growth of -2.2% for the first quarter of 2015, as compared to the first quarter of 2014, which was regarded as a success of Western sanctions in terms of the proximate goal of inflicting damage on the Russian economy. Under this great pressure, it is no surprise that the Kremlin turned to the East and sought cooperation opportunities from China. Though China didn't support Russia's annexation of the Crimea and basically held a neutral position, it did have a great deal of interest in strengthening bilateral cooperation with Russia in economic, military and other areas because China also faced pressure from the West and needed political support from Russia. Admittedly, joining OBOR cannot bring enough benefits to Russia to offset its losses from the sanctions, nor can the closer relations with China.

However, a positive attitude to OBOR is vital for Russia if it hopes to get more financial support from China, whether under the OBOR initiative or other bilateral projects. It is hard to image that the $400 billion USD gas deal between the two countries, which was signed shortly after Russia annexed the Crimea and other cooperation projects can be implemented smoothly if Russia eventually declines this initiative that China attaches the most importance to.

On the whole, the benefit of OBOR seems more symbolic than substantial for Russia and thus Russia still sticks to the

EEU project, which can help to bolster its economic and political dominance in Eurasia. This has been evidenced by the wording used when Lavrov mentioned that the Russia-China relations were at the best of all time this January. He emphasized "aligning" the two projects, instead of "joining" OBOR. Nevertheless, Russia still cannot neglect OBOR because the latter is closely related to China, who is able to provide key support to Russia. This support was vital to Russia when it suffered from the sanctions from the West and is expected to continue to play an important role in the near future because the relations between Russia and the West have been in a stalemate and chances of lifting the sanctions look very slim in the near future.

Uzbekistan

It is not a coincidence that Xi chose Central Asia to announced the "One Belt" initiative first. One plausible explanation for such is that this is the region where the ancient Silk Road first passed by when it left West China, but the underlying reason may be that the five republics of Central Asia are the countries who best match the ideas of OBOR and support it most as well. Since they gained independence twenty-five years ago, these landlocked countries had to face a common challenge, i.e. how to develop their economies in the Post-Soviet time?

Although Putin showed a strong desire to play an even bigger role in this region, Russia's capabilities alone are not enough to ensure the prosperity of these counties. More importantly, such support is not without a price—overreliance on one big power will risk their independence.

The rise of China provided an alternative to these countries which enabled them to choose partners from a wider range and benefit from both. OBOR is attractive to Central Asian countries because the focuses of this initiative, such as promoting connectivity, facilitating trade and investment, and improving infrastructure are all imperative to them. In this section, Uzbekistan is selected as an example, which can be a representative of the other four countries. In May 2014, one year before the *Vision and Actions* was released, the then Uzbek President Karimov stated that Uzbekistan would actively participate in the building of the Silk Road economic belt when he met with Chinese President Xi. In June 2015 China and Uzbekistan agreed to expand trade and economic cooperation under the framework of the "Belt initiatives".

In June 2016, Karimov and Xi agreed to focus on jointly promoting this initiative. All of which clearly shows Uzbekistan's positive attitude to OBOR.

The main areas of cooperation under the OBOR framework include economic and trade cooperation, gas pipeline, railway tunnel construction, people-to-people exchange, etc. and much progress has been witnessed since a series of pacts were signed. For example, the Qamchiq Tunnel in Uzbekistan, which is a part of the Angren-Pap railway line that connects Tashkent and Namangan, was completed on June 22, 2016 as a major achievement of OBOR.

There is also some uncertainty about the implementation of OBOR in this country, which not only comes from the death of Karimov in last September, but also comes from local Uzbekistanis' insufficient knowledge and recognition of OBOR, and too even China's overall model of economic development. In spite of this, cooperation related to OBOR still seems to be on track and there is no sign that it has been set aside by Uzbekistan.

Admittedly, the five republics in Central Asia differ from each other in terms of levels of democracy, natural resources, economic development levels, even in terms of domestic tensions or conflicts. Nevertheless, their common feature in geographic location cannot be overlooked. Being landlocked states, their trade connectivity with the rest of the world is limited, but they are also the overland juncture between East Asia and Europe, which gives them the potential to become a transportation hub that can connect the East and the West. OBOR looks like a perfect solution to this situation.

If properly managed, it can better the connectivity within their individual country and that with other countries, which will bring triple benefits to them. First benefit is in meeting their local needs. Second is in facilitating their own export and import, and the third is to make profit by providing transshipment services. Also, appealing to Central Asian countries is China's "no intervention in domestic politics", "business-is-business" and economic oriented approach. When compared to Russia or other powers, China "is more inclined to perceive the local situation in terms of a sophisticated win-win scenario rather than in terms of aspirations of geopolitical dominance in the region" and such this policy has been approved to be successful.

Overall, OBOR is beneficial to Uzbekistan and joining this initiative can be a reasonable choice. In fact, Uzbekistan can be a typical case with regards to OBOR from two different angles. One is that it represents the other four Central Asian countries which have similar geographic advantages as well as disadvantages and economic status quo. The other is that it can represent many medium or small developing states which have little direct conflicting interest with China in terms of geopolitics and thus can focus more on the economic cooperation they are mutually interested in. Basically, it is not difficult for them to find some areas in which they can cooperate with China on and benefit from them together.

Malaysia

Being an important part of 21st century Maritime Silk Road, or "One Road", the other half of the OBOR, Malaysia, has its significance in two aspects. First, it is sitting on a strategic spot, in that Kuala Lumpur is quite close to the Malacca Strait, the second busiest waterway in the world. Trade statistics show that almost half of the world's total annual seaborne cargo passed through this passage, which is jointly administered by Malaysia, Singapore and Indonesia. Second, Malaysia is now China's largest trading partner in ASEAN and the third largest in Asia and its policy option can be used as reference for some other countries. In addition, Malaysia is able to help China expand markets in other ASEAN and neighboring countries. All these factors together make Malaysia's position key to the prospects of "One Road".

In fact, Malaysia is perhaps the most active country regarding the OBOR in ASEAN, or Southeast Asia. In October 2014, Malaysian Prime Minister Najib Razak voiced his country's readiness to support both OBOR and AIIB when meeting with Chinese State Councilor Yang Jiechi. In addition, many other high-ranking governmental officials also echoed Najib's position on OBOR. For example, Liow Tiong Lai, the Minister of Transport of Malaysia reiterated that the OBOR was a win-win project and indicated that Malaysia was ready for that in his speech at the Boao Forum for Asia in June 2015.

Several key areas and projects have been highlighted by both Malaysia and China under the umbrella of OBOR, including infrastructure, transportation, energy, property and even education and some progress have been made on each to date. For example, 60% of the equity of the 1MDB-owned Bandar Malaysia project in Kuala Lumpur was sold to a consortium led by a Malaysian company and China Railway Engineering Corp (CREC, a stated owned Chinese company) at RM7.41 billion in early 2016.

In November of the year, following an official visit to China by Najib, Malaysian and Chinese companies saw the signing of fourteen agreements on several iconic and mega agreements worth RM144 billion. Another eye-catching project which China hopes to incorporate into OBOR is the High Speed Rail (HSR) connecting Malaysia and Singapore. Though the final result of HSR bidding will not be available until 2018, it is a general consensus that a Chinese-led consortium is one of the two most promising competitors (the other is Japanese-led consortium) because of its successful precedent as set in Indonesia.

There are several reasons that can explain the positive attitude of both government and business sectors. First, Malaysia has basically maintained friendly relations with China over the past few decades.

In fact, Malaysia was the first country in Southeast Asia to build formal ties with China in 1974. Such good relations are also based on the fact that there was little strategic conflict between the two countries after 1980s whereas there was also a frequent people-to-people exchange that occurred because of the large Chinese ethnic population present in Malaysia. It should be noted that territory disputes between the two countries do exist, which is about the waterways in the South China Sea.

However, both Malaysia and China seem to be restrained about such and downplay this dispute, which is unlike the situation between the Philippines and China in the last several years. As a result, this dispute didn't impede the bilateral relations. Second, both Malaysia and China have benefited a lot from previous economic cooperation and thus there is a strong driving force for them to maintain such development. A closer look at the bilateral economic cooperation between the two countries shows that two-way investment and trade involves different sectors, from manufacturing to construction, and different regions in these two countries, which reflects the in-depth and successful cooperation of both. Third, Malaysia believes that much of its needs in infrastructure, transportation and investment can be met by joining OBOR. As Najib notes, for instance,

"[The double-track East Coast Rail Line] will spur socio-economic growth in specific areas and bring great benefit to the people in the East Coast [of Malaysia]".

OBOR can be a good opportunity for Malaysia too because it is more likely to succeed in this country than in some other developing countries along the OBOR. Aside from the strategic significance, Malaysia has a relatively stable political environment, well-established legal system and sound economic framework and good infrastructure. Its unique advantages include its large Muslim population as well as its Chinese ethnic population. The latter can help Chinese businesses easily enter into the local market and the former provide a possibility to connect the Chinese halal industry to the Muslim world.

Though geopolitical consideration is not frequently and publicly emphasized when Malaysian high-ranking officials talk about OBOR, there is good reason to believe that Malaysia is trying to seek a balance between the two big powers of the United States and China. While actively getting involved in OBOR, Malaysia is also a member of TPP, a US-led trade agreement. Since OBOR and TPP are widely considered to be part of a rivalry between China and the US, the involvement of both projects clearly shows that Malaysia hopes to benefit from both but not to overly rely on any. In a sense, the choice of "OBOR or TPP" reflects the choice of "US or China", which is a common issue facing almost all the ASEAN countries, which is largely due to the geographic location of these countries. Although ASEAN countries try to speak with one voice, each of them have different responses to the "US or China" issue — some are more pro-American and others seem more pro-China. Of course, such is subject to change depending on their leadership and certain circumstances and the dispute over the South China Sea plays a key role in the policy option.

Last but not least, skepticism and concerns about OBOR can also be found in Malaysia. In addition to the dispute concerning the South China Sea, the "indifference" of Malay ethnic people as opposed to the "enthusiasm" of Chinese ethnic people and the exaggeration of the potential effect of OBOR are also challenges. However, it seems that the Malay-Chinese cooperation on OBOR hasn't been influenced much by such opinions.

Germany

China became the biggest trading partner of Germany in 2016 for the first time, overtaking France and the US, and Germany has long been China's biggest trading partner in Europe. This clearly shows the even closer economic relations between the two countries. From China's perspective, Germany's significance for OBOR primarily lies in its geographic location as one of the destinations of OBOR as well as its identity as an important actor among Western countries, which means that cooperation on OBOR, if successfully implemented, may set an example for other Western countries in Europe and attract more Western partners. Overall, the German government holds a relatively positive position towards OBOR and its focus is mainly on the areas of improving connectivity and trade and investment facilitation. Germany's Chancellor Angela Merkel has welcomed the initiative to secure more Chinese investment in Europe. At the same time, reservations and ambiguity can also be read from German government positions. German Consul General in Hong Kong when asked about the position of Germany on OBOR, said that Germany welcomed China's openness to the rest of the world but he also highlighted that "any roads and any belts should be and will be in both directions".

Although German government is not very willing to provide clear and strong support to OBOR, it didn't refuse the relevant business opportunities that came with such. However, when compared to the Central Asian countries or some Southeast Asian countries, the result yielded in Germany under OBOR seems rather limited. The most prominent progress related to OBOR made in Germany is the Sino-European freight trains. In fact, the only five big projects to be undertaken by the end of 2016 were those linking the existing railroads. But it should be noted that several of them had been planned long before the announcement of OBOR and were just included in this initiative later.

Unlike some countries which are China's immediate rivals or have territory disputes with China, Germany can stay away from such tricky problems. As a result, the responses of Germany regarding OBOR, especially those positive ones, including the statements of the government or business sectors and projects discussed or agreed to are almost all based on economic calculations. In fact, the realistic or foreseeable benefits for Germany may also lie in this area. For one thing, the operation of Sino-German freight train provided a new option for the transportation of goods between China and Germany, and other European countries with a shorter timeline and more affordable cost. According to the China Railway, the total freight volume of the Sino-European railway reached 42 million tons in 2016, an increase of 12% and Germany was the main destination. It should be noted that there are other destination countries of eastbound freight trains aside from China, such as Kazakhstan. This demonstrates that the connectivity achieved can be beneficial to all the countries along OBOR. For the other, it did attract more Chinese investors to Germany. So far around seventy enterprises have settled in Duisburg, one of the destinations of Sino-German freight train, and most of them entered the European market within the last two years. Overall trade and investment statistics show a very positive trend for the past three years and OBOR did play "some" positive role in such, though it may not be easy to measure precisely to what extent OBOR contributed to this trend.

Admittedly, the challenge facing OBOR in Germany is huge, and such a challenge is quite different from that in the developing countries or in China's neighboring rivals. For a Westernized developed economy like Germany's, infrastructure, one of the key pillars of OBOR, which is also a focus for many of the countries in Central Asia and Southeast Asia, is not a priority, nor even a concern of Germany's because infrastructure is well-established throughout the country. Foreign investment is generally welcomed but not a pressing need. The cooperation on manufacturing capacity which has been in operation by China and some developing countries along OBOR is not applicable to Germany at all. This explains why the major benefit, if not the only benefit, that is attractive to Germany may be the connectivity created by OBOR and the resultant trade and investment opportunities.

In addition to the mismatch as mentioned, the obvious divergence between Germany and China regarding China's markets, transfer of cutting-edge technology to Chinese companies, Chinese state-owned enterprises, or ultimately, China's model of economic development is also a big obstacle for OBOR. For example, Berlin became seriously concerned that Chinese acquisition of hi-tech German companies would make China an even more aggressive competitor while Chinese officials criticized this new protectionist tendencies in Germany in response. Needless to say, this is a common issue between almost all the EU countries and China. Furthermore, the EU's approach has, to a large extent been based on a democratization and human right paradigm, which can be viewed as one of the root causes of their indifference and skepticism of OBOR. As a result, Germany's involvement with OBOR is limited and the influence of OBOR to this country is drastically weakened.

For years Germany's policy on China has been split between the economic interests and ideological considerations. On the one hand, it cannot ignore the Chinese markets and cooperation with China, which has brought huge benefit to its economy. On the other hand, Germany's free market capitalism and values can hardly accommodate China's development and expansion based on the Chinese model and thus deterrence is required. This dilemma has inevitably influenced how Germany looks at OBOR and what impact OBOR will bring to Germany.

The result is, not surprisingly, a temporary balance between the two objectives. Of course, such a balance is not unchangeable and the struggle over economic interests and ideological principles will continue.

A recent and noticeable event that occurred which may sway Germany's position might be US president Trump and his isolationism. Before Merkel's meeting with Trump, Merkel and Xi stressed a commitment to free trade during a telephone call. This move signals that Germany may have to attach more importance to achieving economic cooperation with China, which means OBOR will probably have a more favorable environment in Germany in the future.

The case of Germany can reflect the general European situation to some degree and it basically coincides with European Commission President Jean-Claude Juncker's statement, who also emphasizes the importance of investment and links and holds that this initiative can bring huge benefit to both China and the EU, if it works well. However, the representation of Germany shouldn't be overestimated. On the one hand, there is no official EU position on OBOR as of yet and EU countries also lack a collective voice. On the other hand, the Germany case is more applicable to Western Europe than Eastern, Central and Southeastern Europe. Unlike Germany, most countries in the Central, Eastern and Southeastern parts of Europe are less developed and thus need more infrastructure building assistance and foreign investments, which brings them more opportunities to cooperate with China under OBOR. And this has been evidenced by a series of cooperation between two parties, such as the China Ocean Shipping Company (COSCO)'s purchase of the Greek port of Piraeus and China's building of a high-speed railway from Hungary to Serbia.

Conclusion

The analysis of the four countries, though fragmented and not adequate to provide a whole picture of the impact of OBOR for those countries within the scope as well as their response, to some extent reveals the trend of the relations between OBOR and the relevant countries, because each of the four countries can represent a group of countries, or at least reflects some key consideration of the countries with the same features.

First, big powers are more inclined to put OBOR in the context of power rivalry and this inevitably reinforces OBOR as a challenge and usually leads to distrust of this initiative. Russia's response initially reflected this relationship but China's immense move towards making concessions and Russia's plight in the Ukraine eventually changed Russia's position. By comparison, India is a case in point to show how another power is wary of China's OBOR initiative. Since India positions China more as a rival than a partner, and there are no key drivers that emerged like those which occurred in Russia's case that could reverse the trend, to date India hasn't endorsed this initiative and there is little hope it will in the future. To some degree, the benefits or losses that OBOR can yield have become secondary to geopolitical considerations. Small or medium states, such as the Uzbekistan and Malaysia cases suggest, however, don't want to get involved in the great power games and tend to focus on the tangible and immediate gains that can be derived from OBOR. They don't seem to care whether or not China can get more from the bilateral cooperation than they do. In reality, many of them tend to seize the opportunity as it presents itself and transform it to improve their own country's economy.

Second, developing countries are meant to benefit more from OBOR. Overall, the trade and investment facilitation, one of main goals of OBOR is universally welcomed by both developed countries and developing countries alike. But only the developing countries have huge demands for infrastructure building and requirements for relevant funding to be invested, which can probably be met by the implementation of OBOR. Then it should come as no surprise that developing countries along OBOR show relatively more positive attitudes towards it.

Third, political and economic institutions and too even ideology can play a important role in the assessment of OBOR as well as the position a country takes on it. Western counties are more concerned about the role of the Chinese government and state-owned enterprises in OBOR and are prone to link the implementation of this initiative outside China to the market environment within China. By contrast, non-Western countries have less concern in this regard partly because some of them are also practicing state capitalism, rather than free market capitalism. Therefore, their judgment is basically centered on what result OBOR can yield and to what degree such is beneficial to them.

In general, the idea of enhancing connectivity and promoting trade, which constitutes the main rationale of OBOR, is positive and this explains why OBOR won quite a bit of recognition after three years of intensive promotion, though it has always been accompanied by skepticism and challenges outside China. However, this initiative is still not a one-size-fits-all solution because its real effect relies heavily on the different situation of each country. Then it is no surprise that each country has different positions, all depending on the consideration of various factors, including economic, geopolitical, ideology, etc. Roughly speaking, OBOR is more of an opportunity for small and medium developing states than big powers or Western countries.

In a sense, Trump's new policy, Brexit and even the rise of right-wing political force in West Europe provided an unexpected opportunity for China's OBOR initiative because most countries in the world are still in favor of open and free trade. In the meantime, they also need some kind of mechanism and project to materialize this conception. Intentionally or unintentionally, OBOR may probably play a positive role in this regard, but we also need to realize its limit and avoid too optimistic or unrealistic expectation.

CHINA'S ONE BELT AND ONE ROAD STRATEGY AND SILK ROAD

Since India does not have the assets today to set up contending systems, it might be advantageous to take an interest in those parts of the OBOR which may enhance Indian network to significant markets and asset supplies

The surely understood geopolitical scholar Halford Mackinder proposed in 1904 that the inward zone of Eurasia – described by inside or polar waste and impervious via ocean power – was bound to be the "Turn Area" of world legislative issues. It was his view that the tenet over the heart of the world's most noteworthy landmass would turn into the premise for global control, inferable from the prevalence of rail over boats as far as time and reach. Russia and China, in the event that they met up, he anticipated, could defeat the sea world.

The course of the First World War led him in later years to modify his initial perspective. In looking at the shape of the post-World War II order, he foresaw a world geopolitically balanced between a combination of the North Atlantic, or what he termed as Midland Ocean, and the Asian heartland powers. In effect, he conceded that geopolitical dominance required both a continental as well as a maritime dimension. Another important geopolitical theorist, Alfred Mahan, also had a Eurasian centred global perspective, but his emphasis was on maritime power mediating between a two-fold global framework – a Western and an Oriental system. Against this backdrop, what we may currently be witnessing is a carving out by China of a continental-maritime geo-strategic realm constituted by its initiative labeled 'One Belt and One Road', also known as the Belt-Road Initiative and the abbreviation OBOR.

The belt manifests the continental dimension of this geo-strategic realm. It consists of a network of rail routes, overland highways, oil and gas pipelines and other infrastructural projects, stretching from Xian in Central China, through Central Asia and Russia, with one artery crossing Kazakhstan and the other through Mongolia but both linking up with the trans-Siberian railway and going on to Moscow, Rotterdam and Venice.

The road is the maritime dimension and consists of a network of ports and other coastal infrastructure from China's eastern seaboard stretching across South East Asia, South Asia, the Gulf, East Africa and the Mediterranean, forming a loop terminating at Piraeus (Greece), Venice (Italy) and Rotterdam (Netherlands) in Europe and Mombasa (Kenya) in Africa.

Both the Road and the Belt include regional loops and branches which extend the reach of the emerging transportation networks but also serve to tie the Road to the Belt at critical points. Thus the China-Pakistan Economic Corridor is significant precisely because the port of Gwadar is one of the points where the Road and the Belt intersect. Of interest to India is the branch constituted by the BCIM corridor, which proposes to connect Yunnan in southern China with Myanmar, Bangladesh and eastern India.

More than just routes

The OBOR is not only about putting in place physical infrastructure, although this is an indispensable component of the initiative. The 'Vision and Actions on Jointly Building the Silk Road Economic Belt and 21st-Century Maritime Silk Road' document – announced by the China National Resource and Development Commission and the Ministry of Foreign Affairs in March this year – sets out the overall rationale behind the initiative.

According to Zhang Gaoli, Vice Premier and head of the high level group charged with piloting the project, its objectives are:

- Enhancing policy coordination across the Asian continent;
- Trade liberalisation;
- financial integration; and
- Connectivity including people to people links.

The document describes OBOR as "a systematic project which should be jointly built through consultation to meet the interests of all and effort should be made to integrate the development strategies of the countries along the Belt and the Road".

Thus the initiative is seen as an instrument to create a contiguous land and maritime zone where countries pursue convergent economic policies, underpinned by both physical infrastructure and supported by trade and financial flows. The inclusion of people to people links is a recognition that soft power will play an important role in creating a congenial political environment for the sustained roll-out of the ambitious initiative.

The document further states, "The initiative to jointly build the Belt and the Road enhancing the trend towards a multi-polar world, economic globalisation, cultural diversity and greater IT application, is designed to uphold the global free trade regime and the open world economy in the spirit of open regionalism".

Thus the OBOR may also be seen as China's response to the more exclusive mega-economic blocks in the making, the Trans-Pacific Partnership (TPP) in Asia and the Transatlantic Trade and Investment Partnership or T-TIP, both of which are led by the United States. The Road, for example, is explicitly oriented towards South East Asia, while Europe is the destination of the Belt. The OBOR, therefore, represents an alternative and supposedly more inclusive economic architecture led by China, competing with that promoted by the United States. The document says:

"The Belt and the Road run through the continents of Asia, Europe and Africa, connecting the vibrant East Asia economic circle at one end and developed European economic circle at the other, and encompassing countries with huge potential for economic development."

It should be apparent from these Chinese pronouncements that China sees the twin-dimensional initiative as a long-term project to secure its geo-strategic realm, which has both a continental and a maritime dimension. It is not just an economic initiative. It has obvious political and security implications. In any case, China's strategists do not draw lines separating economic and security objectives. Each dimension reinforces the other, even though the economic dimension may sometimes mask the security imperative.

A key road map for the Chinese economy too

Having spelt out its vision and a broad plan of action, China is now focusing on the deployment of the next phase, identifying "key directions, key countries and key projects".

It may be worth mentioning at this point another major Chinese strategic plan labeled as "Made in China 2025" which seeks to transform the country from a "world factory to a world manufacturing power, complete with innovative products and manufacturing processes". Made in China 2025 fits in neatly with the OBOR initiative. Li Teng, the CEO of Bank of China International claimed recently that OBOR "will push China to transform from low-end commodity export to high-end commodity exports, capital and technology exports".

The OBOR is therefore part of an economic strategy that will enable China to deal with the problem of massive overcapacity in its industry. The infrastructure to implement OBOR will require vast amount of construction materials and capital equipment, sectors where China has vast unused capacity.

There will also be an incentive to export skilled and semi-skilled labour employed in these sectors, also rendered surplus by a slowing Chinese economy. Furthermore, such infrastructural investment will require significant financial flows. The OBOR initiative is underpinned by the Chinese led Asian Infrastructure Investment Bank (capital of $100 billion), the BRICS New Development Bank (capital of $50 billion but may rise to $100 billion) and a proposed Shanghai Cooperation Organisation Financing Institution.

A dedicated Silk Road Fund of $40 billion has also been established to finance projects under the initiative. Part of the China-Pakistan Economic Corridor project comprising of roads, railways and Gwadar port totalling $11 billion will be financed from this Fund. The Chinese business paper, *Caixin*, reports that China will draw upon its substantial foreign exchange reserves to inject $62 billion of capital into the state-owned "policy banks" in support of the OBOR initiative. Half of the amount will go to the China Development Bank and $30 billion to the China Exim Bank. The residual amount will be available to the Agricultural Development Bank of China. Therefore, a significant stream of finance is available to fund projects under the OBOR.

One important motivation behind OBOR is to accelerate the development of the country's relatively poorer western and southern provinces. It has been reported that a sum of $20 billion is available for infrastructure and cross-border projects in the provinces which will be linked to the 'Belt' component of the initiative, in particular Sichuan, Gansu and Qinghai on China's western flank and Yunnan on the southern flank. Thus Chongqing in Sichuan is being established as the starting point of one of the branches of a rail freight corridor linking it with the German city of Duisburg. Another freight corridor will link Beijing with the port city of Hamburg, while a third corridor is proposed linking Wuhan with an as yet unidentified terminus in Europe. It is apparent that China has managed to secure the participation of Russia in the Eurasian component of the initiative, overcoming the earlier hesitations in Moscow about

China muscling Russia aside in what the latter regards as its "near neighbourhood". China has attempted to fold the OBOR into the Russian-led Eurasia Economic Union, which currently groups together Russia, Armenia, Belarus, Kazakhstan and Kyrgyzstan as well as into the Shanghai Cooperation Organisation. A Russian statement has welcomed the initiative, claiming that Siberia, Kazakhstan, Central Asia and the western provinces of China "are the natural centre of Eurasia". At the last SCO summit, Chinese President Xi Jinping said that his country would push for the completion of 4,000 kms of railways and 10,000 kms of highways within the region and that $16 billion of the Silk Road Fund would be dedicated to projects in Central Asia.

There are two significant energy projects linking Russia and China. One is the much publicised $400 million "Power of Siberia" pipeline and the other is the Altai gas pipeline connecting west Siberia to China. However, it is reported that both these projects may be delayed due to shortage of funds promised by China.

Why Europe matters for China

An important aspect of OBOR which has not been much in focus so far is the European end of the Belt and the Road, which is integral to securing China's influence both on the eastern and western flanks of Eurasia. There are carefully selected nodal points along the land corridor and terminal points along the maritime corridor. For example, Hungary has been chosen as a key logistics hub on the trans-Siberian link. It may serve as a distribution point for Chinese exports to Europe and an aggregating point for imports from Europe.

China has taken advantage of the Greek economic crisis to establish itself at the strategic port of Piraeus. The Chinese Shipping Company, COSCO, has a 35-year concession to expand the port by adding two modern container terminals.

It is likely to bid for the 67% Greek government stake in the port, when it is fully privatised. Greek shipping tonnage is one of the largest in the world and most ships for Greek shipping lines are built in China, which has the world's largest ship building industry. Piraeus will thus serve as a major logistics hub for Chinese trade with Europe. China is planning a Land-Sea Express which will link Piraeus with points on the European mainland. A $2.5 billion project is envisaged to build a key high speed rail link from Piraeus into Western Europe.

Another major European terminus is the Dutch port of Rotterdam, which is one of the most important cargo hubs for the entire continent. Like Gwadar in Pakistan, Rotterdam is the other point where the Belt and the Road on the land and maritime corridors come together. This, too, is projected as a major logistics centre for China-Europe trade.

The third terminal is Hamburg in Germany, although details of Chinese activities or investments there are not known yet. In addition, to Piraeus and Rotterdam, China has set up three major logistics and transport hubs, one at Wigan (Manchester) in the UK and two more at Schiphol airport, Amsterdam in the Netherlands. The latter will connect with the nearby port of Rotterdam.

Recently, during Premier Li Keqiang's visit to Brussels, China announced its readiness to invest in Europe's new infrastructure. It may contribute funds to the Juncker-sponsored Euro 315 billion European Fund for Strategic Investment. It should come as no surprise if China invests in those projects which are aligned to its OBOR objectives.

One should also add that the OBOR project also includes a Digital Silk Road and a Silk Road in Cyber Space. There is a proposal for a cooperative Internet Plus Plan which would link the OBOR countries to a super-fast broadband network.

China attaches great importance to promoting financial integration among countries along the OBOR It seeks to do this both through the setting up of institutions (such as the AIIB and the NDB) and the deployment of substantial sums. In this context, the UK has become a key platform for the internationalisation of the renminbi, the creation of an off-shore yuan bond market and the spread of Chinese banking in Europe. Apart from the Wigan logistics hub referred to earlier, London has become China's preferred centre for the launch of yuan-denominated bonds. China has invested in the redevelopment of real estate in the British capital and will guarantee $3 billion for the proposed nuclear power station in Hinckley. Several British banks have been favoured with licenses to operate in China. The British head start is leading to competitive courting by other European financial centres such as Frankfurt and Paris. Thus China sees Europe as helping it to put in place a sophisticated financial network which could underpin the ambitious physical networks that will bind Eurasia together.

This aspect is important because it could – and probably already has – weakened the trans-Atlantic alliance which has been a stable and predictable feature of geopolitics since the end of the Cold War. The British rush to join the AIIB followed by several other European powers, against US opposition, was a clear indication of this emerging trend. The longer it takes for the TTIP to be actualised, the greater the chances of China's Eurasian project succeeding.

What's in this for India?

While looking at the emerging geo-political landscape, Saul Bernhard Cohen, in his book*Geopolitics*, envisages the emergence of three strategic realms this century. One is the US-dominated maritime world of the North Atlantic and the North Pacific Basin; there is the second realm of Maritime Europe, organised around the European Union, and a Continental Asia geo-strategic realm covering the Eurasia landmass with Russia as the original core. But, as pointed out earlier, China has emerged as a separate Continental Maritime realm, shrinking the space for Russia in Central Asia and for the US in the North Pacific. There is an incipient effort to co-opt Russia on the one hand and Europe on the other to confine the US to the American hemisphere. The playing out of this story has major implications, because in case China succeeds with the global strategy underlying OBOR, India may well be consigned to the margins of both land and maritime Asia or become, by compulsion or by choice, a subordinate component of the Chinese-dominated network that is, in the words of Foreign Secretary S. Jaishankar, "hard-wiring" the new world.

Interestingly, Cohen foresaw a time when India, like China, could carve out a fourth geo-strategic realm also continental/maritime in nature. This it would do by dominating the eastern and western reaches of the Indian Ocean and the sub-continental landmass, south of Eurasia but linked to it. If this were indeed possible then India would have an opportunity to deal with the challenge of the Chinese geo-strategic realm on its doorstep with greater room for manoeuvre. I have argued before and do so again: If there is one country which has the potential to catch up with China and even overtake it, it is India. The current asymmetry is not riven in stone. What it will take India to achieve this long-term goal is well-known and I will not repeat it.

Currently, India has neither the resources nor the political and economic weight to put in place competitive and alternative connectivity networks on a global scale. Therefore, for the time being, it may be worthwhile to carefully evaluate those components of the OBOR which may, in fact, improve India's own connectivity to major markets and resource supplies and become participants in them just as we have chosen to do with the AIIB and the NDB.

For example, building a road/rail link to Central Asia through Iran using the port of Chahbahar could then use Chinese built routes to access both Central Asian and Russian destinations as well as Europe. It may be more important to deploy our limited resources to build an Indian Ocean network of ports, with connecting highways and rail routes such as exemplified by the planned Mekong-Ganga corridor and the Sittwe-Mizoram multi-modal transport corridor. There have been longstanding plans to develop the deep water port on Sri Lanka's eastern coast, Trincomalee, as a major energy and transport hub and yet, despite the warning message in the shape of Chinea building the Hambantota port in southern Sri Lanka and expanding the Colombo port, virtually no work has been undertaken since Indian Oil acquired the tank farm located at the port. The Andaman and Nicobar Islands lie at the very centre of the Bay of Bengal and could be developed to serve as a regional shipping hub for the littoral states and beyond. And yet, India continues to treat these islands as a distant outpost rather than leveraging their unique location at the very centre of one of the most strategic stretches of ocean space. There has been much talk about India launching a Spice Route, a Cotton Route and even a Mausam project tying the countries around the Indian Ocean bound together by the monsoon winds. Instead of spreading our limited resources thinly over these mostly rhetorical ripostes to China's OBOR, it may be more prudent to focus on limited but strategically key routes and ports along our adjacent seas and islands to safeguard our most important equities.

To recapitulate, the first priority would be developing our own Andaman and Nicobar Islands as a modern transport and shipping hub for the Bay of Bengal Basin. At the next level would be Chahbahar port to the west with road/rail links to Central Asia; Trincomalee port to the east, with shipping links to the Bay of Bengal littoral ports and beyond; the Mekong-Ganga corridor linking India's east coast with Indo-China; and the Kaladan multi-modal transport corridor in Myanmar's Rakhine province, including the port of Sittwe. The proposed BCIM corridor could then become part of this broader network. Once this primary circle has been secured one could move on to progressively expanding circles as resources become available. What is important to note is that in this 21st century strategy, security and economics go together. Creating a dense web of economic and trade relations itself becomes an assurance of security.

It is fair to say that China, in deploying the OBOR initiative, has demonstrated a level of ambition and imagination which is mostly absent in India's national discourse. It is time both scholars and practitioners started to think and act strategically on issues such as OBOR which will have a significant impact on India's vital interests.

A DIVERSITY OF ROUTES AND CARGOS: SILK PRODUCTION AND THE SILK TRADE

Silk is a textile of ancient Chinese origin, woven from the protein fibre produced by the silkworm to make its cocoon, and was developed, according to Chinese tradition, sometime around the year 2,700 BC. Regarded as an extremely high value product, it was reserved for the exclusive usage of the Chinese imperial court for the making of cloths, drapes, banners, and other items of prestige. Its production was kept a fiercely guarded secret within China for some 3,000 years, with imperial decrees sentencing to death anyone who revealed to a foreigner the process of its production. Tombs in the Hubei province dating from the 4th and 3rd centuries BC contain outstanding examples of silk work, including brocade, gauze and embroidered silk, and the first complete silk garments.

The Chinese monopoly on silk production however did not mean that the product was restricted to the Chinese Empire – on the contrary, silk was used as a diplomatic gift, and was also traded extensively, first of all with China's immediate neighbours, and subsequently further afield, becoming one of China's chief exports under the Han dynasty (206 BC –220 AD). Indeed, Chinese cloths from this period have been found in Egypt, in northern Mongolia, and elsewhere.

At some point during the 1st century BC, silk was introduced to the Roman Empire, where it was considered an exotic luxury and became extremely popular, with imperial edicts being issued to control prices. Its popularity continued throughout the Middle Ages, with detailed Byzantine regulations for the manufacture of silk clothes, illustrating its importance as a quintessentially royal fabric and an important source of revenue for the crown. Additionally, the needs of the Byzantine Church for silk garments and hangings were substantial. This luxury item was thus one of the early impetuses in the development of trading routes from Europe to the Far East.

Knowledge about silk production was very valuable and, despite the efforts of the Chinese emperor to keep it a closely guarded secret, it did eventually spread beyond China, first to India and Japan, then to the Persian Empire and finally to the west in the 6thcentury AD. This was described by the historian Procopius, writing in the 6th century:

Beyond Silk; a diversity of routes and cargos

However, whilst the silk trade was one of the earliest catalysts for the trade routes across Central Asia, it was only one of a wide range of products that was traded between east and west, and which included textiles, spices, grain, vegetables and fruit, animal hides, tools, wood work, metal work, religious objects, art work, precious stones and much more. Indeed, the Silk Roads became more popular and increasingly well-travelled over the course of the Middle Ages, and were still in use in the 19th century, a testimony not only to their usefulness but also to their flexibility and adaptability to the changing demands of society. Nor did these trading paths follow any one trail – merchants had a wide choice of different routes crossing a variety of regions of Eastern Europe, the Middle East, Central Asia and the Far East, as well as the maritime routes, which transported goods from China and South East Asia through the Indian Ocean to Africa, India and the Near East.

These routes developed over time and according to shifting geopolitical contexts throughout history. For example, merchants from the Roman Empire would try to avoid crossing the territory of the Parthians, Rome's enemies, and therefore took routes to the north, across the Caucasus region and over the Caspian Sea. Similarly, whilst extensive trade took place over the network of rivers that crossed the Central Asian steppes in the early Middle Ages, their water levels rose and fell, and sometimes dried up altogether, and trade routes shifted accordingly.

Maritime trade was another extremely important branch of this global trade network. Most famously used for the transportation of spices, the maritime trade routes have also been known as the Spice Roads, supplying markets across the world with cinnamon, pepper, ginger, cloves and nutmeg from the Moluccas islands in Indonesia (known as the Spice Islands), as well as a wide range of other goods. Textiles, woodwork, precious stones, metalwork, incense, timber, and saffron were all traded by the merchants travelling these routes, which stretched over 15,000 kilometres, from the west coast of Japan, past the Chinese coast, through South East Asia, and past India to reach the Middle East and so to the Mediterranean.

The history of these maritime routes can be traced back thousands of years, to links between the Arabian Peninsula, Mesopotamia and the Indus Valley Civilization. The early Middle Ages saw an expansion of this network, as sailors from the Arabian Peninsula forged new trading routes across the Arabian Sea and into the Indian Ocean. Indeed, maritime trading links were established between Arabia and China from as early as the 8th century AD. Technological advances in the science of navigation, in astronomy, and also in the techniques of ship building combined to make long-distance sea travel increasingly practical.

Lively coastal cities grew up around the most frequently visited ports along these routes, such as Zanzibar, Alexandria, Muscat, and Goa, and these cities became wealthy centres for the exchange of goods, ideas, languages and beliefs, with large markets and continually changing populations of merchants and sailors.

In the late 15th century, the Portuguese explorer, Vasco da Gama, navigated round the Cape of Good Hope, thereby connecting European sailors with these South East Asian maritime routes for the first time and initiating direct European involvement in this trade. By the 16th and 17th centuries, these routes and their lucrative trade had become subject of fierce rivalries between the Portuguese, Dutch, and British. The conquest of ports along the maritime routes brought both wealth and security, as they effectively governed the passage of maritime trade and also allowed ruling powers to claim monopolies on these exotic and highly sought-after goods, as well as gathering the substantial taxes levied on merchant vessels.

The map above illustrates the great variety of routes that were available to merchants bearing a wide range of goods and travelling from different parts of the world, by both land and sea. Most often, individual merchant caravans would cover specific sections of the routes, pausing to rest and replenish supplies, or stopping altogether and selling on their cargos at points throughout the length of the roads, leading to the growth of lively trading cities and ports. The Silk Roads were dynamic and porous; goods were traded with local populations throughout, and local products were added into merchants' cargos. This process enriched not only the merchants' material wealth and the variety of their cargos, but also allowed for exchanges of culture, language and ideas to take place along the Silk Roads.

Routes of Dialogue

Perhaps the most lasting legacy of the Silk Roads has been their role in bringing cultures and peoples in contact with each other, and facilitating exchange between them. On a practical level, merchants had to learn the languages and customs of the countries they travelled through, in order to negotiate successfully. Cultural interaction was a vital aspect of material exchange. Moreover, many travellers ventured onto the Silk Roads in order to partake in this process of intellectual and cultural exchange that was taking place in cities along the routes. Knowledge about science, arts and literature, as well as crafts and technologies was shared across the Silk Roads, and in this way, languages, religions and cultures developed and influenced each other. One of the most famous technical advances to have been propagated worldwide by the Silk Roads was the technique of making paper, as well as the development of printing press technology. Similarly, irrigation systems across Central Asia share features that were spread by travellers who not only carried their own cultural knowledge, but also absorbed that of the societies in which they found themselves.

Indeed, the man who is often credited with founding the Silk Roads by opening up the first route from China to the West in the 2ndcentury BC, General Zhang Qian, was on a diplomatic mission rather than a trading expedition. Sent to the West in 139 BC by the Han Emperor Wudi to ensure alliances against the Xiongnu, the hereditary enemies of the Chinese, Zhang Qian was captured and imprisoned by them. Thirteen years later he escaped and made his way back to China. Pleased with the wealth of detail and accuracy of his reports, the emperor sent Zhang Qian on another mission in 119 BC to visit several neighbouring peoples, establishing early routes from China to Central Asia.

Religion and a quest for knowledge were further inspirations to travel along these routes. Buddhist monks from China made pilgrimages to India to bring back sacred texts, and their travel diaries are an extraordinary source of information. The diary of Xuan Zang (whose 25-year journal lasted from 629 to 654 AD) not only has an enormous historical value, but also inspired a comic novel in the sixteenth century, the 'Pilgrimage to the West', which has become one of the great Chinese classics. During the Middle Ages, European monks undertook diplomatic and religious missions to the east, notably Giovanni da Pian del Carpini, sent by Pope Innocent IV on a mission to the Mongols from 1245 to 1247, and William of Rubruck, a Flemish Franciscan monk sent by King Louis IX of France again to the Mongol hordes from 1253 to 1255. Perhaps the most famous was the Venetian explorer, Marco Polo, whose travels lasted for more than 20 years between 1271 and 1292, and whose account of his experiences became extremely popular in Europe after his death.

The routes were also fundamental in the dissemination of religions throughout Eurasia. Buddhism is one example of a religion that travelled the Silk Roads, with Buddhist art and shrines being found as far apart as Bamiyan in Afghanistan, Mount Wutai in China, and Borobudur in Indonesia. Christianity, Islam, Hinduism, Zoroastrianism and Manicheism spread in the same way, as travellers absorbed the cultures they encountered and then carried them back to their homelands with them. Thus, for example, Hinduism and subsequently Islam were introduced into Indonesia and Malaysia by Silk

Road merchants travelling the maritime trade routes from India and Arabia.

CONCEPTUAL FRAMEWORK: BELT AND ROAD INITIATIVE

The Belt and Road Initiative alludes to the Silk Road Economic Belt and 21st Century Maritime Silk Road, a noteworthy improvement system dispatched by the Chinese government with the expectation of advancing financial co-operation among nations along the proposed Belt and Road courses.

The Initiative has been intended to improve the methodical free stream of financial variables and the effective allotment of assets. It is additionally proposed to further market combination and make a provincial financial co-operation structure of advantage to all.

The National Development and Reform Commission (NDRC) issued its Vision and Actions on Jointly Building the Silk Road Economic Belt and 21st Century Maritime Silk Road on 28 March 2015. This delineated the system, key territories of co-operation and co-operation instruments with respect to the Belt and Road Initiative.

Conceptual Framework

The Belt and Road Initiative aims to connect Asia, Europe and Africa along five routes. The Silk Road Economic Belt focusses on: (1) linking China to Europe through Central Asia and Russia; (2) connecting China with the Middle East through Central Asia; and (3) bringing together China and Southeast Asia, South Asia and the Indian Ocean. The 21st Century Maritime Silk Road, meanwhile, focusses on using Chinese coastal ports to: (4) link China with Europe through the South China Sea and Indian Ocean; and (5) connect China with the South Pacific Ocean through the South China Sea.

Focussing on the above five routes, the Belt and Road will take advantage of international transport routes as well as core cities and key ports to further strengthen collaboration and build six international economic co-operation corridors. These have been identified as the New Eurasia Land Bridge, China-Mongolia-Russia, China-Central Asia-West Asia, China-Indochina Peninsula, China-Pakistan, and Bangladesh-China-India-Myanmar.

The New Eurasia Land Bridge Economic Corridor

The New Eurasia Land Bridge, also known as the Second Eurasia Land Bridge, is an international railway line running from Lianyungang in China's Jiangsu province through Alashankou in Xinjiang to Rotterdam in Holland. The China section of the line comprises the Lanzhou-Lianyungang Railway and the Lanzhou-Xinjiang Railway and stretches through eastern, central and western China. After exiting Chinese territory, the new land bridge passes through Kazakhstan, Russia, Belarus and Poland, reaching a number of coastal ports in Europe. Capitalising on the New Eurasia Land Bridge, China has opened an international freight rail route linking Chongqing to Duisburg (Germany); a direct freight train running between Wuhan and Mìlník and Pardubice (Czech Republic); a freight rail route from Chengdu to Lodz (Poland); and a freight rail route from Zhengzhou to Hamburg (Germany). All these new rail routes offer rail-to-rail freight transport, as well as the convenience of "one declaration, one inspection, one cargo release" for any cargo transported.

The China-Mongolia-Russia Economic Corridor

Linked by land, China, Mongolia and Russia have long established various economic ties and co-operation by way of frontier trade and cross-border co-operation. In September 2014, when the three country's heads of state met for the first time at the Shanghai Co-operation Organisation (SCO) Dushanbe Summit, agreement was reached on forging tripartite co-operation on the basis of China-Russia, China-Mongolia and Russia-Mongolia bilateral ties. At the same meeting, the principles, directions and key areas of trilateral co-operation were defined. The three heads of state also agreed to bring together the building of China's Silk Road Economic Belt, the renovation of Russia's Eurasia Land Bridge and the proposed development of Mongolia's Steppe Road. This commitment will strengthen rail and highway connectivity and construction, advance customs clearance and transport facilitation, promote cross-national co-operation in transportation, and help establish the China-Russia-Mongolia Economic Corridor. In July 2015, the three leaders held a second meeting in the Russian city of Ufa. This second summit saw the official adoption of the *Mid-term Roadmap for Development of Trilateral Co-operation between China, Russia and Mongolia.*

China-Central Asia-West Asia Economic Corridor

The China-Central Asia-West Asia Economic Corridor runs from Xinjiang in China and exits the country via Alashankou to join the railway networks of Central Asia and West Asia before reaching the Mediterranean coast and the Arabian Peninsula. The corridor mainly covers five countries in Central Asia (Kazakhstan, Kyrgyzstan, Tajikistan, Uzbekistan and Turkmenistan) as well as Iran and Turkey in West Asia.

At the third China-Central Asia Co-operation Forum, held in Shandong in June 2015, a commitment to "jointly building the Silk Road Economic Belt" was incorporated into a joint declaration signed by China and the five Central Asian countries. Prior to that, China had signed bilateral agreements on the building of the Silk Road Economic Belt with Tajikistan, Kazakhstan and Kyrgyzstan. China had also concluded a co-operation document with Uzbekistan on the building of the Silk Road Economic Belt.

This was aimed at further deepening and expanding mutually beneficial co-operation in such areas as trade, investment, finance, transport and communication. The national development strategies of the five Central Asian countries – including Kazakhstan's "Road to Brightness", Tajikistan's "Energy, Transport and Food" (a three-pronged strategy aimed at revitalising the country), and Turkmenistan's "Strong and Happy Era" – all share common ground with the establishment of the Silk Road Economic Belt.

China-Indochina Peninsula Economic Corridor

During the Fifth Leaders Meeting on Greater Mekong Sub-regional Economic Co-operation, held in Bangkok in December 2014, Chinese Premier Li Keqiang put forward three suggestions with regard to deepening the relations between China and the five countries in the Indochina Peninsula. The suggestions included: (1) jointly planning and building an extensive transportation network, as well as number of industrial co-operation projects; (2) creating a new mode of co-operation for fundraising; and (3) promoting sustainable and co-ordinated socio-economic development. Currently, the countries along the Greater Mekong River are engaged in building nine cross-national highways, connecting east and west and linking north to south. A number of these construction projects have already been completed. Guangxi, for example, has already finished work on an expressway leading to the Friendship Gate and the port of Dongxing at the China-Vietnam border. The province has also opened an international rail line, running from Nanning to Hanoi, as well as introducing air routes to several major Southeast Asian cities.

China-Pakistan Economic Corridor

The concept of the China-Pakistan Economic Corridor was first raised by Premier Li Keqiang during his visit to Pakistan in May 2013. At the time, the objective was to build an economic corridor running from Kashgar, Xinjiang, in the north, to Pakistan's Gwadar Port in the south. At present, the two governments have mapped out a provisional long-term plan for building highways, railways, oil and natural gas pipelines and optic fibre networks stretching from Kashgar to Gwadar Port. According to a joint declaration issued by China and Pakistan in Islamabad in April 2015, the two countries will proactively advance key co-operation projects, including phase II of the upgrade and renovation of the Karakoram Highway (the Thakot-Havelian section), an expressway at the east bay of Gwadar Port, a new international airport, an expressway from Karachi to Lahore (the Multan-Sukkur section), the Lahore rail transport orange line, the Haier-Ruba economic zone, and the China-Pakistan cross-national optic fibre network.

Bangladesh-China-India-Myanmar Economic Corridor

In a series of meetings during Premier Li Keqiang's visit to India in May 2013, China and India jointly proposed the building of the Bangladesh-China-India-Myanmar Economic Corridor. In December 2013, the Bangladesh-China-India-Myanmar Economic Corridor Joint Working Group convened its first meeting in Kunming. Official representatives from the four countries conducted in-depth discussions with regard to the development prospects, priority areas of co-operation and co-operation mechanisms for the economic corridor. They also reached extensive consensus on co-operation in such areas as transportation infrastructure, investment and commercial circulation, and people-to-people connectivity. The four parties signed meeting minutes and agreed the Bangladesh-China-India-Myanmar Economic Corridor joint study programme, establishing a mechanism for promoting co-operation among the four governments.

Key Areas of Co-operation

The five major goals of the Belt and Road Initiative are: policy co-ordination, facilities connectivity, unimpeded trade, financial integration, and people-to-people bonds.

In terms of specifics, policy co-ordination means that countries along the belt and road will, via consultation on an equal footing, jointly formulate development plans and measures for advancing cross-national or regional co-operation; resolve problems arising from co-operation through consultation; and jointly provide policy support to practical co-operation and large-scale project implementation.

Facilities connectivity refers to prioritising areas of construction as part of the Belt and Road strategy. Efforts will be made to give priority to removing barriers in the missing sections and bottleneck areas of core international transportation passages, advancing the construction of port infrastructure facilities, and clearing land-water intermodal transport passages. The connectivity of infrastructure facilities, including railways, highways, air routes, telecommunications, oil and natural gas pipelines and ports, will also be promoted. This will form part of a move to establish an infrastructure network connecting various Asian sub-regions with other parts of Asia, Europe and Africa.

In order to facilitate unimpeded trade, steps will be taken to resolve investment and trade facilitation issues, reduce investment and trade barriers, lower trade and investment costs, as well as to promote regional economic integration. Efforts will also be made to broaden the scope of trade, propel trade development through investment, and strengthen co-operation in the industry chain with all related countries.

With regard to financial integration, action will be taken to enhance co-ordination in monetary policy, expand the scope of local currency settlement and currency exchange in trade and investment between countries along the route, deepen multilateral and bilateral financial co-operation, set up regional development financial institutions, strengthen co-operation in monitoring financial risks, and enhance the ability of managing financial risks through regional arrangements.

In terms of people-to-people bonds, efforts will be made to promote exchanges and dialogues between different cultures, strengthen friendly interactions between the people of various countries, and heighten mutual understanding and traditional friendships. This will all form the basis for the advancement of regional co-operation.

Co-operation Mechanisms

The Belt and Road Initiative upholds the principles of jointly developing the programme through consultation with all interested parties. Existing bilateral and multilateral co-operation mechanisms will be utilised to promote the integration of the development strategies of the countries along the route. Steps will be taken to advance the signing of co-operation memorandums of understanding or co-operation plans for the establishment of a number of bilateral co-operation demonstration projects. Efforts will also be made to set up a sound bilateral joint work mechanism, and to devise an implementation plan and action roadmap for advancing the Belt and Road strategy.

The Silk Road Fund

The US$40 billion Silk Road Fund has been established to finance the Belt and Road Initiative. It will invest mainly in infrastructure and resources, as well as in industrial and financial cooperation. The Fund was set up as a limited liability company in December 2014 with its founding shareholders including China's State Administration of Foreign Exchange, the China Investment Corp, the Export-Import Bank of China and the China Development Bank. The Fund will comply with market rules and the international order of finance, and welcome participation from domestic and overseas investors, such as the China-Africa Development Fund and the Asian Infrastructure Investment Bank.

The Asian Infrastructure Investment Bank (AIIB)

The AIIB, a new multilateral development bank (MDB), has been set up with a view to complementing and cooperating with the existing MDBs in order to address infrastructure needs in Asia. AIIB will focus on the development of infrastructure and other productive sectors in Asia, including energy and power, transportation and telecommunications, rural infrastructure and agriculture development, water supply and sanitation, environmental protection, urban development and logistics.

As of December 2015, all of the 57 Prospective Founding Members of AIIB had signed the Articles of Agreement. The initial signatories were Australia, Austria, Azerbaijan, Bangladesh, Brazil, Brunei Darussalam, Cambodia, China, Denmark, Egypt, Finland, France, Georgia, Germany, Iceland, India, Indonesia, Iran, Israel, Italy, Jordan, Kazakhstan, Republic of Korea, Kyrgyz Republic, Kuwait, Lao PDR,

Luxembourg, Malaysia, Maldives, Malta, Mongolia, Myanmar, Nepal, Netherlands, New Zealand, Norway, Oman, Pakistan, Philippines, Poland, Portugal, Qatar, Russia, Saudi Arabia, Singapore, South Africa, Spain, Sri Lanka, Sweden, Switzerland, Tajikistan, Thailand, Turkey, the United Arab Emirates, the United Kingdom, Uzbekistan, and Vietnam.

The AIIB Articles of Agreement entered into force on 25 December 2015. On 16 January 2016, the Board of Governors held its inaugural meeting, declaring the Bank open for business and electing Mr. Jin Liqun as President for an initial five-year term.

5

OBOR and the Central Asian Stans

Endowments of natural resources (gas, uranium, petroleum, etc.) attracted the Chinese presence in Central Asia well before the launch of the OBOR initiative. China has secured its supplies to fuel the strong growth of its economy. China's participation in the development of the energy sectors contributed to the strong growth of trade. Over the past decade, trade between China and Kazakhstan has increased from $ 5 billion to $ 20 billion, from $ 0 to $ 10 billion with Turkmenistan, from a few hundred million to nearly $ 5 billion with Kyrgyzstan, Uzbekistan, Tajikistan's $ 2 billion. Over the same period, Russia's trade with Kazakhstan grew from $ 8 billion to $ 20 billion; They have made very little progress, or even stagnated, with the other Stans (Financial Times 2015).

For these countries, cooperation with China is also a means of relaxing the dependence on Russia which was at the initiative of the creation of the Eurasian Economic Union (EEU). The countries of the region, notably Kazakhstan, are hard pressed to cope with this dual dependency: devaluation of the currency, the impact of the Russian economic crisis, and Chinese pressure to obtain benefits (leasing of lands). Today, in hydrocarbons, China represents more than 30% of investments in the country. For other countries such as Kyrgyzstan, cooperation with China allows for infrastructure development, reducing dependency with Russia. The Kyrgyz economy is also strongly affected by the Russian crisis, especially with the drastic decline in transfers of remittances from Russia.

The relationship with Russia is certainly the most problematic because of the competition / cooperation relations that stem from the strong economic presence of China in this Union, and in the strong asymmetries that follow. China imports raw materials, it brings capital, infrastructure and actually integrates these economies, reducing the scope of the economic choices of each country, and their specializations.

To the contrasting economic dynamics are added the level of resources available, the geopolitical stakes, the desired coherence between the construction of a new economic space (Eurasian Economic Union) and the linkage to the OBOR project. Recent negotiations between China and the Economic Commission of the new Union have addressed a number of issues related to trade and investment, leaving aside the issue of a free trade agreement, which is still a very sensitive issue for Russia and the countries of Central Asia because of the high level of protectionism. For Russia the benefits of EEU cooperation with the OBOR project are greater than the risks involved even though it is inevitable that China will become the main investor in Central Asia and the main market for the region's vast natural resources.

In addition, Chinese objectives, including the construction of fast rail lines to reach Europe, compete with the existing lines (Trans-Siberian). Russia intends to integrate in this project the development of the eastern regions of Siberia, as far as Vladivostok. The construction of a high-speed Moscow-Kazan train by China (originally to be financed by Russia and built by Germany) is the cornerstone of this cooperation between the UEE and the OBOR project. This high-speed train should link, in the future, Moscow to Beijing.

At the moment, the Asian pivot envisaged by Russia does not yet translate into an increase in trade flows. Trade remains at a relatively low level, unbalanced in favor of China. Foreign direct investment also shows a strong imbalance, with the Chinese investing in more diversified sectors, reflecting the practice in other parts of the world, notably in Europe (Richet 2016). Agreements for the conveyance of Russian gas to China involve large investments, notably the construction of a gas pipeline (Power of Siberia 2), but there are still differences of view on the roads to be borrowed. Ultimately, Russia should become China's gas supplier up to 30% of its needs. Strictly speaking, these agreements relate to bilateral relations between the two countries and not necessarily within the framework of the OBOR project.

Finally, further west, but still in the EEU, Belarus intends to benefit from the customs union established by the EEU, since trains from China and heading to Europe will only have to cross two customs posts (China-Kazakhstan, Belarus-Poland).

THE OBOR ROUTINGS

Reflecting at the land and sea routes of the old Silk Road linkages, the OBOR has land and sea dimensions that converge at certain points, which together constitute an extraordinary seamless connectivity that embraces all of Eurasia and the Indian Ocean littoral. The Eurasian land connection, known as the "New Silk Road Economic Belt" or simply the "Belt," is made up of railways, highways, oil and gas pipelines, and major energy projects.

Beginning at Xian, the legendary starting point of the old Silk Road, the OBOR will have two routings: one, across China to Kazakhstan and then Moscow, and the other through Mongolia and southern Russia to Moscow. Both routes will merge and then go on to European cities — Budapest, Hamburg and Rotterdam. The southern route will branch into one that will cross Iran and Turkey, and end at Budapest. It will have another branch from the Pakistani port of Gwadar to the Chinese city of Kashgar in the western province of Xinjiang.

The sea route, known as the "Maritime Silk Road" or simply the "Road," made up of ports and coastal development, begins from China's eastern ports and goes on to Southeast Asia, South Asia, East Africa and then on to West Asia and the

Mediterranean, embracing Greece and Venice and ending at Rotterdam. Both routes, again recalling the old Silk Road, will have a series of loops and branches, with the two main routes also meeting at important junctions, such as Gwadar, Istanbul, Rotterdam and Hamburg. According to Korean scholar Jae Ho Chung, when completed, the OBOR will include 60 countries, with two-thirds of the world's population, 55 percent of the global GDP and 75per cent of global energy reserves. It will consist of 900 infrastructure projects, valued at about 1.3 trillion US dollars. Much of the funding is expected to come from Chinese banks, financial institutions and special funds. The Hong Kong-based South China Morning Post has described the OBOR as "the most significant and far-reaching project the nation has ever put forward".

Promoting the OBOR

The OBOR initiative has captured world attention for the sheer range and audacity of the concept, the extraordinary ambition that lies at its base and the significant resources — technological, human, financial and political — that will need to be garnered globally to realise the vision. Since the first announcement, Chinese officials and commentators have debated the project, fleshed out several loose ends and sought to bring as many countries as possible on board as partners.

These have included a series of engagements with policymakers in countries on the OBOR routes. The OBOR was of course initiated in Central Asia and China has obtained the support of these republics with promises of massive investment for regional development. Xi has said China will support the construction of 4000 kilometres of railways and 10,000 kilometres of highways in Central Asia, with nearly 16 billion US dollars of Chinese funding.

When completed, the OBOR will include 60 countries, with two-thirds of the world's population, 55 per cent of the global GDP and 75 per cent of global energy reserves. It will consist of 900 infrastructure projects, valued at about 1.3 trillion US dollars. The next most important interaction China has had on the OBOR is with Russia. China has benefited from Russian estrangement from the West following the events in Ukraine – and the consequent abandoning of the Russian "Greater Europe" project that would have linked Vladivostok with Lisbon – and developed energy, financial, technological and defence ties with Moscow. This has led to Russian acceptance of China's presence in Central Asia and the merging of Russian President Vladimir Putin's Eurasian Economic Union project with the OBOR.

In October 2013, Xi reached out to the ASEAN countries and sought to bring them within the fold of the maritime route by invoking 14th century Chinese mariner Zheng He (1371-1433/35), who explored South and Southeast Asia, and proposing the building of a close-knit China-ASEAN community. Following this, Xi met a Gulf Cooperation Council delegation in January 2014 and attempted to make West Asia a partner in the OBOR as well.

The drivers of the OBOR

In promoting the OBOR, China is being driven by domestic and foreign considerations. The urge to achieve development in all of China's 31 provinces is a major factor and all provinces have already affirmed their active participation in different aspects of the enterprise. The western province of Qinghai has indicated that it will build a rail, highway and aviation network to link the provinces and countries along the OBOR; Guangdong province along the coast will execute some major infrastructure projects, such as a power plant in Vietnam and an oil refinery in Myanmar.

The realisation of the OBOR will of course see the western province of Xinjiang playing a major role — its cities of Urumqi, Kashgar and Khorgos will be at the centre of many of the proposed routes. OBOR-related projects will also provide an outlet for China to use its overcapacity in steel, cement and construction materials, as also its surplus financial reserves.

Chinese scholar Tingyi Wang of Tsinghua University has explained that while the OBOR is prompted by China's interests in energy, security and promotion of economic ties, it is actually driven by the vision of a "greater Eurasian idea" that calls for "strengthening economic and cultural integration" across this whole swathe of territory and building "a new type of international relations underpinned by win-win cooperation". Wang summarises the Chinese strategy as "to guarantee its interests in this region and at the same time cooperate with the other powers". Former Indian Foreign Secretary Shyam Saran sees the OBOR not just as economic initiative but one that has clear political and security implications; it is for Saran "a carving out by China of a continental-marine geo-strategic realm".

The China-Pakistan Economic Corridor

The one aspect of the OBOR that has caused the greatest concern in India, both in regard to its land and maritime implications, is the China-Pakistan Economic Corridor (CPEC). Finalised in April 2015 on the basis of 51 agreements, the CPEC consists of a series of highway, railway and energy projects, emanating from the newly developed port of Gwadar on the Arabian Sea, all of which taken together will be valued at 46 billion US dollars. These projects will generate 700,000 jobs in Pakistan and, when completed, add 2-2.5 per cent to the country's GDP. The CPEC has been described as a "flagship project" for the OBOR.

Gwadar will be developed as a deep-water port capable of handling 300-400 million tonnes of cargo per year. A new 1100-kilometres motorway from Karachi to Lahore will be completed, while the Karakoram Highway from Rawalpindi to the Chinese border will be re-constructed. Railway lines across the country will be thoroughly upgraded and expanded, with the road and railway network reaching Kashgar in Xinjiang.

Oil and gas pipelines will be constructed, including a gas pipeline from Gwadar to Nawabshah, carrying gas from Iran. Most of the money will be spent on energy projects — about 10,400 MW of electricity will be developed between 2018-20, besides renewable energy, coal and liquefied natural gas projects.

An 800-kilometres optic fibre link to boost telecommunications in the Gilgit-Baltistan region is already under construction. These projects will promote national economic development through industrial parks and special economic zones. Washington-based Council on Foreign Relations described CPEC as "part development scheme, part strategic gambit" in a recent report.

By investing heavily in Pakistan's development, particularly in its backward regions, China is clearly addressing its own concerns relating to security problems whose roots are in Pakistan. The most important of these is the threat from the East Turkestan Islamic Movement (ETIM), made up of Chinese-dissident Uighur militant groups that have taken sanctuary in the Pakistan-Afghanistan border areas and are said to be linked to al-Qaeda and the Taliban. The ETIM aims its violence at targets in China and also at Chinese interests in Pakistan.

Gwadar port, which will be developed and operated by Chinese companies will have both economic and strategic advantages for China. It will enable China to route the oil and gas purchases from the Gulf through pipelines that would bypass the West-dominated Malacca Straits, thus providing China with one more alternative route, besides the Sittwe-Kunming pipeline in Myanmar. Again, control over Gwadar would give China a permanent naval presence in the western Indian Ocean and a commanding position at the mouth of the Gulf. This dramatic expansion of the Chinese naval forces into what India sees as its home-ground is a matter of long-term concern for India.

CHINA'S CURRENT SECURITY POLICY

In response to the attacks in Africa during the last five years, China has confronted the problem of nontraditional security threats in several ways.

The PRC's initial reaction is to work with local governments. "China will cooperate closely with immigration departments of African countries in tackling the problem of illegal migration, improve exchange of immigration control information, and set up an unimpeded and efficient channel for intelligence and information exchange," China's 2006 *Africa Policy* stated.

"In order to enhance the ability of both sides to address nontraditional security threats, it is necessary to increase intelligence exchange, explore more effective ways and means for closer cooperation in combating terrorism, small-arms smuggling, drug trafficking, transnational economic crimes, etc." Beijing has instructed its embassies in Africa to keep a close watch on local security. The swift and successful evacuation of Chinese citizens from Chad also demonstrated that China has developed operational scenarios to deal with these emergencies. The Chinese government has also started issuing travel advisories.

In Sudan and Kenya, state-owned companies receive protection from local armed forces against attacks by rebels. Beijing has signed an agreement with South Africa to prevent the Chinese diaspora from turning into a target for armed gangs. Such measures are designed to help Chinese citizens and companies avoid some of the risks related to operating in Africa, but they do not provide any guarantee for safeguarding China's economic activities if the situation keeps deteriorating. In the case of Sudan, China learned the hard way that prodding instable governments can have drastic consequences. If problems start to occur at the regional level, supporting these emerging states might prove even riskier.

Nor does this narrow security response address China's uncertainty about the military capability of African nations. The dilemma reverts back to the realistic supposition of self-help. Is the PRC trying to safeguard its interests by building up its own military presence in Africa?

Bilateral military exchanges are a first indicator to test whether this assumption holds true. According to the Chinese government, interaction with other armed forces expanded significantly, with 174 high-level visits in 2001 and more than 210 in 2006. This upward trend was not maintained in Africa, however, where such bilateral exchanges have remained stable at an annual average of 26. Beijing has established a permanent military dialogue only with South Africa. Interviews with European diplomats in ten randomly chosen African countries also reveal that the number of accredited military officers in Chinese embassies, i.e., military attachés and their support staff, has barely or not expanded at all in the last few years. In fact, only in 15 countries are Chinese military attachés assigned on a permanent basis. China's military diplomacy in Africa remains modest, and it has not kept up with the impressive number of Chinese trade officials posted in African nations to strengthen economic ties in the last few years. Military aid is another indicator. Providing military hardware to partner nations can serve various objectives. In a context of competition, it helps to thwart defence cooperation with other states or to prevent other powers' attempts to alter the regional military balance. Defence aid might help a privileged political partner to safeguard economic interests. Whereas these three objectives are motivated by security issues and long-term economic interests, defence aid may well be the result of more short-sighted aspirations. There is no evidence that China's military aid successfully counterbalances other powers, such as the United States.

Apart from Sudan and Zimbabwe, most countries that have received Chinese military aid in the last few years are also supplied by Washington. In 2007, Beijing temporarily froze the supply of heavy arms to Khartoum after pressure from the West. When Nigeria's Vice President, Atiku Abubakar, announced that his nation would turn to China instead of the United States for arms, Beijing's response was reluctant, and no major supply operations materialized. China's military aid programs should not be considered as support for its forays into the mining industry. For instance, between 2004 and 2008, resource-rich Nigeria received only half as much military aid as Ghana or Uganda. During this period, China provided more military assistance to Angola than to Sudan, even though the security challenges in the latter were much greater.

Although violence in Somalia has threatened China's oil exploration activities in both Ethiopia and Kenya, China only made a commitment to Kenya to help in protecting its border. China has, at times, provided military aid, but such assistance does not seem to be part of any coherent strategy related to protecting its security interests.

Finally, self-help would imply the deployment of military forces whenever China's interests are threatened, possibly in an attempt to train friendly armed forces and dissuade any challengers. Yet, such a Chinese military presence is negligible. China has no bases in Africa, as does the United States and France, nor has it trained African soldiers to counter threats to its national interests.

In Sudan, Zimbabwe, Cameroon, and Gabon, China has employed teams of three to ten instructors, but they are assisting in the maintenance of equipment, rather than providing training for combat missions. In Zambia and Algeria, similar examples of cooperation exist but are limited to medical activities. Other major powers deployed naval vessels in an effort to combat piracy and to maintain the maritime supply lines surrounding Africa. During such operations, the Chinese Navy has rarely shown its flag.

In 2000, China sent its newest *Luhai*-class guided missile destroyer and a supply ship to Tanzania and South Africa. A 2002 fleet composed of a guided missile destroyer, the *Qingdao*, and a supply ship, the *Taicang*, visited Egypt. These voyages were gestures of courtesy rather than a reaction to security challenges. They were limited in duration, and no actions were attempted against pirates or poachers. In December 2008, however, the Chinese government did deploy two destroyers and a replenishment ship in the Gulf of Aden to participate in the United Nations-backed mission against piracy. A mission that was only undertaken after receiving a positive signal from US Pacific Command chief Admiral Timothy Keating.

Instead of dealing with security threats unilaterally, China has resorted to bandwagoning. Although in the 1980s and early 1990s, Beijing opposed attempts by the international community to intervene in African security issues, nowadays it tends to join them. Beijing is increasingly recognizing the United Nations' role in resolving the numerous conflicts and safeguarding the sovereignty of developing nations. In the 1990s, China began supporting United Nations (UN) missions designed to implement peace agreements between rivalling parties, on the condition that a well-defined and restricted mandate was included. Traditional peacekeeping operations such as those in Somalia (UNSOM I), Mozambique, Rwanda, and Sierra Leone all were supported. When the UN Security Council decided to dispatch forces to Liberia in 2003, China offered to support the mission and gradually increased the number of its peacekeepers to 1,300 in 2007.

At the same time, however, failed states and national governments that had actively participated in atrocities challenged the efficacy of many of the traditional UN operations. China's focus on the primacy of sovereignty, requiring at a minimum the state's consent, collided with the willingness of other nations to intervene aggressively under the UN Charter's Chapter VII mandate.

Beijing loudly opposed the move by European countries to push for Operation Turquoise in Rwanda, Washington's call to broaden the UNSOM mandate, or France's demand for a troop increase in the 2004 UN operation in Ivory Coast. Despite its strong concerns, China did not veto these interventions at the UN Security Council, but rather abstained and remained aloof from implementation. Sudan was the first instance where China actively lobbied an African government to permit a UN mission on its soil. Via active brokering and indirect pressure, China succeeded in neutralizing the incompatibility between its economic interests and the principle of noninterference on the one hand, and western appeals for intervening in Darfur and the need for long-term stability on the other.

That Beijing recognizes the importance of collective security became apparent in 2006, when China was the first nation to ask the UN Security Council for a peacekeeping mission in Somalia. In June that year, at a Security Council meeting in Addis Ababa, China's Permanent Representative to the UN, Wang Guangya, scolded other diplomats for neglecting Somalia and urged them to support the deployment of peacekeepers. "I was reluctant to take on this role," said Wang, explaining that African governments had been pushing China to raise the issue in the Council, "but there was a lack of interest by the other major powers."

Initially, the proposal was tentatively received by Great Britain and the United States, but after various talks in New York, Beijing and Washington jointly sponsored a resolution for the deployment of a UN mission. In 2007, in early consultations with France, China supported a French draft resolution on Chad calling for the dispatch of mainly European peacekeepers under the auspices of Chapter VII. It was significant that China approved the "close liaising" with the Hybrid Operation in Darfur (UNAMID), where earlier it had objected to the development of links between UNAMID and UN missions. "Our support for the resolution on Chad shows that we are prepared to cooperate to tackle security issues at a regional level and that our awareness on the increasing complexity of violent conflicts in Africa grows," a Chinese diplomat explained.

China is also turning to African regional organizations to collaborate on security issues. In the China-Africa Action Plan, approved in November 2006, Beijing vowed "to support Africa in the areas of logistics" as well as "to continue its active participation in the peacekeeping operations and demining process in Africa and provide, within the limits of its capabilities, financial and material assistance as well as relevant training to the Peace and Security Council of the African Union." In June 2006, the Chinese government granted the African Union's Mission in Sudan $3.5 million in budgetary support and humanitarian aid. Earlier, it provided financial and technical support to the Association for West African States.

Slowly but surely, China is showing itself ready to participate in international efforts to prevent conflicts, fuelled by the easy availability of small arms and illegally exported natural resources. In 2002, for instance, Beijing revised its regulation on the control of military products for export and published the

"Military Products Export Control List" supplying guidelines for the export of military-related products. In the same year, it signed the "Protocol Against the Illicit Manufacturing of and Trafficking in Firearms," which committed the People's Republic to control the manufacturing, marking, import, and export of firearms, and to confiscate and destroy all illicit firearms. In 2005, the government launched a national information management system for the production, possession, and trade of light arms, and it introduced a system to monitor end-users of Chinese-made weapons to prevent the arms from finding their way to "sensitive regions" around the world via third parties. In 2006, China supported a draft UN resolution on the illicit trade of small arms and light weapons, in contrast to the United States. In 2002, China joined the Kimberley Process, a joint government, international diamond industry, and civil initiative designed to stem the flow of conflict diamonds originating from Africa. In 2005, China allowed a voluntary peer review of its support for the Kimberly Process. Although these actions still have many flaws, they seem to prove that China wishes to do more than just put "boots on the ground" in response to Africa's internal conflicts.

Despite the strategic importance of Africa, China does not try to safeguard its foothold in the region by unilaterally projecting military power. In Africa, its military diplomacy remains limited when compared with defence initiatives in other regions. If the PRC does pursue bilateral cooperation programs, these are more likely to be a part of its diplomatic charm offensive, rather than addressing threats to China's economic and security interests. Instead of relying on a military presence to counterbalance other powers, the PRC tends to join collective security efforts within the framework of the United Nations and African regional organizations. Over the past few years, this strategy of joint ventures has evolved from passive support to active cooperation. Beijing has softened its devotion to noninterference. While maintaining the primacy of sovereignty, it has become willing to support interventions whenever regional stability is at stake.

Although China has become a revisionist power in terms of its economic aspirations on the continent, it is acting as a status-quo power in terms of security objectives. There are several explanations for this stance. First, China only recently began its economic focus on the African continent. For the past two decades, China concentrated on curbing the military and diplomatic influence of Taiwan; the focus on "economization" of its Africa policy only began in the late 1990s.

Hence, the security challenges it is facing now are a recent phenomena, and solutions to these challenges are just starting to be explored. The PRC is going through the early stage of resecuritization of its Africa strategy, and joining with other nations in an allied strategy can be considered the easiest immediate response. Second, and related to this point, China has not developed sufficient means to back up its security policy with military power. This is a matter of budgetary constraints. Building an independent and sustained military presence is a costly affair and would, at present, overstretch the PLA's capabilities, while Asia remains its primary focus. The PLA does not possess the logistical capacity to support sustained region wide deployment in Africa. Its long-range airlift and sealift, as well as its intelligence and command capabilities, are not up to the task. Third the Chinese government wants to avoid the People's Republic being perceived as a hegemonic power.

In the initial stage of its economic charm offensive, the PRC tried to pursue a business-as-usual approach, maintaining a low profile and steering clear of political entanglements. That approach is no longer possible now that China stands at the forefront of Africa's political scene, actively altering the economic balance of power. Beijing is well aware of the dichotomy between its weak and strong identities and is reluctant to demonstrate any independent military capacity. Such a show of strength might reduce its diplomatic maneuverability, increase resistance from African nations-just as Washington is now experiencing-and raise suspicions elsewhere regarding Chinese intentions. Yet, as interests, perceptions, and capacities are susceptible to change, the question remains whether China will stay on this track of cooperative security.

China's interests in Africa have changed over the past decades and will undoubtedly continue to evolve. The concept for its security policy in the region will depend on the role that Africa plays as a supplier of natural resources. Africa currently supplies approximately 30 percent of China's oil imports. Beijing and its African partners announced that they are preparing to increase bilateral trade to $100 billion by the year 2010. Most of this increase will come from the import of raw commodities. In recent years, Chinese companies have laid the foundation for a substantial increase in the production of resource industries. Exploration in the Gulf of Guinea, Angola, and the Horn of Africa have the potential for an increase in oil exports to China of more than 80 percent in the next ten years. Chinese companies are just starting to tap the large mines that were recently acquired in Gabon, the Democratic Republic of Congo, Namibia, and elsewhere on the continent. Given the fact that other emerging markets such as India and Brazil are shifting the use of their raw materials from export to domestic consumption, the economic relevance of Africa to China cannot be overstated.

How necessary it is to back up these Chinese economic ventures with more overt security measures is yet to be seen. The incidents described in the first section of this article, the persistent instability in nations, as well as the weak position of amicable political leaders will undoubtedly position Africa higher on Beijing's foreign security agenda and require a more complete approach. The question again arises whether it is in China's best interest to apply its African policy independently or in synergy with other nations.

The short-term costs of any unilateral action would certainly exceed those of collective action, but long-term uncertainty about the intentions of other major players might influence any concerns related to cost-effectiveness. If Washington or Delhi decides to change course and contain China's expanding influence in Africa by pursing a strategy of counterbalancing and sea denial, the repercussions for the People's Republic will be dramatic.

The concerns of the national security establishments in India and the United States and their expanding military presence in Africa are not unnoticed in China, and they highlight the necessity for the PRC to build a legitimate capacity to deal with crises unilaterally. China's diplomatic identity will help shape policy decisions in support of a more active and autonomous security strategy.

Beijing is realizing that the comfortable cloak of frailty it previously presented to the world no longer fits. African partners do not attach much value to China's diplomatic schizophrenia and the complex image of an economic giant, political dwarf, and minor military player it projects. When mayhem erupts, China automatically ends up on the frontline, finding itself hounded by African governments asking it to exercise its leverage.

The cases of Chad and Somalia are not the only examples of this. South Africa has accosted China regarding illegal immigrants from Zimbabwe. Central Africa has carefully examined the violent incursions from Sudan. The African Union has called upon China several times to play a more active role in promoting security. The possibility exists that individual countries may be compelled to form a closer alliance with China in order to reduce their current reliance on the European Union and United States for security. Nigeria's announcement that it would rely on China instead of the United States for military support hints at this direction. The ability of the PRC to keep a low military profile is diminishing.

On the other hand, China's self-perception is also in transition. The "Century of Humiliation" is far behind and is being replaced by a national attitude of confidence and assertiveness. Chinese leaders have built on the success of their policy of good neighbour diplomacy that resulted in fewer frictions and more influence in Asia. The People's Republic has drawn confidence from the successful launch of a number of new defence systems. As China sees its diplomatic leverage expanding geographically from the Strait of Formosa, via Asia to the rest of the developing world, its ability to deal with emerging security issues is likely to follow suit.

Finally, there is the factor of capacity. China is gearing its military for a greater deployment capability. Its large immobile army is gradually being converted into a highly specialized and flexible organization. Simultaneously, the PLA is launching new military systems that will enhance its capacity to transport these forces.

In 2007, the Chinese government approved the development of large passenger jets, including military transport variants similar to the American C-17 Globemaster III. Beijing has also ordered several new ships in an effort to enhance its naval transport capacity. In 2006, the hull of the first T-071 vessel was laid.

This landing-platform dock has a range that goes far beyond Taiwan, with the aim of providing sea-based support to operations on land, humanitarian aid, and assisting in evacuations and disaster management. These vessels will be supported by a new generation of large replenishment ships and could be escorted by advanced frigates and destroyers. The Chinese flotilla that was sent to Somalia demonstrates China's new blue-water capacity.

The type 052C *Lanzhou*, for instance, is a showcase of the advanced detection capacity for China's Navy. Its multifunction, active phased-array radar has a detection range of 450 kilometres and is complemented with a long-range, two-dimensional air search radar that has a 350-kilometer range and three additional systems to detect incoming missiles and aircraft. China is advancing its ability to pursue a more confident and independent security policy in Africa.

Will all this newfound military activity be sufficient to offset the antagonistic response it is likely to provoke? Probably not. If China decides to go solo and to pursue a more aggressive security policy in Africa, it is improbable that it will be able to overcome countermoves by India and the United States. It will be difficult for China to safeguard maritime trade with

Africa if India exercises its naval dominance in the Indian Ocean.

The sheer geographical divide between the PRC and the African continent makes it extremely difficult to support military activities if the United States or India opposes them. Contrary to China's revolutionary phase of the 1950s and 1960s when trade and economic interests only played a small part, China's increasing reliance on Africa renders it highly vulnerable to sea denial operations or a *guerre de course*. The fragile Cold War balance between the United States and the Soviet Union that allowed Mao to meddle with America's interests in Africa without having to fear political or economic reprisals can no longer be counted on. These days China has much to lose if it provokes Washington or Delhi.

"THE HEGEMONY GAMES": THE USA AND THE PEOPLE'S REPUBLIC OF CHINA

This relationship between Washington and Beijing has existed somewhat uneasily since the early 1970s after the PRC broke with the Soviet Union mainly over intense ideological differences within the communist movement. In effect the Communist Party of China (CPC) joined with capitalist America in an informal tacit alliance against Russia. This was a geopolitical triumph for the U.S. but not for China. In the last couple of years Beijing and Moscow have developed a close relationship, largely as a repost to Washington's expressions of hostility toward both countries.

China was considered a revolutionary communist country from the 1949 revolution until the deaths of party leader Mao Zedong and Premier Zhou Enlai in 1976. The left wing of the CPC was then crushed, and the leadership in 1977 went to "paramount leader" Deng Xiaoping, a long time revolutionary and high government official in many posts who had earlier been purged twice "for taking the capitalist road."

Deng set about in 1980 to develop a dynamic capitalist economy under the slogan of "using capitalism to build socialism." By 1990, after the U.S. and others imposed sanctions against China for the Tiananmen Square confrontation with students seeking certain democratic changes, Deng issued the following instruction to the CPC: "Observe calmly; secure our position; cope with affairs calmly; hide our capacities and bide our time; be good at maintaining a low profile; and never claim leadership."

The Chinese economy after 35 years is one of the wonders of the capitalist world, particularly since it is still maintained by the CPC, as are all other aspects of Chinese society. The PRC's political system is officially described as being "socialism with Chinese characteristics," though the socialist aspect has been abridged.

For many of these decades the U.S. superpower and global hegemon has gradually sought to position China within America's extensive orbit of states that look to Washington for leadership.

Beijing came closer with warmer relations, joining the World Trade Organization, respecting the World Bank and IMF, even sharing war games with the Pentagon — but never so close as to be stifled by Washington's dominant embrace. This didn't inconvenience the U.S. as long as China was mainly involved with internal growth, building huge cities, massive infrastructure projects and becoming the global manufacturing center.

But then two things changed. 1. By the time Xi Jinping became general secretary of the CPC and president of China less than three years ago, the PRC was about to surpass the U.S. as the world's economic giant and was universally recognized as a significant major power. It had plenty of cash, ideas, supporters and incentives to contemplate a larger independent role for itself on the international stage. 2. Given China's growth, it evidently seemed that strict compliance with Deng Xiaoping's defensive suggestion to hide China's light under a bushel was outdated.

The Obama Administration is not pleased with China's more forward stance. Relations between Washington and Beijing are cooling quickly but both countries have a mutual desire to prevent this situation from getting out of hand. The key difference, and it is of great significance to both parties, is that China opposes hegemony in principle, and the U.S. is determined to remain the global hegemon.

Contradiction is ever present in U.S. foreign/military policy, and things are rarely as they seem to an American people largely uninformed or misinformed about the realities of international affairs. This observation is occasioned by the extremes to which U.S. policy and interference around the world are being taken by the Obama Administration and its Republican congressional alter ego, obstructive on domestic matters but complicit with President Obama's principal international monomania — the retention of Washington's unilateral global hegemony.

The Obama Administration appears to be preoccupied day and night gallivanting throughout the world issuing dictates, administering punishments, rewarding friends, undermining enemies, overthrowing governments, engaging in multiple wars, subverting societies not to its liking, conducting remote control assassinations, listening to every phone call and examining the daily contents of the Internet lest someone get away with something, jailing honest whistleblowers, upgrading its nuclear stockpile and delivery systems, moving troops and fleets here and there, and that's only the half of it.

This is happening for one main reason. The U.S. has arrogated world rule to itself, without authority, competition, or oversight, since the implosion of the Soviet Union nearly 25 years ago. There is nothing more important to America's ruling elite. Every possible danger to Washington's hegemony must be neutralized. And looming in East Asia is the cause of Washington's worst anxieties — China.

In his victory speech after winning the 2008 election, Barack Obama — a humdrum one-term U.S. Senator with no foreign policy experience after serving several years as an obscure Illinois state legislator — announced that with his assumption to the presidency "a new dawn of American leadership is at hand." He was referring to his own leadership restoring U.S. international domination greater than ever after eight years of blundering President George W. Bush and Vice President Dick Cheney.

No one seemed to think twice about this. Democrats applauded; Republicans nodded. After all, isn't that what the United States is supposed to do?

Expanding global supremacy is a popular political promise in America. Extreme nationalism often wildly inspires the masses of a powerful country as it blinds them to the equality of nations and humanity, and guides them to another proposed conquest; and the prospect of greater profits through intensified world domination compensates the powerful corporations and families that contributed to Obama so generously in both elections.

The President frequently repeats his jingoist mantra about the necessity of American "leadership," at times accompanied by pandering clichés such as "I believe in American exceptionalism with every fiber of my being." Speaking at an Air Force Academy graduation in 2012 Obama told the cadets, "never bet against the United States of America... [because] the United States has been, and will always be, the one indispensable nation in world affairs." Applause, hats in air, now go out and kill.

Since the vast corporate capitalist mass media is entirely in agreement with the sacrosanct principle that only the United States is morally, politically and militarily equipped to rule the world, Obama's flag-waving imperial intentions are rarely if ever criticized by the press, Democrat or Republican. At least 90% of the American people obtain virtually all their scatterings of information about foreign affairs from a propagandistic ultranationalist media powerhouse controlled by just six billionaire corporations.

Many millions of Americans have opposed Washington's frequent and usually disastrous imperialist wars. But far fewer challenge the concept of U.S. global "leadership" — the euphemism for ruling the world that allows Washington carte blanche to engage in wars or bullying whenever its perceived interests appear to be challenged. It may seem like a century, considering the carnage, but it is important to remember that Washington only obtained solo world power when the Soviet Union imploded less than a quarter century ago. The next quarter century, as a new world order is beginning to take shape in the very shadow of the old, will be rough indeed as the U.S. government resists inevitable change.

The days of American hegemony over the nations of the world are numbered. This is perhaps the main and certainly the most dangerous contradiction deriving from America's determination to lead the world as carried forward by President Obama and undoubtedly to be continued by the next and the next administrations. There are many secondary contradictions strewn throughout the world, but almost all are related to first.

The U.S. government is recklessly flailing its arms and interfering in all the global regions to impose its will in order to indefinitely continue enjoying unilateral domination and the sensation of luxuriating in the extraordinary advantages derived from being the world's top cop, top judge, only jury, mass jailer and executioner extraordinaire. If you doubt it, just look about at the human, structural and environmental anguish created in the last 15 years by the action or inaction of Bush-Obama world leadership. Think about the trillions of U.S. dollars for destruction and death, and the paucity of expenditures for construction and life. A better world can only emerge from a better and more people-friendly political and economic global order.

Obama's policy of enhanced American "leadership" has created havoc these last six years as a result of the collusion between the Democratic White House and the Republican Congress — partners in the projection of American armed power around the world. The main target — despite all the elbowing and ranting about Russia, Putin, Ukraine, Syria, Iraq, Libya, Saudi Arabia, Israel, Iran, Yemen, Islamic State, ad infinitum — is and will remain China. The U.S. does not want a war with China, though one is certainly possible in time. It would prefer warm, friendly and mutually beneficial relations, under one condition: The U.S. is boss, and leads, while China — rich and powerful if it wishes — is subordinate, and follows, even in its own natural sphere of influence. Beijing does not seek hegemony, but it will not kowtow to the United States.

In the midst of all this rumbling and grumbling from the White House, it may be interesting to become acquainted with the enormous but modest main national strategic goal of the Communist Party of China. It is "to complete the building of a moderately prosperous society in all respects by 2021; and the building of a modern socialist country that is prosperous, strong, democratic, culturally advanced and harmonious by 2049. It is a Chinese Dream of achieving the great rejuvenation of the Chinese nation." So goes the Chinese "menace."

China is not a newcomer to world politics and economic power, as the U.S. government has at times suggested of one of the world's oldest and most creative civilizations. As James Petras has written:

"The study of world power has been blighted by Eurocentric historians who have distorted and ignored the dominant role China played in the world economy between 1100 and 1800."

This period ended because of Western imperialist intervention and plunder, including the Opium War, which brought about the humiliation and decline of Imperial China's final dynasty, which fell in 1911. A form of semi-democracy/semi-feudalism prevailed until the Communist revolution of 1949, when, in the words of Mao Zedong announcing victory, "The Chinese People have stood up." In these last 66 years China removed about 700 million citizens from poverty, and has become the world's manufacturing center and a major economic power.

The Chinese Communist government is calibrating its rise very carefully, intent upon avoiding offense to the crouching, tail twitching American imperial dragon. On May 21, Peoples Daily quoted a recent talk by President Xi Jinping: "China aims to become stronger but not seek hegemony; the strategic choice of cooperation and win-win [for all sides] is the path that China chooses. China has always been a peace-loving nation that cherishes harmonious relations. Its adherence to the five principles of peaceful coexistence and anti-hegemonism has shown China's determination to stick to peaceful development."

The five principles have governed New China since the revolution. They are: "Mutual respect for each other's sovereignty and territorial integrity; mutual non-aggression; non-interference in each other's internal affairs; equality and mutual benefit; and peaceful co-existence." There have been a few minor lapses, but these principles have remained stable and effective all these years. China's concept of harmonious relations is of ancient philosophical extraction. Frankly, in this writer's view, there are times when China's criticism of an extremely inhumane aspect of one or another state's internal affairs would do some good — but non-interference, much less non-aggression, is vastly superior to Washington's endless interference and aggression.

Xi's statement is an accurate representation of China's foreign relations. This is the PRC's long-term global strategy of development. It needs and wants peace. Washington knows all this, but that's not the point. Xi declared that Beijing opposed the very concept of global hegemony by any nation, including itself, and, of course, the U.S.. President Obama's primary foreign policy objective, and assuredly that of succeeding administrations, is the retention of global rule. This contradiction will eventually have to be resolved through negotiation or hostilities.

China will certainly not confront the U.S. on this matter within the foreseeable future. Beijing's reading of the tea leaves suggests that world trends will encourage the incoming tide of multipolar world order and displace the outgoing tide of unipolar dominion. Such thinking emerges from America's evident decline, the imminent rise of the developing nations, and the mounting dissatisfaction with the results of Washington's global rule among countries not dependent upon Fortress Americana.

Writing in Time June 1, Ian Bremmer noted: "Emerging countries are not strong enough to overthrow U.S. dominance, but they have more than enough strength and self-confidence to refuse to follow Washington's lead." This is a recent development that will continue to unfold in the next decade or two.

At this point, equipped with the seven league boots only possessed by a superpower, the U.S. is far ahead of its detractors in the emerging competition to determine whether only one, or many nations in combination, will shape the future. The UN may figure in this, but only after the preponderant influence of the U.S. and certain other countries is reduced and more evenly shared with the rising countries, a number of which surely realize it's time for a change. They wish to avoid a dreadful future of devastating wars, rampant climate change, poverty and scandalous inequality.

The fact remains: Washington is determined to keep the keys to the kingdom, and it is taking measures daily to strengthen its intention to constrain China by depriving it of exercising even the regional power to which it is entitled on the basis of its huge economy, a population of 1.4 billion people, and its peaceful rise and intentions.

President Obama is quite visibly seeking to confront China, politically, militarily, and economically and politically in the Asia/Pacific region. This is what the "pivot" to Asia is about, containing Chinese influence within its own geographical environment.

The U.S. is at least two decades ahead of China in war technology, equipment, nuclear weapons, various missiles, planes, ships — everything. John Reed wrote in DefenseTech a few years ago: "Even China's newest military gear is reminiscent of Western or Soviet technology from about 20 years ago, or more." People's Liberation Army (PLA) leaders certainly want to catch up and are making progress, but they can only approach near proximity if Pentagon scientists decide to sleep for the next two decades. Instead, Washington's immense military, several times that of China, is increasing the gap in real time. U.S. military spending this year will amount to 4.5% of GNP, and that does not count a number of military expenses concealed in nonmilitary budgets such as the new 20-year multi-billion dollar program to modernize U.S. nuclear weapons and delivery systems (charged to the Department of Energy). China's spending this year, with four times the American population, is 1.5% of GDP. China's extremely important cyber warfare advances may or may not be equal to those of the U.S., but it is the only area of relative equivalence, and it's causing headaches in the Pentagon.

The U.S. is frantically surrounding China with military weapons, advanced aircraft, naval fleets and a multitude of military bases from Japan, South Korea and the Philippines through several nearby smaller Pacific islands to its new and enlarged base in Australia and, of course, intercontinental ballistic missiles from the United States. The U.S. naval fleet, aircraft carriers and nuclear submarines patrol China's nearby waters. Warplanes, surveillance planes, drones and spying satellites cover the skies, creating a symbolic darkness at noon. By 2017, the Pentagon plans to encircle China with "the most advanced stealth warplanes in the world," according to RT. "The Air Force's F-22s and B-2s, as well as a fleet of the Marine Corps' F-35, will all be deployed. This buildup has been going on for three years and it is hardly ever mentioned in the U.S.

Washington seems to fear China's military defense capability more than its potential offensive abilities, though that remains a serious concern. In the Pentagon's annual report to Congress May 8, all 31,000 words were devoted to "Military and Security Developments Involving the People's Republic of China 2015," including these:

"China is investing in capabilities designed to defeat adversary power projection and counter third-party — including U.S. — intervention during a crisis or conflict.... The PLA is developing and testing new intermediate- and medium-range conventional ballistic missiles, as well as long- range, land-attack, and anti-ship cruise missiles that extend China's operational reach, attempting to push adversary forces—

including the United States — farther from potential regional conflicts. China is also focusing on counter-space, offensive cyber operations, and electronic warfare capabilities meant to deny adversaries the advantages of modern, informationized warfare.... China's military modernization has the potential to reduce core U.S. military technological advantages." Concern was also expressed for "China's development and testing of missile defense."

Much of the Pentagon report is far more objective and informative about China than statements from the White House, Congress and the provocative corporate mass media: First of all it describes China's political goal realistically: "Securing China's status as a great power and, ultimately, reacquiring regional preeminence." Question — Why is the Obama Administration doing everything possible to thwart China's regional preeminence? Answer — Because it is unwilling to share a regional portion of its own world preeminence with any country that will not bend a knee to Washington's supremacy.

The report says accurately: "China continues to regard stable relations with the United States and China's neighbors as key to its development. China sees the U.S. as the dominant regional and global actor with the greatest potential to both support and, potentially, disrupt China's rise. Top Chinese leaders, including President Xi Jinping, continued to advocate for a 'new type of major power relations' with the United States throughout 2014. China's 'new type' of relations concept urges a cooperative U.S.- China partnership based on equality, mutual respect, and mutual benefit."

Most interestingly, the Pentagon also recognized that "Chinese leaders see a strong military as critical to prevent other countries from taking steps that would damage China's interests and to ensure China can defend itself, should deterrence fail. China seeks to ensure basic stability along its periphery and avoid direct confrontation with the United States in order to focus on domestic development and smooth China's rise. Despite this, Chinese leaders in 2014 demonstrated a willingness to tolerate a higher level of regional tension as

China sought to advance its interests, such as in competing territorial claims in the East China Sea and South China Sea."

The Wall Street Journal May 13 defined the South China Sea as "one of the world's busiest shipping routes and a strategic passage between the rich economies of Northeast Asia and the Indian Ocean. As much as 50% of global oil-tanker shipments pass through its waters.... China often intercepts and protests over U.S. naval ships and aircraft conducting surveillance near its coastline in the South China Sea.... Six governments – China, Vietnam, Brunei, Malaysia, Taiwan and the Philippines — claim the waters, islands, reefs and atolls in whole or in part, making the area a potential flashpoint."

Two countries, Japan and South Korea, have claims in the East China Sea to the northwest, so eight nations are involved. China has long claimed authority over almost all the islands on the basis of evidence the other states consider inadequate.

The Obama Administration is navigating with abandon and roiling the political waters throughout both seas, enthusiastically supporting the claims of all the smaller nations against China's claims.

This is a very important and delicate matter because verified claimants are entitled to exploit energy, mineral and other abundant resources in the proximity as well as to deploy them for military purposes, if large enough, but most are tiny. This is clearly a complex matter that should be resolved over time through peaceful negotiations, and give and take dispute resolution. The continuation of America's self-appointed role as advocate and protector of the counter-claims of smaller countries against China will only cause more trouble.

The U.S. has absolutely no authority in this matter, and it even refuses to ratify the United Nations Convention on the Law of the Sea, which is equipped to mediate territorial disputes in the South and East China Seas. Actually, Obama doesn't give a fig about the claims. The only purpose of his intervention against China's claims is to consolidate and expand Washington's large and growing cheaper-by-the dozen gaggle of regional client states — some of which (Japan, S. Korea, the Philippines) have been U.S. protectorates since the end of World War II. All these countries will support America's global political, economic and military intentions in East Asia, including that of confining China's influence within its own borders to the extent possible. If not, they will be escorted to the door.

In this connection the U.S. is also exaggerating the fact that China is involved in land reclamation efforts in five small reefs in the Spratly Islands. It's expanding them by adding sand and making infrastructure additions, including an airfield in one. The White house says up to is about 2,000 acres are at issue. Obama said a month ago that China was "flexing its muscles" to browbeat smaller nations into accepting Beijing's sovereignty over disputed islands, and more recently Washington implied it might send navy ships and aircraft to the islands — but soon backed off because China's actions were entirely legal.

In mid-May, Assistant Secretary of State for East Asia Daniel Russel told the Washington Post: "Reclamation isn't necessarily a violation of international law, but it's certainly violating the harmony, the feng shui, of Southeast Asia, and it's certainly violating China's claim to be a good neighbor and a benign and non-threatening power." At that point, the heavens finally intervened with a lighter moment. Wrote the Wall Street Journal May 21: "Chinese Taoist priest Liang Xingyang is rebutting the U.S. official's understanding of feng shui. The term, which translates directly as 'wind water,' refers to the Chinese philosophical system of harmonizing the human being with the surrounding environment. In fact, claims Mr. Liang, China's reclamation efforts are improving the region's feng shui.... Mr. Liang maintained that feng shui 'belongs to the whole world, but the power of interpretation stays with China.'"

Soon after the Pentagon report, China outlined a new military strategy to boost its naval reach May 26. In a policy document issued by the State Council, China vowed to increase its "open seas protection," switching from air defense to both offense and defense, and criticized neighbors who take "provocative actions" on its reefs and islands. A statement in the document declared: "In today's world, the global trends toward multipolarity and economic globalization are intensifying.... The forces for world peace are on the rise, so are the factors against war.... There are, however, new threats from hegemonism, power politics and neo-interventionism." China will speed up the development of a cyber force to tackle "grave security threats" to its cyber infrastructure. Cyberspace is highlighted as one of China's four "critical security domains", other than the ocean, outer space and nuclear force.

In addition to military threats, and encouraging allies to assist in containing China, Washington's "pivot" includes strong intervention intended to increase America's economic clout in East Asia and reduce Beijing's. Obama's chosen vehicle — the Trans Pacific Partnership — so favors corporations at the expense of U.S. jobs, the interests of working people, the environment and national sovereignty that many Democrats in Congress, led by Sen. Elizabeth Warren, are sharply opposed. In the words of Public Citizen:

"The TPP is a massive, controversial 'free trade' agreement currently being pushed by big corporations and negotiated behind closed doors by officials from the United States and 11 other countries – Australia, Brunei, Canada, Chile, Japan, Malaysia, Mexico, New Zealand, Peru, Singapore, and Vietnam.(The TPP would expand the North American Free Trade Agreement (NAFTA) "trade" pact model that has spurred massive U.S. trade deficits and job loss, downward pressure on wages, unprecedented levels of inequality and new floods of agricultural imports.

"The TPP not only replicates, but expands NAFTA's special protections for firms that offshore U.S. jobs. And U.S. TPP negotiators literally used the 2011 Korea FTA – under which exports have fallen and trade deficits have surged – as the template for the TPP.((In one fell swoop, this secretive deal could: offshore American jobs and increase income inequality, jack up the cost of medicines, sneak in SOPA-like threats to Internet freedom (i.e., Stop Online Piracy Act), and empower corporations to attack our environmental and health safeguards, expose the U.S. to unsafe food and products, roll back Wall Street reforms, and ban Buy American policies needed to create green jobs."

The Japan Times sounded like recalcitrant U.S. Democrats when it reported May 15: "One big problem with the TPP talks is the secrecy of the negotiating process. The participants are required not to publicize developments in the talks and draft agreements while they are still being negotiated. The talks are going forward without the Japanese public and lawmakers being given relevant information on what is being discussed or agreed upon. For example, it is impossible to know the details of discussions on regulations the TPP nations can adopt for environmental protection and food safety. Even when the trade pact takes effect, the participants will be forbidden from disclosing internal documents on the negotiation process for four years." Japan has not signed the TPP deal yet. It is demanding concessions on automobiles and agricultural products.

The Senate rejected Obama's demand for a fast track arrangement in mid-May, 52 to 45, but after corporate howls, promises and dollars it was passed days later 62-37. Most Republicans supported the trade plan from the beginning. Winning over his own party has proven so difficult that Obama has introduced the false patriotism of anti-China rhetoric to shame recalcitrant Democrats into changing their views. Speaking in May he said: "If we don't write the rules for trade around the world, guess what? China will." Actually, China is far more cooperative with U.S. trade proposals than obstructive. On the TPP Beijing simply understands that it is aimed against China and that it has many shortcomings, as Warren has repeatedly pointed out.

Although China earlier appeared deeply concerned about the TPP, it now seems indifferent. Over the last several months, President Xi has combined a well-financed, spectacular package of trade, banking, and infrastructure projects that are bound to significantly advance China's power and prestige in Asia, Europe and North Africa as well.

The two most important and far reaching projects are the Asian Infrastructure Investment Bank (AIIB), and the visionary, immensely expensive One Belt, One Road (OBOR) project. The latter initiative is also referred to as the New Silk Road after the 4,000-mile trade route between China and the West that developed from 114 BCE to the 1450s. The accompanying maritime trade lanes were called the Spice Route. OBOR, too, consists of a land and sea route. When New China does things it's often in a big way, often with a touch of long-past history in mind.

China's recent creation of the Asian Infrastructure Investment Bank (AIIB) — an exceptionally powerful economic initiative destined to benefit all of Asia and the world — was perceived by the White House as a humiliating affront. Washington worked for months to undermine the impending venture, advising allies and underlings far and near to keep out.

Beijing proposed the AIIB in October 2013; a year later, 21 nations, all Asian, gathered in Beijing and signed the memorandum establishing the bank. Six months later, the membership has expanded to 57.

In mid-March, Washington's closest ally, the United Kingdom, was among the first major western economies to join the bank, prompting an extraordinary outburst by an anonymous high official of the Obama Administration, who declared for publication: "We are wary about a trend toward constant accommodation of China, which is not the best way to engage a rising power." President Obama had to give permission for "anonymous" to deliver so petulant and insulting a remark.

Within a couple of weeks all the major world nations had joined except Japan and the U.S. The rest knew a good deal when they saw it in the midst of prolonged economic stagnation, particularly in Europe. Remember Willy Sutton's answer when asked why he robbed banks? "That's where the money is." Their economies will profit.

The international news analyst M.K. Bhadrakumar reported in Asia Times May 26: " The AIIB Charter is still under discussion. The media report that China is not seeking a veto in the decision-making comes as a pleasant surprise. Equally, China is actively consulting other founding members (UK, Germany, France, Italy, etc.).

These would suggest that Beijing has a much bigger game plan of scattering the U.S. containment strategy. Clearly, the Trans-Pacific Partnership free-trade deal is already looking more absurd if China were to be kept out of it. The point is, AIIB gives financial underpinning for the 'Belt and Road' initiative, which now the European countries and Russia have embraced, as they expect much business spin-off."

China benefits immensely, in terms of international prestige and politically as well, from the new venture. The AIIB has become a strong rival to the International Monetary Fund and the World Bank, two powerful U.S.-controlled financial organizations, as well as the regional Asian Development Bank, ruled by Japan and America. China is not interested in debasing these associations but in collegial modernization with Beijing having a voice.

What's the oddly named named One Belt, One Road (OBOR) project stand for? The "Belt" refers to the Silk Road Economic Belt, largely composed of countries situated on the original Silk Road from China through Central Asia, West Asia, the Middle East and Europe. The "Road" refers to the new maritime Silk Road. The initiative calls for the integration of the region into a cohesive economic area through building infrastructure, increasing cultural exchanges and broadening trade. Many of the countries that are part of the "belt" are also signed up with the AIIB. The Maritime Road is aimed at investing and fostering collaboration in Southeast Asia, Oceania, and North Africa through several contiguous bodies of water.

Journalist Binoy Kampmark points out in Global Research:

"The economic belt, as Xi terms it, features such concrete manifestations as high-speed rail lines [including one between Beijing and Moscow], highways, bridges, and Internet connectivity. These, in turn, will be complemented by port development that is already seeing a presence in the

Mediterranean and Indian Ocean. Spearheading the drive are China's state-owned enterprises."

Two other countries play important supporting roles in the U.S.-China exchange — Russia and Japan.

President Xi said recently that China is devoted to "promoting a new model of major-country relationship with the U.S., keeping its comprehensive strategic partnership with Russia, [and] strengthening its partnership with the EU." China's partnership with Europe involves trade, investment, environmental issues and the like. With Russia it's broader, specifically: Energy, Business and Trade, High Technology and Industry, Finance, Military and Political/Diplomatic.

China has military and political/diplomatic relations with the U.S. as well, but of a different character. According to Russian Insider: "Military: China and Russia are engaging in military exercises of increasing scale and frequency. Their respective General Staffs closely coordinate with each other. Russia has resumed arms and technology sales to China. Political and Diplomatic: China and Russia are joint founder members of the Shanghai Cooperation Organization. They actively coordinate their foreign policy positions with each other. They also work closely together and support each other in the UN Security Council."

Moscow's partnership with Beijing has become much stronger in recent years. Russia is a major nuclear power, roughly equivalent to America, with sophisticated military technology and hardware exceeding that of China, to which it is now selling offensive and defensive weaponry after a lapse of decades. The world's two biggest countries (size and population) have long been wary of each other, but a perceived need to strengthen their defenses brings them closer. Whether they will ever form a binding formal alliance is not known, but Russia's power adds to that of China and vice versa. Commenting on the relationship a couple of weeks ago Xi declared: " We are strong if united but weak if isolated."

At the same time the PRC is trying to calm an aroused Washington. Michael Swaine, a China expert at the Carnegie

Endowment for International Peace in Washington recently told the press: "The Chinese are trying to convey a more moderate and softer message. They are trying to promote the image of a more flexible power." Chinese Vice Premier Wang Yang recently declared in a widely publicized speech that that the PRC "does not have any ideas or capabilities" with which to challenge or displace America's global command.

Russia shares with China the threat of U.S. military power on its periphery. Stratfor noted March 30: "From the Baltics to the Black Sea and now the Caspian, the United States is on the search for recruits to encircle Russia. Romania threw its lot in with the United States last year, but this year, Turkey and Turkmenistan are the ones to watch.

"All along Russia's frontier with Europe, the U.S. military is bustling with activity. Bit by bit, the United States is expanding various military exercises under the banner of Operation Atlantic Resolve. The exercises began in the Baltics and Poland and, as of last week, expanded into Romania with plans to move into Bulgaria. So far, most of these missions are on the smaller side, consisting of only a few hundred troops at any given time, and are meant to test the U.S. ability to rapidly deploy units to countries that can then practice receiving and working with these forces. Additionally, various headquarter units from U.S. Army infantry brigades have been rotating in and assuming control of Operation Atlantic Resolve in order to practice joint command and control." Several hundred American troops are in Ukraine training Kiev's military.

It was symbolically significant that that Xi Jinping was seated next to President Putin at the May 9 Victory Day Parade in Moscow and that a Chinese military detachment was part of the event celebrating the 70th anniversary of the allied victory in Europe. Putin and Russian troops have been invited to participate in China's celebration of Japan's defeat in September. The U.S., Britain and France, Russia's former allies, boycotted the Moscow event.

The new U.S.-Japan expanded military guidelines for "defense cooperation" that was agreed in Washington between

Japanese Prime Minster Shinzô Abe and the Obama Administration April 27 is of major geopolitical significance. Tokyo will now increase its military role in the region and assume a "more robust international posture," in response to growing Chinese influence. The guidelines allow for global Washington-Tokyo cooperation militarily, ranging from defense against ballistic missiles, cyber and space attacks as well as maritime security.

China has sharply criticized the new guidelines, calling them an attempt to undermine Beijing, as well as the geopolitical architecture of the Asia-Pacific. Global Times, which is affiliated with the CPC, declared: "The new guidelines have struck a threatening pose toward China, which is the strongest driver for East Asia's development. They should know that their aggression has sent a dangerous signal to regional stability."

Washington also renewed and strengthened America's "iron-clad" commitment to support Japan and all territories "under Tokyo's administration." Japan and China are locked in a sharp disagreement about their rival claims to tiny East China Sea islets and reefs, some no more than large rocks sticking out of the water. Should the conflict become a serious confrontation the Obama Administration evidently will intervene on behalf of Japan.

The daily Indian newspaper The Hindu reported May 1:

"Officials from the United States have been quoted as saying that the latest guidelines — updated for the first time since 1997 — end the geographic limits on the Japanese military to operate. Following permission from Parliament, Japanese forces can participate in military operations across the globe. 'The current guidelines are unrestricted with respect to geography,' U.S. Defense Secretary Ash Carter has been quoted as saying. 'That is a very big change — from being locally focused to globally focused,' he observed. Analysts point out that the changes to the U.S.-Japan pact inject more substance into President Barack Obama's 'Pivot to Asia' doctrine, which the Chinese say lays the military groundwork for containing Beijing's peaceful rise."

Heretofore the terms of the "pacifist" constitution imposed on Japan after it was defeated in World War I" confined the Japanese military to fight only in Japan and in self-defense. The right wing Abe government has sought to dispense with this constitution entirely, but a majority of the Japanese people strongly oppose such a step. Abe envisions Japan once again becoming a major military power in Asia. Actually Tokyo already wields the ninth largest military force in the world, replete with high technology weaponry.

China has just made an amazing overture to Japan in an effort to reduce tensions. M.K. Bhadrakumar reported May 27 that China has decided to extend the "hand of friendship to Japan," describing a precedent-breaking event in Beijing May 23.

"A heavyweight politician from Japan's ruling party leads a 3,000-member delegation (yes, 3,000) to Beijing; the Chinese hosts spread out a grand dinner for the 3,000 Japanese guests at the Great Hall of People; President Xi Jinping makes an apparently surprise but carefully choreographed appearance at the dinner; Xi makes an extraordinarily warm speech full of conciliatory sentiments belying his fame as an assertive leader, stressing the imperatives of Sino-Japanese friendship not only for the two countries but for the region and the world at large; the heavyweight Japanese politician steps forward in front of his 3,000-strong delegation and hands over to Xi a hand-written letter from Prime Minister Shinzo Abe; Xi reciprocates by conveying his best regards to Abe – a thaw in China-Japan ties seems to be at work.

"Cynics might say Abe has a habit of sending hand-written letters to counterparts in countries with which Japan has strained relations, such as South Korea. But there is something beyond the calls of public diplomacy here, as is apparent from the contents and tone of the speech Xi made while addressing the goodwill delegation from Japan. A Xinhua commentary noted,

'The onus is now on the leaders of Japan to reciprocate the friendly tone and take concrete actions to mend frayed ties with

China.' The two neighbors are showing a spirit of pragmatism that was considered unthinkable as recently as last November when on the sidelines of the Asia Pacific Economic Cooperation summit Xi and Abe held a frosty meeting."

The Financial Times reported April 30 "Washington is giving up on the idea that a risen China can be co-opted as a stakeholder in the present global order," implicitly suggesting that Washington is going to adopt a much tougher stance toward China to preserve its geopolitical superiority. The article references a new report on China from the Council on Foreign Relations, the leading establishment voice in foreign affairs. Titled, "Revising U.S. Grand Strategy Toward China," the newspaper reports it "outlines a plan to draw together all the elements of U.S. power with the goal of maintaining America's 'primacy' in East Asia.... But balancing Beijing's weight is one thing. Nervous as they are, China's neighbors have a powerful economic interest in getting on with Beijing. A U.S. that sought permanent preponderance would be inviting a collision. Unstoppable forces and immovable objects come to mind."

Both China and the United States want to keep their disputes within bounds in the proximate future, if possible. This was demonstrated after weeks of public squabbling May 16 and 17 when Secretary of State John Kerry paid his fifth visit to China. According to a May 26 report in China-U.S. Focus by Zhang Zhixin, chief of American Political Studies at the China Institutes of Contemporary International Relations, this is the meaning:

"As the highest-level American official who visited China this year, with a hot China policy debate going on in the U.S., and the Obama administration strongly criticizing China's reclamation in South China Sea, [Kerry's] visit has been regarded as a trip aimed at denouncing Beijing. However, judging from the result, Kerry's visit is better characterized as a trip of in-depth communication.

"Early this year, American strategic circles started another round of China policy debate. From the so-called 'cracking up' of the CPC to the familiar rhetoric of the 'China threat' it made some American China watchers believe the consensus underlying the U.S. China policy is collapsing."

Kerry's constructive visit,

"has been of great importance at this critical moment. First, it shows that both countries would like to manage differences before crises occur.... Chinese leaders tried to reassure the U.S. side they are still committed to building a new major power relationship....

"Second, this visit made timely preparation for the coming bilateral and multilateral events — including President Xi Jinping's first State visit to the U.S. in September — that could shape the following two year's Sino-U.S. relations....

"Third, Secretary Kerry's visit is a success as it deepened the understanding between two countries at this critical time, but it reminds both countries consensus is easy to reach but hard to actualize. The disputes between two countries highlighted the U.S. misinterpretation of China's plans for future development. The U.S. side should neither overestimate its influence upon China's future, nor underestimate China's ability to explore its own way of development with Chinese characteristics."

Interestingly, a similar situation to the Beijing surprise occurred weeks earlier when Kerry was sent to Moscow for talks with President Putin. Washington's advance leaks suggested that he would read the riot act to the Russian leader because of the Ukraine situation — but the opposite happened, evidently not least because of U.S. concerns of a developing alliance between Russia and China. Kerry turned on a dime just before both meetings, as though receiving late instructions.

Apparently, the White House concluded its policy of pouting and denouncing China is churlish and demonstrably counterproductive. Even some of Washington's allies were beginning to look askance at Oval Office shoot-from-the-hip decisions. However, nothing else has changed. The quest to retain global rule is more pronounced than ever and the danger level is getting higher.

Both the U.S. and China are strong and intelligent countries. But as Darwin said, "It is not the strongest of the species that survives, nor the most intelligent that survives. It is the one that is the most adaptable to change."

Great changes have already started and the pace will intensify in coming decades — politically, economically, environmentally and in terms of social systems and world order. One needed change is replacing single-country global hegemony with multi-country cooperation for the advancement of humankind. The governments of several rising countries will help bring this about, if possible, but it won't be easy.

Systemic changes are needed in our societies, as well. We cannot simply paper over the class exploitation, gross inequality, racism, poverty, state violence and the shredding of our ecology — and say that's "change." Billions of human beings alive today want a world where wealth is sufficiently shared so everyone has at least enough. That's no exaggeration. Billions live in poverty. They all want out. Whether in poverty or not, who prefers to live in a world where the richest 1% of the global population own more than the remaining 99%? That's our world today, and it must change.

THE POST-SOVIET SPACE AND THE NEW SILK ROAD

Among the 65 countries targeted (The Economist, 2016) by this ambitious project, the countries that make up the post-Soviet space are all present (may be with the exception of Ukraine). They are or will be, to varying degrees, concerned with its realization. These countries come today under different institutional configurations. Russia, along with Belarus, Armenia, Kazakhstan and Kyrgyzstan, founded the Eurasian Economic Union. The other former Central Asian Republics, like Tajikistan and Turkmenistan, are not members, neither Georgia nor Azerbaijan, while, in Europe, Ukraine and Moldova are not associated. The former Baltic republics (Latvia, Lithuania, Estonia) joined the European Union with the former

« Eastern countries », which were formerly under Soviet trusteeship (the CEECs). With these countries and those of the former Yugoslavia, China founded, at the end of the road, an association called Cooperation between China and Central and Eastern European Countries (16 + 1).

Finally, in 2001 China initiated the establishment of an Asian regional intergovernmental organization, the Shanghai Cooperation Organization comprising Russia, China, Kazakhstan, Kyrgyzstan, Tajikistan and Uzbekistan, and, since 2016, also India and Pakistan.

6

India's Response to the OBOR

India's official response to the OBOR has been cautious and relatively muted, but a perusal of academic writings and news reports affirm that India has deep concerns about the implications of the OBOR for its strategic interests. India shares the view of several countries in Northeast and Southeast Asia that far from being an enterprise founded on wide and substantial cooperation, the OBOR could in fact be the vehicle for China's influence, if not hegemony, across Asia. After all, China is promoting the OBOR just when it is flexing its muscles in East Asia, particularly in regard to asserting its territorial claims unilaterally in the South China Sea.

India has more immediate and specific concerns, which pertain to the CPEC. The CPEC was announced within a month of the publication of the OBOR vision and action plan document, which had highlighted the need for extensive consultations across Asia. Clearly, no such consultations took place with India and the CPEC was presented as a fait accompli. While India might share China's position that extremism should be countered with development, it cannot accept that the CPEC's logistical projects should pass freely through large parts of Pakistan-occupied Kashmir.

Officially, India has focused on the absence of consultation from the Chinese side. Speaking at the inauguration of the Raisina Dialogue on "Asian Connectivity" in Delhi in March,

Indian Foreign Secretary S. Jaishankar said, "The key issue is whether we will build our connectivity through consultative processes or more unilateral decisions. ... we cannot be impervious to the reality that others may see connectivity as an exercise in hard-wiring that influences choices".

CHINA'S OBOR GOALS

OBOR is focused on addressing two of the Chinese government's existential concerns: one focused inward, the other outward.

The outward focus is more apparent: obviously, OBOR is intended to boost China's regional power. As a very public display of ambition, it may indicate that the Chinese leadership believes that the time has come for the fulfillment of a dictum of Deng Xiaoping, the leader who opened China in the 1980s and set it on its current development path. Deng famously said, "Hide your strength and bide your time." Xi Jinping clearly believes that China's time has come.

OBOR will secure and expand China's regional leadership by tying lesser-developed regional powers more deeply to Chinese capital, Chinese markets, and Chinese infrastructure networks. Indeed, China has been pursuing this kind of "soft power" for some time; we've written about how China has ingratiated itself with various African governments by providing infrastructure capital when Western lenders were more reticent. This year we got the first evidence of what usually follows "soft power" as China began construction of its first foreign military base, in Djibouti. Not surprisingly, this base is near the strategically critical Mandeb Strait between the Red Sea and the Gulf of Aden, one of the eight global chokepoints for seaborne crude oil shipments.

Other energy and port infrastructure tied to OBOR also aims to reduce China's vulnerability to energy shipment disruptions by building pipelines to bypass the Strait of Malacca. This is one of the main potential benefits of one of OBOR's flagship programs, the China-Pakistan Economic Corridor, or

CPEC, which will involve major development of the Pakistani port of Gwadar and could ultimately serve as an energy transshipment point.

Since OBOR was launched at a time when China has been expressing a more assertive regional and global presence, it is easy and natural to see OBOR through that lens. However, it's important not to lose sight of the initiative's core economic significance.

INDIA THINKS ABOUT CHINA'S ONE BELT, ONE ROAD INITIATIVE

The availability activities that China and other Asian nations are seeking after crosswise over Asia and the Indian Ocean locale—fabricating new base, foundations, and interlinkages—is ostensibly redrawing the landmass' guide. That has monetary ramifications, as well as geopolitical ones. India has been generally noiseless on maybe the most discussed of the activities, China's One Belt, One Road (OBOR). In any case, at the inaugural Raisina Dialog, facilitated in New Delhi toward the beginning of March by the Indian Ministry of External Affairs and the research organization Observer Research Foundation, the Indian government flagged Delhi's worry about Beijing's methodology toward availability and the area all the more comprehensively.

In three addresses more than three days, Indian External Affairs Minister Sushma Swaraj, Minister of State for External Affairs (or agent remote pastor) V.K. Singh, and Foreign Secretary S. Jaishankar gave the clearest piece yet of India's legitimate point of view on and approach toward network at home and in the district. Along the lines of policymakers' and investigators' remarks for quite a long time, there was discussion of how availability can unite nations and be commonly advantageous. Yet, there was very little talk—as there might have once been in the locale—of such connections lightening contentions. Without a doubt, a repeating topic in the addresses was about the interaction of geopolitics and availability, and how much the last could either represent the moment of truth provincial security. Availability, once seen as helping nations rise above geopolitics, was rather recognized by the outside secretary as having "developed as a theater of present day geopolitics."

Without once naming China, the Indian officials at the dialogue laid out Delhi's perception of that country's connectivity initiatives and contrasted the Chinese and Indian approaches to connectivity and the region. In her speech, the foreign minister outlined the importance of Asian connectivity and the opportunities and challenges it presents for India. She stressed, notably: "We bring to bear a *cooperative* rather than*unilateral* approach and believe that creating an environment of trust and confidence is the *pre-requisite* for a more inter-connected world." (emphasis added)

In the past, India has indicated that it sees China's OBOR as a "national Chinese initiative." In Singapore last year, the Indian foreign secretary, when asked about OBOR, noted that it was "not incumbent on other countries to necessarily buy" into such unilateral initiatives:

"Because a national initiative is devised with national interest, and an international or regional initiative has other interests, which are reconciled into that. So, where we stand is that if this is something on which they want a larger buy in, then they need to have larger discussions and those haven't happened."

And flipping the idea that economic cooperation and connectivity would have a palliative effect on the China and India's political relationship,Prime Minister Narendra Modi has asserted in the past that the former is a pre-requisite, contingent on the latter: *If* the two countries achieved "a climate of mutual trust and confidence; respect for each other's sensitivities and concerns; and, peace and stability in our relations and along our borders" *then* "we can reinforce each other's economic growth."

Some Indian analysts and a former national security adviser have called for Delhi to see the opportunities that OBOR presents as well, and "use the infrastructure and institutions that are being created to further India's transformation." India is arguably already using some of the infrastructure like Sri Lankan ports developed by China and institutions like the Asian Infrastructure Investment Bank (AIIB), which it is helping shape as a founding member.

But we're unlikely to see a formal endorsement of OBOR as a whole. For one, the Indian government has particular concerns about the China-Pakistan Economic Corridor that is part of OBOR and that includes projects in territory that India claims. This is a crucial reason why Indiapushed for a provision in the charter of AIIB (that is expected to fund some OBOR projects) that requires project financing in disputed territory to have the agreement of the disputants. In addition, there is clearly also concern about the way China is pursuing OBOR, the motivations behind it, and particularly the kind of influence that Beijing might be seeking through it. The foreign secretary elaborated on this at the Raisina Dialogue and also had a message for China, which has sought global multipolarity:

"The key issue is whether we will build our connectivity through consultative processes or more unilateral decisions. Our preference is for the former...But we cannot be impervious to the reality that others may see connectivity as an exercise in hard-wiring that influences choices. This should be discouraged, because particularly in the absence of an agreed security architecture in Asia, it could give rise to unnecessary competitiveness. Connectivity should diffuse national rivalries, not add to regional tensions... Indeed, if we seek a multi-polar world, the right way to begin is to create a multi-polar Asia. Nothing could foster that more than an open minded consultation on the future of connectivity."

The foreign secretary's remarks suggested that Delhi did not object to doing business with Beijing per se, but rather its way of doing business. Giving the example of the AIIB, he noted that when there was a consultative process toward an initiative, India would respond positively. The deputy foreign minister refined this further, noting the preferencefor such consultation to be from "the conception stage itself."

Indian official concern about the Chinese approach in the region beyond connectivity initiatives was also evident at the conference. Without mentioning tensions in the South China Sea explicitly, the foreign secretary stressed the importance of freedom of navigation and peaceful resolution of disputes. The foreign secretary noted that India, in contrast, took "a collaborative and consultative approach to the maritime domain." The foreign minister was more pointed: "India preaches what it practices and the agreement with Bangladesh on our maritime boundary should stand out as an example to others." In his remarks at the dialogue, Admiral Harry Harris, commander of U.S. Pacific Command, also drew attention to the contrast—in blunter words:

"While some countries seek to bully smaller nations through intimidation and coercion, I note with admiration India's example of peaceful resolution of disputes with your neighbors in the waters of the Indian Ocean. India, indeed, stands like a beacon on a hill, building a future on the power of ideas... not on castles of sand that threaten the rules-based architecture that has served us all so very well."

The Defense Department has made this comparison before, highlighting positively in its Asia-Pacific Maritime Security Strategy report India's acceptance of international arbitration (and its verdict) for an India-Bangladesh maritime dispute.

INDIA'S CONNECTIVITY PROJECTS

However, the logistics scenario in Asia is not as bleak from the Indian perspective as it might appear at first sight. While the OBOR captured global imagination when it was first announced over two years ago, it is important to recall that India is itself at the centre of major regional connectivity projects; these might lack the dramatic value of the OBOR, but taken together, they bring a number of solid partners and have the capacity of transforming the regional economic and geopolitical landscape to India's advantage. India, thus, has little need to feel insecure about the OBOR.

The most important Indian connectivity project is of course the trade and transit corridor from Chabahar in Iran to Afghanistan, to link with the highway network of the latter; India has already contributed to this network with the Zaranj-Delaram highway. This project has the greatest economic and strategic value for India since it provides unimpeded access to Afghanistan, enables India and Iran to contribute together to the economic development and political stability of Afghanistan, besides of course confronting the depredations of the Taliban. Over the long term, India would be in position to limit Pakistan's quest for so-called "strategic depth" in Afghanistan, an aspiration that has caused great death and destruction in that country.

But, the importance of this project goes well beyond Afghanistan: it provides a highway across the relatively peaceful northern part of Afghanistan to all the Central Asian republics, culminating at Almaty in Kazakhstan.

The other connectivity project with which India is associated is the International North-South Transit Corridor (INSTC). Initiated in September 2000, over a decade before the OBOR, the INSTC had initially brought together India, Iran and Russia in an effort to create multi-modal links (ship-rail-road) from India to Europe, via the Gulf, Central Asia and Russia. The partnership was later expanded to include Turkey and the other Central Asian republics. A dry-run to check its viability was also successfully conducted in August 2014, after which transit and customs agreements were approved in September 2015.

These connectivity projects received a boost recently when the Indian cabinet approved India's accession to the Ashgabat Agreement. This multi-modal transport agreement, that brings together India, Oman, Iran and the Central Asian republics, was initiated in April 2011, two years before the OBOR was announced. Its routing will be linked closely to the INSTC projects.

Closer home, India is looking at a number of connectivity proposals: these include the development of the Andaman & Nicobar Islands in the Bay of Bengal into a maritime hub, including a dry dock and a ship-building facility. Again, at the Sri Lankan port of Trincomalee, India has been looking at setting up a petroleum hub, besides activating the 80-year old tank farm in the strategically-located port city. India has also announced that it will develop a number of connectivity projects in South Asia, valued at $5 billion.

An OBOR-related project that involves India directly is the "Bangladesh-China-India-Myanmar Economic Corridor," or "BCIM-EC". It will involve a combination of infrastructure and trade facilitation arrangements between the four countries, as road, air and water links are set up from Kolkata to Kunming in Southeast China at a total cost of $ 22 billion. Conceived in the 1990s, the BCIM-EC was formally endorsed by the four countries in December 2013 and is viewed as a part of the OBOR connectivity projects. While India will benefit in terms of the development of the Kolkata port and the opening up of the economic potential of the northeast states, China will obtain one more route bypassing the Malacca Straits.

China clearly does not have the monopoly for envisaging major connectivity projects in Asia, and India is fully capable of leading a number of important projects for its economic and geopolitical benefit.

Other extenuating factors

Besides the fact that India is a major role-player in a number of strategically important connectivity projects in its neighbourhood, there have been a number of developments relating to OBOR-related projects that constitute a reality check on Chinese ambitions and encourage a more cooperative mind-set on its part.

First, there is little doubt that China has recognised the need for more extensive and intensive dialogue with principal role-players such as India, whose participation in the OBOR would be crucial for the success of the project. Thus, Chinese officials and academics are anxious to remind us that the OBOR is still an evolving concept; in a paper presented in August last year at the Cambridge Research Meeting, Wang said, "[The] OBOR is still an unclear and unspecific conception, without an authoritative definition. Actually, lots of debates and discussions about this new Silk Road are still going on inside and outside China." He recognised the numerous challenges that the project faced, particularly from "complex religious and ethnic issues, active terrorism and extremism", historical divisions across the region and competing geopolitical interests.

Similarly, according to Jia Qingguo,member of the standing committee of the Chinese People's Political Consultative Conference and dean of international relations at Beijing University, "the idea is still at the planning stage. It will take years to come to fruition and will face many serious challenges along the way". Finally, Lu Xiankun, a former Chinese trade negotiator, pointed out that the "OBOR is far from a fixed blueprint with detailed actions to be taken by all countries along the OBOR" and that many aspects need to be "developed, designed and consulted" before concrete actions can take place.

Second, China has already begun to understand the daunting challenges that would need to be addressed before the OBOR can become a reality. Wang, in his paper on OBOR's connections with the Arab Gulf countries, noted the deep knowledge-gap between China and the Arab world, and even quoted a western observer who referred to their ties as "unnatural". Besides the geopolitical issues noted above, almost all the OBOR projects will be imbued with operational, financial, legal and regulatory, and sovereign risks on account of the wide diversity in the countries involved, and their geographical, political and economic situations. Thus, the *Economist Intelligence Unit's* April 2015 report on the OBOR pointed out that just changes in governments following elections could place certain approved projects in jeopardy, as in Sri Lanka, or local activist groups could question certain projects on environmental grounds, as has happened recently with dam projects in Cambodia and Myanmar.

Hence, not surprisingly, while early writings on the project seemed to be China-centric, the principal focus of present-day comment by Chinese writers is on the need for participating countries to work closely together. Thus, Huang Yiping, a journalist for *Caijing,* and Chu Yin, associate professor of international relations at Tsinghua University, warned that the vision would not move forward if China were to adopt crude "great-power diplomacy" and excessive centralised planning.

Zhang Yuanyuan, speaking at a conference in Ulaanbaatar in October 2015, emphasised the "three togethers" in implementing OBOR – designing together, working together and sharing benefits together. Xiankun made this point robustly when he said, "OBOR emphasises a lot the need to integrate itself with the development strategy of OBOR countries, instead of imposing dragon claws on them."

These considerations have led Yuanyuan to note that five points will govern China's approach to project execution – policy coordination, infrastructure connectivity, free movement of goods, financial integration and people-to-people bonds. Thus, Yuanyuan is echoing the remarks of Jaishankar who said Asian connectivity would need to take into account "institutional, regulatory, legal, digital, financial and commercial connections", besides "the common cultural and civilisational thread that runs through Asia".

Third, the problems that are already hampering the CPEC projects in Pakistan should reassure India that it is much easier to draw lines on the map than it is to realise projects on the ground. As of now, almost every aspect of the CPEC is mired in some controversy or difficulty. There have been criticisms in provincial assemblies over the routing of the railways and highways, and over non-transparency in financial matters. There has also been opposition from Baloch nationalists and Gwadar residents. While the Balochis fear large-scale migration of outsiders and have attacked Chinese projects and workers, the people of Gwadar fear eviction from their homes. A dedicated force of 10,000 personnel has been deployed to protect the Chinese workers.

While both China and Pakistan remain committed to the successful completion of the proposed projects, this "flagship" proposal does exemplify the daunting difficulties that other OBOR projects will face as well. To divert attention from these problems, Pakistan's army chief General Raheel Sharif declared that India has "openly challenged" the CPEC and is "blatantly involved in destabilising Pakistan". Fourth, interactions with other countries appear to have made clear to China that there are misgivings about the OBOR in several Asian capitals. Hence, Chinese writers are at pains to assert that the OBOR is nothing like the Marshall Plan: it is not the result of occupation; it will not be a "tool of geopolitics"; and all countries, the US, Japan, Russia and India, are welcome to join it.

To allay regional misgivings, Yan Xuetong advocated that China needs "to improve its image and expand friendly relationships" through a "new diplomatic approach" in the neighbourhood. Chinese comment now tends to play down the geopolitical aspects of the OBOR: the need for greater sensitivity and accommodativeness is the central feature of the "vision" document and action plan. The paper upholds the centrality of policy coordination across Asia, the need for trade liberalisation and financial integration, and above all, the importance of promoting "people-to-people links". It recognises that the OBOR would be meaningless without policy coordination in crucial areas such trade, finance and investments.

Thus, though initiated by China, the OBOR can no longer be a Chinese project; for its success, it now needs to be an Asian enterprise.

MULTI-POLAR ASIA

In his remarks at the inauguration of the Raisina Dialogue, Jaishankar urged that China eschew the unilateral approach in promoting its connectivity projects on account of their obvious geopolitical implications. In this context, he observed that such a cautious approach was particularly important in Asia "in the absence of an agreed security architecture in Asia". Instead, he advocated a "multi-polar Asia," which he felt would be best achieved through "open-minded consultations on the future of connectivity".

Jaishankar's intervention has placed the connectivity issue at the heart of emerging regional and global strategic scenarios, highlighting the importance of matters such as — the nature of the world order that is taking shape at present, what role India will assume to define it, and where it will finally fit itself in these structures. Unfortunately, the discussion on these issues, in India and in several other world capitals, is often distorted by "zero-sum" thinking, a simplistic view that separates "us" and "them" into firm dichotomous categories. This is also what informs much Indian academic response to initiatives and projects with which China is associated.

There is little doubt that, as a major country, with pride in its history and civilisational values and the sense of its own destiny, China will be India's rival and will compete for influence in different sectors — geographical, political, economic, cultural and ideational. But, this will still leave huge spaces where there will be a convergence of interests, and it is here that the two nations will explore how they can coordinate their capabilities to achieve the best results. Such cooperative efforts will take place both bilaterally and within multilateral fora, such as the BRICS, G-20, the Shanghai Cooperation Organisation and even the UN Security Council; they can also take place in regard to the OBOR.

Both countries accept the importance of expanding connectivities in Asia, a continent that is rich in resources but unable to move these to markets where they are required. If connectivity projects were to be negotiated among the various stakeholders and decisions taken in accordance with the cooperative spirit, the strategic value of the projects would increasingly give way to their more important economic value, which would be the true "win-win" that Chinese policymakers have been emphasising lately. This would open the space for an active Indian role in respect of projects that serve its interests, such as BCIM-EC and those that would promote links to Central Asia and Russia.

This would apply to the security scenario as well. In coming years, it is most unlikely that a neat Asian security architecture will be put in place. At the same time, no sharp, dichotomous lines are likely to divide major world powers immutably. We will continue to have several polarities representing diverse interests, with different poles coming together from time to time to support specific issues. India will of course need to manoeuvre actively among the various interest groups, depending on the issues at stake.

Thus, while India has every reason to watch developments relating to Gwadar with close attention, there is no reason to despair: India is not without assets of its own in the shape of its place at Chabahar and its naval partnership with Oman. Indeed, India enjoys far greater influence in the Gulf than China does and is a more acceptable role-player in addressing the security concerns of that region in conflict. The major powers in the region – Saudi Arabia, Iran and Turkey – will also avoid firm alliances with world powers and, like India, will generally pursue policies of flexible alignment. A multi-polar Asia already exists and India is an important part of it.

GEOPOLITICS OF THE INDIAN OCEAN REGION

The Indian Ocean and the states on its littoral are of significant and growing importance. The region contains 1/3 of the world's population, 25% of its landmass, 40% of the world's oil and gas reserves. It is the locus of important international sea lines of communication (SLOCs). The region is home to most of the world's Muslim population as well as India, one of the world's likely "rising powers." The Indian Ocean also is home to the world's two newest nuclear weapons states, India and Pakistan, as well as Iran, which most observers believe has a robust program to acquire nuclear weapons.

In addition, the region constitutes one of the key centres of gravity of international terrorism - - "the broad incubator of terrorism" in the words of one conference participant. While India and some a few of the other littoral states appear to be on a path of sustained economic progress, most of the region is characterized by high levels of poverty. The Indian Ocean region suffers from a high level of international and internal conflict and is a key venue for international piracy. It also is the locus of some 70% of the world's natural disasters.

The regional strategic environment is volatile and dangerous. In addition to some of the conditions enumerated above, recent developments in Iraq and Afghanistan now pose additional challenges of violence, terrorism, and instability across the entire Indian Ocean region. A Malaysian conference participant, for example, argued that the foregoing conflicts have been bad for Malaysia and have "played into the hands of local terrorists." For these reasons and others, the region - - an "insecurity community" - - has been an arena of increased diplomatic and military activity on the part of a variety of littoral states as well as external powers in last few years.

Military power, including weapons of mass destruction and their delivery vehicles, is looming larger in the region. Conference participants pointed to the ongoing insertion of military power in the region by the United States and - - to a much lesser extent - - Japan. At the same time, it was emphasized that India, Malaysia and a variety of other littoral states are strengthening their militaries. We also will see "a resurgent Iranian naval capability eventually." Moreover, many of these states are emphasizing power projection capabilities, often through the acquisition of more advanced military hardware and the construction of new bases intended for forward defence. For example, one Indian participant claimed that India's relatively new Andaman and Nicobar Command - - which New Delhi almost decided to name "Southeast Asia Command" - - is intended to "stop the Chinese east of the Malacca Strait."

Quite a few conference participants underscored the growing role of nuclear weapons in the region. The Israeli scholar pointed to Israel's growing emphasis on strategic reach and on the development of a maritime second-strike nuclear capability with respect to both the Indian Ocean - - to deal with Iranian and Pakistani contingencies - - and the Mediterranean. The Indians, similarly, emphasized their intention to develop a full triad of nuclear weapons capabilities to include, in the words of one scholar, "high yield nuclear weapons in the Indian Ocean."

India remains concerned about the role of external powers (or some of them) in the Indian Ocean region. Most of this concern relates to China and - - to a lesser extent, the United States. On the other hand, some conference participants - - to include some Indian participants - - believe that key littoral countries like India, Pakistan, Iran, and Malaysia have gained substantial space and strategic autonomy because of the desire of external powers to forge alliances and coalitions in the region. One Indian, moreover, commented: "asking outside powers to stay away is a pipedream."

The Indians present also seemed comfortable with, and appreciative of, Israel's expanding security perimeter and its growing strategic involvement in the Indian Ocean region. The Indians present welcomed the evolving Indo-Israeli security nexus and were pleased by a presentation by an Israeli scholar, which placed India and Israel in a common democratic and civilizational community. Similarly, one Indian - - referring to Moscow's recent naval foray into the Indian Ocean - - stated: "India is pleased that Russia is back in the Indian Ocean."

The region is characterized by growing strategic competition involving both external powers and the littoral states. In this regard, most conference participants emphasized the continuing rivalry between India and China, the "peer powers of Asia," and the potential for this problem to worsen. The Indians at this conference were especially vocal and alarmed about Beijing's evolving role the Indian Ocean region. One Indian, for example, asserted that the 21st century would be the "template for Sino-Indian rivalry." Pointing to Chinese proliferation of WMD, provision of conventional arms to various South Asian states, "ruthless subordination of its neighbours", "special relationships" with Pakistan and Burma, "growing presence of the PLA" in areas adjacent to India's borders, and developing naval capabilities, most of the Indians present made it clear that China, in their view, is India's number one security problem. Commenting on India's insertion of naval forces into the South China Sea last year, one Indian said it was a "good thing if China felt threatened by our exercise. We intended to send a message and they got the message." The Chinese scholar present strongly countered these assertions and argued that Chinese strategy in the Indian Ocean is benign and has three dimensions: trade and development, good neighborliness and friendship, and security and cooperation. In his view, China has re-oriented its overall security strategy since the end of the Cold War, but India has not done so. He argued that China is no longer preoccupied by fears that other states are "encircling" China, but Indian national security strategists remain fixated on fears of encirclement of India.

Some of the Americans at the conference also attempted to calm Indian fears, arguing, for example, that China's security strategy is oriented mainly east, not south. The Indians generally reacted to such interventions with skepticism. In addition, on the matter of Burma, one conference participant argued that fears about Chinese influence in Burma are overdrawn and it is not Beijing, but Rangoon, that holds the "whip hand" in the China-Burma relationship.

Paralleling this concern with China, there also is some Indian worry about the growing role of the United States and, to a lesser extent, Japan in the region. At the extreme, one Indian argued strongly for the need for Indian military - - and nuclear - - contingency plans with respect to a potential U.S. threat. This worry about the United States and U.S. power is so notwithstanding the reality that almost all of the Indians at the conference welcomed the development of closer Indian ties with the United States.

According to an Indian naval officer, "the United States is unquestionably the most dominant player in the Indian Ocean in modern history." The United States has the capability to project military power in the region and a well-defined strategy to pursue its policy of preeminence. The U.S. maritime strategy of the 1980s envisioned a war at sea won by sea control. The new U.S. strategic thrust aims to move away from classical sea control/sea denial to influencing events further ashore as exemplified by Afghanistan. He observed: "if the U.S. objective is to share with ...other nations ...(the) enduring objective...(of) stopping the emergence of a hostile coalition, then it must remain engaged in the region. Its policies must work towards engagement rather than adopt unilateralist approaches." The Indians present also seemed anxious about how the United States will "manage" China when the PLA navy or other military forces start to operate in the Indian Ocean, as New Delhi believes likely. India will be increasingly attentive to its interests in the Indian Ocean region in the coming years. This is suggested by a variety of considerations. All Indian participants in the conference stressed the importance of the Indian Ocean to India from economic, political, legal and military perspectives. India's political and naval leadership is convinced that matters maritime are going to play an increasingly important and critical role. India needs a secure maritime environment to achieve sustained national development. In addition, many Indians see the Indian Ocean as India's backyard and see it as both natural and desirable for India to function as the leader and the predominant influence in this region - - the world's only region and ocean named after a single state.

To this end, there was broad agreement among the Indian delegation that India's security perimeter - - its "rightful domain" - - extends from the Strait of Malacca to the Strait of Hormuz and from the coast of Africa to the western shores of Australia. India, according to a senior Indian naval officer at the conference, "will have to play a very large role (in the Indian Ocean) if the prospects for peace and cooperation are to grow."

India will try to exert a strong hand in this region for fundamental national security reasons. Protecting India's EEZ of over 2.3 million square kilometers, securing India's energy lifelines, promoting overseas markets and fulfilling international commitments are some of the interests to which India is sensitive. As expressed at the conference, New Delhi's "Look East" policy, its growing ties with Israel and Africa, and even Iran, and its naval, air and nuclear weapons modernization efforts, all are related to these concerns. Aside from India, many of the other littoral states are acquiring a more pronounced maritime orientation and developing closer links with one another.Malaysia, for example, is more focused now than ever before on the potential strategic importance of the Indian Ocean approaches to Peninsula Malaysia. Not long ago, Malaysia's navy chief said that the country's strategic location in the waterways of the South China Sea and the Indian Ocean exposes the country to serious dangers. Reacting to this challenge, the Malaysian navy has inaugurated construction of a new navy base and command centre at Langkawi, Kuala Lumpur's only port directly fronting the Indian Ocean.

Thailand, similarly, is now more aware of its status as an Indian Ocean littoral state. Arms trafficking in southern Thailand, which has fueled conflicts in Sri Lanka and northeast India, has come under scrutiny as Thailand's neighbours have urged a more robust response from Bangkok. In recent years, Bangkok also has joined a plethora of Indian Ocean regional organizations - - including BIMSTEC and IOR-ARC, and has pursued the so-called "Look West" policy of cultivating Indian Ocean states, especially India. Thailand lately has also shown new interest in building a canal across the Kra Isthmus to forge a shorter direct route between the Pacific and Indian Oceans. However, large obstacles stand in the way of this dream being realized any time soon, not the least of which is Singapore's implacable opposition to a Kra Canal.

Sub-regional efforts to promote Indian Ocean peace and security are more likely to bear fruit than are region-wide schemes. To this end, conference participants were of one mind that confidence-building and similar measures would be most successful if attempted in Bay of Bengal (the area of operations of BIMSTEC) or the Arabian Sea or between the Indian and Pakistani navies. On the other hand, large region-wide efforts such as the "Indian Ocean Zone of Peace" concept or even the Indian Ocean Region Association for Regional Cooperation are much less likely to succeed.

INDIA'S PEARLS IN THE INDIAN OCEAN

Over the last decade or so, India has developed good security relationships with many states throughout the Indian Ocean, with particular focus on the maritime choke points of the Mozambique Channel in the southwest Indian Ocean, the Persian Gulf in the northwest and the Malacca Strait in the northeast. India is also developing a security presence in the central Indian Ocean astride the east-west SLOCs across the Indian Ocean.

Southwest Indian Ocean

The southwestern Indian Ocean forms the gateway between the Atlantic and Indian Oceans. India's security relationships in the region are anchored by its close relationship with Mauritius, the island territory that lies around 900km to the east of Madagascar. India has long-standing and close political, economic and security associations with Mauritius. Some 70% of the Mauritian population is of Indian ethnic origin and for several decades Mauritius has acted as the primary gateway for international investment into India

(originating from the United States, Europe and elsewhere), largely due to favourable tax arrangements. Former Mauritian Prime Minister Paul Berenger described the bilateral relationship as "umbilical and sacred" and security relations as "intense". The current President Anerood Jugnauth describes the connection in terms of "blood relations".

The Mauritian elite see India in largely benign terms and appear to have accepted India as having a special role in Mauritian security. Cooperation is formalised in a 1974 defence agreement under which India has transferred patrol boats and helicopters to Mauritius (including the supply of a patrol vessel in 2010) and provides training to Mauritian personnel and officers for the Mauritian National Coast Guard and Police Helicopter Squadron (effectively the Mauritian navy and air force). Since 2003, the Indian Navy has also provided maritime security through periodic patrols of Mauritian waters including anti-piracy patrols in 2010. India also backs Mauritius' territorial claims to Diego Garcia which was separated from Mauritian administration in the 1960s. Mauritian political leaders have publicly indicated on several occasions that India would be permitted to establish naval facilities on Mauritius if it so wished and there are claims that India already operates a signals intelligence station. In 2006 and 2007 there were reports of discussions between the Mauritian and Indian governments over the long term lease to the Indian government of the Agalega islands (which lie between the island of Mauritius and the Seychelles), ostensibly for tourism. It has been speculated that India's intention was to upgrade the Agalega airstrip to service Indian manned and unmanned surveillance aircraft. Discussions over the proposal reportedly ended due to political sensitivities concerning the local creole population (contemplating, perhaps, the complaints of the Diego Garcians who were dispossessed from their islands following a deal between the British and Mauritian governments).

India also has growing security relationships with Madagascar, Mozambique and the Seychelles, littoral states in and around the crucial Mozambique channel, the SLOC used by shipping transiting the Cape of Good Hope. The security of the Seychelles was highly contested during the latter half of the Cold War as the United States and the Soviet Union competed to maintain or establish a security presence there. At the same time, India was seen by the Seychelles as a benign regional protector. In the early 1980s, Seychelles' leftist President Albert Rene sought commitments from Indira Gandhi to intervene in the case of an attempted coup. Although Gandhi declined to provide public commitments, India did contribute two helicopters and training to the Seychelles security forces. The Indian Navy has assisted with maritime security in the Seychelles EEZ under a 2003 defence cooperation agreement under which it provided anti-piracy patrols in early 2010. In 2005 India gifted a patrol boat to the Seychelles—reportedly in a hurried effort to pre-empt offers of Chinese assistance. In July 2007 the Indian Navy opened an electronic monitoring facility in northern Madagascar at the head of the Mozambique Channel and reportedly has also been granted "limited" berthing rights in Madagascar for Indian naval vessels. The Indian Navy has also acted as a maritime security provider for Mozambique, including taking responsibility for maritime security during the 2003 African Union and 2004 World Economic Forum summits held in Maputo. In 2006, India and Mozambique entered a defence cooperation agreement that envisages joint maritime patrols, supply of military equipment, training and technology transfer in repairing and assembling military vehicles, aircraft and ships.

India's maritime security relationships in the southwestern Indian Ocean are also buttressed by growing maritime security relations with France and South Africa. Since 2001 the Indian Navy has conducted annual exercises with the French navy, which operates out of Reunion and Djibouti. India has also sponsored the "IBSA" trilateral security dialogue among India, Brazil and South Africa, pursuant to which trilateral naval exercises have been held in 2008 and 2010 off the Cape of Good Hope. Further south, India also has a growing presence in Antarctica, with one active research station and a second due to open in 2012.

While some might see India as holding a strong security role in the southwest Indian Ocean, there are fears in New Delhi that China might undermine or pre-empt Indian's relationships. According to the former Indian Chief of Naval Staff, Admiral Prakash, India "cannot afford to have any hostile or inimical power threatening the island states in this region". Political and economic relations between China and Mauritius and Seychelles are closely watched by New Delhi and it has been claimed that a so-called Chinese "thrust" towards these states presages Sino-naval rivalry in the western Indian Ocean. While China may develop better economic and political interests in the area, it seems unlikely that it would be able to dislodge India as the dominant security provider to Mauritius and there are no indications at present that it would be able to seriously challenge India's maritime security role elsewhere in the southwest Indian Ocean.

Northeast Indian Ocean

India has placed considerable emphasis on developing a security presence in the northeast Indian Ocean. There are several dimensions to this: first, India's direct security presence in the Andaman Sea, second, its bilateral security relationships in the region and third, its aspirations to gain a security role in the Malacca Strait. While India aspires to play a significant security role in Southeast Asia it has given particular focus to the Malacca Strait, the key maritime choke point between the Indian and Pacific Oceans.

India's Andaman and Nicobar islands, which run north-south through the Andaman Sea form a natural base for projecting power into the Strait and beyond into the South China Sea. In the mid-1990s, India commenced development of military facilities in the Andaman Islands for a new tri-service Andaman & Nicobar Command. This chain of bases now includes extensive port facilities to service elements of the Indian Eastern Fleet and several bases for surveillance and strike aircraft. The operational radius of aircraft based there encompasses the Malacca Strait and large portions of the South China Sea. The Andaman Islands have particular significance for the security of the Strait and have been described by one Chinese naval writer as constituting a "metal chain" that could lock the western end of the Strait tight.

India's security relationships in the region are anchored by Singapore. During colonial times Singapore effectively acted as the eastern anchor to British India's political and security sphere. On gaining independence in 1965, Singapore courted India to act as its "natural" security provider, including requests for the stationing of Indian naval vessels. However India, under Prime Minister Indira Gandhi, declined any security role in the region. With the end of the Cold War India renewed its links with Singapore, which now acts as India's primary economic, political and security partner in Southeast Asia. Singapore sees India as having an important security role in the region, acting as a balance to other extra-regional powers, including China, the United States and Japan. India and Singapore conduct extensive security cooperation, including broad-based security dialogues, joint exercises, intelligence sharing and cooperation in defence technology. The two have conducted annual bilateral naval exercises since 1993 and now stage annual large-scale exercises between all three armed services. In a first for India, Singapore has been granted long term use of Indian facilities to conduct air and army training. It has been reported that there is an arrangement allowing for "frequent visits" of Indian naval vessels to Singapore's Changi Naval Base, and the development of an Indian naval logistical presence in Singapore seems not beyond the realms of possibility.

India has also been developing its security relationship with Indonesia, although more slowly. While Indonesia has been very supportive of India developing its political and economic links with ASEAN states over the last two decades, it is only in recent years that the relationship has developed a security element. A Defence Cooperation Agreement was signed in 2001.

In 2002 concerns about the potential use of the Andaman Sea as a communication route with extremist groups in the region (including claimed links between Jihadist terrorists and Aceh separatists) led to the commencement of biannual "coordinated" naval patrols between the Indian and Indonesian navies in the Six-Degree Channel at the northern entrance to the Malacca Strait. These patrols comprise Indian and Indonesian vessels and aircraft, co-ordinated out of India's Joint Operations Command in the Andaman Islands. In recent years India has been pressing Indonesia to extend naval cooperation into the Strait itself.

The Strait of Malacca, which represents a key choke point between the Indian and Pacific Oceans, forms a focus of India's maritime security ambitions in the northeast Indian Ocean. Arguably, the potential to exercise a significant degree of control over shipping movements through the Strait is a prerequisite of effective control of the eastern Indian Ocean. Some have argued that for India the Strait represents a rough counterpart to the importance of the Panama Canal to the United States in terms of its ability to maintain regional hegemony. Others place it as the mid-point in an "arc of rivalry" between India and China stretching from the Persian Gulf to the Sea of Japan.

The Malacca Strait is one of the world's busiest waterways, with over 62,000 ship movements in 2006. It is the key trade route between East Asia and Europe, carrying an estimated one third of global trade and the bulk of energy supplies from the Middle East to East Asia (including an estimated 70-80% of China's energy imports and 90% of Japan's).

The Strait is considered to be particularly prone to piracy and terrorist attacks. In the early years of last decade there were widely-held concerns about the level of sea-robbery of ships transiting the Strait, although reported cases of sea robbery in the Malacca Strait and surrounding areas have fallen significantly in recent years due to improved land policing, improved economic conditions and the end of the insurgency in Indonesia's Aceh province. Since 2001, politically motivated piracy or terrorism has also been of concern, although no such attacks have eventuated. The Strait is largely within the territorial waters of Singapore, Indonesia and Malaysia, with the latter two states in particular being highly sensitive to the presence of any "external" maritime security providers in the Strait.

In the wake of September 2001, at the invitation of the United States, India took a security role inside the Strait through the provision of naval escorts for high value commercial traffic, as part of the U.S.-led Operation *Enduring Freedom*. Since then, India has been careful to position itself as a benign security provider in the Strait, and to ensure that any naval presence was seen as "non-intrusive, cooperative and benign" by the littoral states.

According to one Indian naval officer: "Our role [in the Malacca Strait] is being perceived as that of a responsible nation, which can create a balance in the region. Also, everyone realises that India has no ambitions of hegemony." India has regularly pressured littoral states over the last decade to take an active security role in the Strait and in June 2006 the Indian Defence Minister Mukherjee reaffirmed India's offers to provide assistance. However, India's official justification for its interest in the Strait—that is, securing the Strait from threats of piracy and terrorism—holds little water. Not only are these primarily policing rather than military issues, the reported statistics in recent years clearly demonstrate that there is no crisis requiring external intervention. It is evident that India's interest in the Strait is primarily motivated by a desire to enhance its role as the leading maritime security provider in the Indian Ocean and potentially control access to the Indian Ocean.

However, the littoral states (and in particular, Malaysia) have resisted giving India a formal security role in the Strait, either on a bilateral basis or in the various cooperative security arrangements that have been put in place (including the MALSINDO coordinated naval patrols, the ReCAAP information sharing centre, and the so-called Cooperative Mechanism). It remains to be seen whether there are circumstances in which the littoral states would agree to India's requests for a direct security role in the Strait.

Northwest Indian Ocean

India historically exercised a special political and economic role in the northwest Indian Ocean. During the nineteenth and early twentieth centuries, British India was the dominant economic, political and military force in the region. The Trucial States (now United Arab Emirates) and Aden (now Yemen) were administered from British India and British Indian Army garrisons were stationed throughout the Persian Gulf until 1947. India's influence in the region diminished significantly following independence.

Although India generally adopted a pro-Arab foreign policy, its ties in the region were regularly strained as a result of the India-Pakistan conflict. Pakistan's close political, economic and military ties with many states continue to this day. Some argue that the ability of India to extend its security presence in the northwest Indian Ocean has also been constrained by US predominance in the Gulf, leaving little room for India to develop its own relationships, and that the United States has not encouraged an increased Indian security presence there. This perception is reinforced by the fact that the US military relationship with India is the responsibility of US Pacific Command, based in Hawaii, while the US security presence in the northwest Indian Ocean is administered by the US Central Command (which also has responsibility for the US military relationship with Pakistan).

Arun Prakash, 'Security and Foreign Policy Imperatives of an Emerging India', p. 7. Including an announced $700 million investment by China in a special economic zone in Mauritius. James Lamont, 'Beijing Edges aside Delhi to Woo Mauritius as Africa Hub', *Financial Times,* 26 January 2010. C. Raja Mohan, 'Sino-Indian Rivalry in the Western Indian Ocean', *ISAS Insights,* no. 52 (24 February 2009). Pakistani military personnel have key roles in the armed forces of Saudi Arabia and many Gulf states.

Despite these constraints, India is developing security relations in the region, particularly with Qatar (which sits inside the Persian Gulf), and Oman (which sits on the Strait of Hormuz at the head of the Persian Gulf). They may see India as partially balancing their security relationships with the United States. Since 2003, India has entered into several defence agreements with Oman dealing with training, maritime security cooperation and joint exercises. The Indian Air Force uses the Thumrait air base for transit purposes and Oman has offered the Indian Navy berthing facilities in support of anti-piracy patrols. In 2008 India also entered into a security agreement with Qatar which, according to some reports, includes Indian security guarantees. The agreement, which was reportedly entered following "persistent" efforts of Qatar, deals among other things with maritime security and intelligence sharing. One Indian official commented that, "The agreement is just short of stationing troops (in the region)", while another was reported as commenting that "We will go to the rescue of Qatar if Qatar requires it, in whatever form it takes." The Indian Navy has also sought to play an active role in Somali-based piracy and since October 2008 has one or two vessels in anti-piracy patrols off Somalia. India's contribution has been made separately from the US-sponsored Combined Task Forces 150 and 151, in which Pakistan has played an active role.

Central Indian Ocean

The two island chains that dominate the central Indian Ocean are the British-administered Indian Ocean Territory (which hosts the US air and naval base on Diego Garcia) and the Maldives. These island chains run north-south, astride the major east-west SLOCs between East Asia and the Middle East.

India has long regarded the Maldives as falling within its South Asian sphere of influence. In 1988, with the apparent blessing of the United States and Britain, India sent troops and naval forces to the Maldives to support President Gayoom in an attempted coup by Sri Lankan mercenaries. Since that time, India has supplied the Maldivian armed forces with equipment and training and the Indian Navy has provided maritime security. In August 2009, a security agreement was formalised that will significantly enhance India's capabilities in the central Indian Ocean. India has been granted use of the former British naval and air base on Gan Island, part of the southernmost group of islands in the Maldives (lying around 1,000 km south of India and around 700 km north of Diego Garcia). India is reportedly planning to base Dornier aircraft and helicopters at Gan, although it is unclear to what extent the Indian Navy will establish a permanent presence at the associated Gan naval facilities. India also reportedly plans to station aircraft and naval vessels at Male in the central Maldives and at Haa Dhalu Atoll in the north. As part of the agreement, India is also building a system of 26 electronic monitoring facilities across the Maldives archipelago. According to the Maldivian President, the installations are to protect the Maldives' large EEZ from illegal fishing.

CHINA'S RESPONSE TO INDIA'S GROWING STRATEGIC INFLUENCE

Indian Primer Minister Manmohan Singh once said that India as "a super regional power", its strategic footprint "covers the region bounded by the Horn of Africa, West Asia, Central Asia, Southeast Asia and beyond, to the far reaches of the

Indian Ocean". China is conscious of New Delhi's intentions in Asia, as well as its ambitions to project its power into and beyond the Indian Ocean. India's ambitious geopolitical expansion strategy and its economic potential might not only turn India and China into competitors over oil supplies, but might as well increase their concerns over the opportunity for 'relative economic gains' in the short term when weighed against the threat of increased geopolitical competition in the long term.

In South Asia, India is competing with China to woo energy-rich nations such as Bangladesh and Myanmar that are politically closer to China. In the case of Myanmar, India's interest goes well beyond simply getting control over gas supply. Good relations with Myanmar will also help open up the northeast to trade, solve a number of political and ethnic problems in the region, and enhance India's relations with the rest of Southeast Asia through ASEAN.

India has moved from voicing its opposition to the military junta's crackdown on pro-democracy activists and the arrest of Aung San Suu Kyi, the leader of the National League for Democracy, to a more pragmatic, non-interventionist and ostrichlike policy to the current crisis in Mayanmar. This change in policy by India has been prompted by its desire to access the region's energy resources, gain access to the vast markets of Southeast Asia, balance the influence of China and counter Indian insurgent groups operating from Myanmar. In the face of India's growing strategic influence, China's approach is to develop economic and strategic ties with South Asian nations, ensuring that India is surrounded by countries friendly toward China. China's trade with SAARC (South Asian Association for Regional Cooperation) rose from US$ 4.2 billion to US$ 34.7 billion; while China's bilateral trade with India rose from US$ 2 billion to US$ 24.9 billion. Similarly, bilateral trade between China and Pakistan has been increasing by 45% on a year-on-year basis, reaching US$ 5.3 billion in 2006.

China's increasingly economic and strategic ties with major South Asian nations paved the way for its entry into the SAARC as an observer at the 13th SAARC summit held in Dhaka on November 12-13, 2005. India tried to keep Beijing out of the SAARC in vain. Pakistan saw China's entry into the SAARC an opportunity to "counterbalance India's design to act as a regional power and dominate SAARC".

Strategically, China has built a naval port at the Arabian Sea Coast in Gwadar, Pakistan. This would lead not only to Gwadar emerging as a transit terminal for oil imports but also as a pretext for China's naval presence in the Indian Ocean, thereby enabling China to "monitor US naval activity in the Persian Gulf, Indian activity in the Arabian Sea, and future US-Indian maritime cooperation in the Indian Ocean". Similarly, Bangladesh has offered China naval access to its prized Chittagong port, which New Delhi has long sought but to no avail. India would like to gain access to Chittagong port to help ship its planned natural gas imports from Myanmar to its northeast region. In April 2005, China also signed a comprehensive agreement with Sri Lanka which provides access to Colombo's ports, and thereby the Indian Ocean.

In response to India's changing relations with Myanmar, China has been increasing economic and military support to the military regime in Myanmar. Statistics showed that by the year 2005, China's total aid to Myanmar reached about US$100 million. From 1991 to 2005, the Bank of China and China Import-Export Bank provided Myanmar with seller's credits worth over US$1 billion. In 2006, China provided another US$85 million of low-interest loans to Myanmar for purchasing two new oil-drillers.

From the perspective of security, China's assistance to Myanmar in constructing and improving port facilities on two islands in the Bay of Bengal and Andaman Sea is significant as this can be used as a listening post to gather intelligence on Indian Naval operations and as a forward base for future Chinese naval operations in the Indian Ocean. China's interest also includes plans for constructing a gas pipeline across Myanmar from the offshore gas reserves in the Bay of Bengal to Yunnan province and an oil pipeline for crude from the

Middle East. Myanmar's strategic location also becomes an important outlet for Chinese exports via the Bay of Bengal and serves as an alternate trading and shipping route to the Malacca Strait.

Chinese scholars hold that China's interests and goals in South Asia and Indian Ocean are mainly focused on economy, aiming at establishing more trade partnerships and ensuring oil shipment security. But economic interests need to be protected and maintained by friendly political relationships and stable security environment. They believe that "China's military relationships with South Asian countries are mainly developed for economic interests, and should not be understood as targeted at India." In recent years, Central Asia is attracting more and more attention from big powers not only because of its geo-strategic position and rich natural resources, but also because of its specific role in global campaign against terrorism. Being a common strategic neighbour to China and India, the importance of Central Asia has been fully recognized by both governments. India considers Central Asia as its "immediate and strategic neighbourhood" for historical/cultural as well as geopolitical and economic reasons. 28 India has been conducting bilateral anti-terrorism military excises with some Central Asian countries, and has established its first overseas military base near Dushanbe – the capital of Tajikistan, indicating that it is getting involved in Central Asian affairs.

China has also reached out to Central Asia. It joined Kazakhstan, Kyrgyzstan, Russia, Tajikistan, and Uzbekistan as founding members of the Shanghai Cooperation Organization (SCO) on June 15, 2001. Under the SCO umbrella, China has strengthened its economic and strategic cooperation with these Central Asian countries. Chinese trade with these five Central Asian countries had risen from US$9.8 billion in 2000 to US$37.7 billion in 2005. China has also spent over US1 billion to construct a 1,000 km-long oil pipeline from the Karazhanbas field to Xinjiang. The pipeline, which began operation in 2006, has a 200,000 bbl/d (barrels of oil per day) capacity. Chinese scholars believed that, compared with the situation in South Asia and

Southeast Asia, China and India's China and India's interests in Central Asia are relatively limited. Neither country has the desire or drives to dominate this region, which has traditionally been Russia's "backyard."

Instead, there is for China and India more potential for cooperation rather than competition in Central Asia. In terms of security cooperation, Chinese scholars refer to terrorism, separatism and religious extremism the so-called "three evil forces" in Central Asia and believe these forces are common threats to both countries. One study suggests that the "*East Turkestan Islamic Movement,*" which is considered a threat to the security of China's Xinjiang autonomous region, has penetrated South Asia from Central Asia and might be seeking to establish a terrorism base there to attack Chinese diplomats and citizens in South Asian countries.

If true, developments along this dimension will become a new factor of instability in South Asia. In economic terms, both China and India are developing economies and need to import a large amount of oil and natural gas to meet their domestic increasing demand. This makes it possible for these two countries to cooperate and compete as well in this region. In recent years, Chinese and Indian oil companies entered Central Asian energy market by forging new alliance and synergies in the energy sector.

Some Indian scholars proposed that these two countries jointly build an oil and gas "energy highway" from Central Asia to the north of India through the west of China. The state-oil companies from China and India have cooperated in some cases. But what is more important is to promote economic integration in Central Asia, realizing common development and prosperity in this region. This is the best way to ensure and maintain regional peace and stability. China and India could play their roles in this regard. For instance, there exist great economic complementarities between Central Asian countries and China and India. China and India can provide various sorts of equipments and facilities, including transportation, electricity and telecommunication equipments which are badly needed in these countries; China and India own many developed seaports, thus can provide outlets for these landlocked Central Asian countries' imports and exports. China and India can achieve win-win result if they could manage their interests and influence in Central Asia properly while bearing more responsibility as two big regional powers.

ONE BELT, ONE ROAD: CHINA'S RESPONSE TO THE US "PIVOT"

At two top-level gatherings in Asia last month—the Asia Pacific Economic Cooperation (APEC) and the East Asia Summit—US President Barack Obama again exploited maritime disputes in the South China Sea to press his "pivot to Asia" agenda—consolidating an economic bloc through the Trans Pacific Partnership (TPP) and military ties and alliances throughout the region, all directed against China.

Even before the "pivot" was formally announced in 2011, the Obama administration, in response to the deepening global economic breakdown, began shifting focus to the Indo-Pacific region in a bid to counter the perceived threat posed by a growing China to American hegemony. Simply by virtue of its sheer economic size, China is cutting across the longstanding economic and strategic relationships established after the end of World War II based on US pre-eminence.

Confronted with the TPP, from which China is excluded, and an extensive US military build-up throughout the region, the Chinese regime has been forced to react. Its response is conditioned by the class interests it represents—the tiny super-wealthy oligopoly that enriched itself through the processes of capitalist restoration during the past three decades. Broadly, Beijing has sought to appease Washington while at the same time engaging in an arms race that can only end in one way.

In 2013, the new leadership of President Xi Jinjing and Premier Li Keqiang elaborated an extensive geo-political strategy that drew together and extended existing strands of foreign policy. Its aim is to extricate China from its strategic encirclement by the US and its allies, while opening up further trade and investment opportunities for Chinese capitalism. Known as the Silk Road Economic Belt and the 21st Century Silk Road, or One Belt One Road (OBOR), the scheme envisages massive infrastructure development to link the Eurasian landmass, as well as Africa, both by land and sea.

By offering substantial investment in infrastructure as well as burgeoning trade and economic benefits, Beijing is hoping to draw countries across Eurasia, the Middle East and Africa into its plans and thereby blunt the US "pivot."

At the East Asia Summit in Kuala Lumpur, Chinese Premier Li made a definite appeal to the Association of South East Asian Nations (ASEAN) leaders, highlighting China's commitment efforts to establish land transport links from southern China throughout South East Asia as well as the upgrading of port facilities in the region. He pledged $US10 billion for the next phase of the China-ASEAN special infrastructure loan.

As well as boosting economic relations between China and ASEAN, with two-way trade projected to reach $1 trillion by 2020, the land linkages have a strategic aim—to lessen China's dependence on shipping lanes through South East Asia to import energy and raw materials from the Middle East and Africa. Beijing is well aware that US military strategists regard a naval blockade, including by control over the Malacca Strait, as a crucial element of their war plans against China.

Last week China hosted the fourth China-Central and Eastern European (CCE) summit at which Li highlighted the role of Eastern Europe, the Balkans and Baltic States as "the east gateway to Europe and along the routes of the Belt and Road initiative." He said he wanted to work with all 16 countries represented "to build the China-Europe land-sea express line and promote connectivity in Europe." China signed a deal with Hungary and Serbia to build a high-speed rail line between their capitals, as part of a broad plan for a rail link to the Greek port of Piraeus. Li also announced investments in port facilities in the Baltic, Adriatic and Black Seas but gave no specifics.

Beijing's pitch is above all directed toward the major European powers—all of which are part of the formal NATO military alliance with the United States. While China's European diplomacy has been developing for years, three key visits in late October and early November—President Xi's trip to Britain, and the visits by French President Francois Hollande and German Chancellor Angela Merkel to China—highlight the economic and strategic issues, as much for Europe as for China.

Britain, France and Germany all have their own imperialist ambitions in Eurasia, which have been further fuelled by the worsening global economic breakdown and the slump in Europe, in particular. With the emergence of China as the world's largest cheap labour platform and second largest economy, all the major powers—the US, Japan and European—are driven to maximise their economic engagement and investment, and thus their influence in Beijing.

In an article published on the *Europesworld.org* website in May, Wang Yiwei, director of the China-Europe Academic Network, openly spelt out China's strategic aims, declaring: "With the rise of the United States, Europe entered into a decline which recent attempts at integration have been unable to reverse. Europe is now faced with a historic opportunity to return to the centre of the world through the revival of Eurasia."

At this stage, the One Belt, One Road initiative remains largely in the realm of grandiose and general ideas. The Chinese government issued a document this March entitled "Visions and Actions on Jointly Building Silk Road Economic Belt and 21st Century Maritime Silk Road." It was short on specifics and long on the rhetoric of "peaceful coexistence," "win-win cooperation" and the advantages of closer economic integration.

Insofar as the broad outlines are known, the land-based Belt involves the construction of 80,000 kilometres of high-speed rail links, with a major route running from the Chinese city of Xian, historically the starting point of the Silk Road, to Europe, through Urumqi in China's western Xinjiang province and Central Asia to Moscow and Europe. Other rail lines include one from southern China through South East Asia to Singapore and another from Xinjiang through Pakistan to the Chinese-built port of Gwadar on the Arabian Sea.

The plans include a major expansion of roads, oil and gas pipelines and digital cables, along with power production and energy grids. As well as providing an impetus for economic growth in China's undeveloped inland regions, the infrastructure proposals are designed to provide an outlet for China's production overcapacities and profitable opportunities for Chinese corporations.

The maritime Road focusses on the expansion of port facilities, particularly in South East Asia to develop sea transport from China to Europe, and in Kenya to integrate Africa.

Beijing has proposed to allocate up to $1.4 trillion to finance the huge array of infrastructure projects and is setting up financial institutions alongside the International Monetary Fund, World Bank and Asian Development Bank. Together with the provision of money, China is calling for measures and agreements to reduce or remove trade barriers, economic red tape and other obstacles to economic integration.

An initial $50 billion has been provided to the recently established Asia Infrastructure Investment Bank (AIIB), which is projected to have at least $100 billion in funds. Another $40 billion has gone into the Silk Road Fund for projects in Central Asia. China has announced $46 billion to finance the China-Pakistan economic corridor. China has also made an initial contribution of $10 billion to the BRICS-led New Development Bank, set up in August. The China Development Bank has declared that it will fund up to $1 trillion in One Belt, One Road projects.

The Chinese government proposes next year to begin a five-year period of planning projects with its OBOR partners with a view to starting the projects' full-scale implementation from 2021 and completion in 2049.

The economic prospects of the One Belt, One Road scheme have already had an impact in Europe. In March, Britain broke ranks with the US and signed up to the Chinese-backed AIIB to take advantage of the financial opportunities that could open up. Other European powers rapidly followed suit. Chinese academic Wang Yiwei commented: "The New Silk Road Initiative could help redirect the centre of geopolitical gravity away from the US and back to Eurasia... The recent decision by France, Germany, Italy and the UK to join the Asian Infrastructure Investment Bank goes in this direction, and represents a major shift in European attitudes towards Asia, and China in particular, that clearly departs from the US position."

US imperialism, however, is not going to stand by and allow moves to integrate Eurasia by China and the European powers, from which it is marginalised or excluded altogether. American strategists have long regarded Eurasia—a region with 70 percent of the world's population and over half of global output—as central to its global hegemony.

In his 1997 book *T he Grand Chessboard*, former US National Security Advisor Zbigniew Brzezinski wrote: "For America, the chief geopolitical prize is Eurasia... Eurasia is the globe's largest continent and is geopolitically axial. A power that dominates Eurasia would control two of the world's three most advanced and economically productive regions... Eurasia is thus the chessboard on which the struggle for global primacy continues to be played."

Since the collapse of the Soviet Union in 1991, the US has sought to bring the vast Eurasian landmass under its domination. Its own Silk Road Strategy, first outlined in 1999, has guided its interventions and intrigues in the former Soviet Republics of Central Asia and the Caucuses. The "war on terror" provided the pretext for the US-led invasion of Afghanistan and the installation of a puppet regime to provide Washington with a base of operations in neighbouring Central Asia.

While not an elaborated or necessarily coherent strategy, the Obama administration's "pivot to Asia," along with its provocations and interventions in Ukraine and Syria, implicitly drives toward the break up and subjugation of China and Russia, in order to bring the Eurasian landmass under US hegemony.

Speaking about the TPP in October, President Obama declared: "When more than 95 percent of our potential customers live outside our borders, we can't let countries like China write the rules of the global economy. We should write those rules." But if the US is unable to dictates terms to the world through the TPP, and its counterpart for Europe, the Transatlantic Trade and Investment Partnership, then as it has done over the past three decades, it will resort to military provocations, interventions and war.

The vision of a One Belt, One Road scheme peacefully integrating Eurasia is no more viable than a united capitalist Europe. Fuelled by the deepening global economic crisis, the divisions and rivalries among the major imperialist powers within Europe and with the United States and Japan, will only intensify as each scrambles to secure its interests. The chief destabilising factor remains US imperialism, which has repeatedly demonstrated its determination to offset its historic decline through the use of military force, even if that could plunge the world into a catastrophic war.

7

OBOR: China's Strategy for a New Global Financial Order

Sit Tsui is an associate professor at the Rural Reconstruction Institute at Southwest University, Chongqing. Erebus Wong is a senior researcher at the Kwan Fong Cultural Research and Development Program at Lingnan University, Hong Kong. Lau Kin Chi is an associate professor in the Department of Cultural Studies at Lingnan University. Wen Tiejun is director of the Rural Reconstruction Center at Renmin University, Beijing. All are founding members of the Global University for Sustainability.

This is the second of three articles by Sit Tsui and her coauthors offering a Chinese perspective on current issues in global political economy. *MR* thanks Zhihe Wang for his assistance in editing this article. Translated from the Chinese by Alice Chan.

In late 2013, Chinese premier Xi Jinping announced a pair of new development and trade initiatives for China and the surrounding region: the "Silk Road Economic Belt" and the "Twenty-First-Century Maritime Silk Road," together known as One Belt, One Road (OBOR).1 Along with the Asian Infrastructure Investment Bank (AIIB), the OBOR policies represent an ambitious spatial expansion of Chinese state capitalism, driven by an excess of industrial production capacity, as well as by emerging financial capital interests.

The Chinese government has publicly stressed the lessons of the 1930s overcapacity crisis in the West that precipitated the Second World War, and promoted these new initiatives in the name of "peaceful development."

Nevertheless, the turn to OBOR suggests a regional scenario broadly similar to that in Europe between the end of the nineteenth century and the years before the First World War, when strong nations jostled one another for industrial and military dominance. The OBOR strategy combines land power and maritime power, bolstering China's existing oceanic hegemony in East Asia.

Historically, at the time of the Tang Dynasty (618—907), China's expanding trade with the West motivated the Islamic world to exert control over the trading routes of Central and West Asia, forcing Europe—under the pressure of a silver crisis caused by continuing trade deficits—to seek eastern trading routes that would allow it to bypass the Islamic regions. One after another, Spain, the Netherlands, the United Kingdom, and eventually the United States became dominant maritime powers, protecting and expanding their trade interests in East Asia. If the OBOR project were merely "one road," it would be little more than a traditional land-power strategy, but OBOR opens up secondary maritime power along China's coast, backed by the vast expanse of country's landmass.

At the turn of the twentieth century, the English geographer Halford John Mackinder proposed that a strong power integrating the transportation and trading channels of Europe, Asia, and Africa into a single "World-Island" would be ready to dominate the globe. In 1919, he wrote that "who rules East Europe commands the Heartland; who rules the Heartland commands the World-Island; who rules the World-Island commands the world." In practice, however, it is still necessary to coordinate control of land routes with maritime transportation along the coast of this World-Island.

OBOR depends on a series of delicate geopolitical calculations. Today only three nations can be considered continental powers: China, Russia, and the United States. China cannot simply open a new inland Silk Road, because it would inevitably have to pass through Russia.

Ever since its emergence as an imperial power in the late eighteenth century, Russian geopolitical strategy has been oriented toward Europe, with only secondary attention given to East Asia. This partly explains why, as its economy benefited from a surge in oil prices several years ago, Russia took little notice of China's Silk Road proposal.

Likewise, Russia took the lead in negotiating the new Eurasian Economic Union, meant to integrate and link Europe with the former Soviet countries of Central Asia. Putting it bluntly, it was not up to China to integrate Central Asia. However, in the aftermath of the Ukraine crisis, Russia faces hostility from Europe and the United States, and with the global drop in oil prices, the country has no choice but to turn east and seriously consider China's proposal for a trans-continental strategic partnership. Yet if relations with Europe were to improve, Russia would promptly turn back toward Europe. No matter how closely tied their regional interests become, neither Russia nor China can put all their eggs in one basket. That is why China's land-power strategy is being presented as OBOR, a distinctly Chinese project.

Nevertheless, China is aware that the United States would counter the OBOR effort by strengthening its alliance with capital interest blocs within China—both inside and outside the ruling clique—to reassert its influence over China's future development policy. Indeed, in this respect the United States has already had much success: the Chinese financial bureaucracy accedes to the unwavering primacy of the United States as the world's central bank, making it unlikely to question, much less undermine, U.S. leadership in the global order.

Nevertheless, there is little doubt the United States will adjust its diplomatic strategy with regard to OBOR. Iran, for example, is an important part of the OBOR proposal, and whatever its other aims, the U.S. nuclear agreement with Iran was a strategic adjustment meant to balance China's influence in the region.

MARITIME POWER AND THE ASEAN REGION

For such a small place, Singapore has long had an outsize influence and strategic importance. With the Strait of Malacca, it controls a vital access point for the maritime trade routes connecting Europe, Africa, and Asia. Singapore clearly understands that its survival depends on a balancing act between the West and China. The West valued Singapore's first prime minister, Lee Kuan Yew, an ardent Cold Warrior determined to stop the spread of Communism in the region. Thus, despite Lee's close ties to Chinese officials and their sympathy for the authoritarian efficiency and corporatism of his "Asian values" ideology, Singapore would never become a Chinese ally. Lee remained loyal to U.S. interests to the end: shortly after Obama took office, he advised the United States on its diplomatic "pivot" to Asia and the Pacific, and opened up military ports to assist with new U.S. military deployment within the Association of Southeast Asian Nations (ASEAN) region. Given this legacy, China harbors no illusions about Singapore's allegiances.

For these and other reasons, China wants to open up another transportation channel from southwest China to the Indian Ocean, bypassing the Strait of Malacca. Another potential southbound route would pass through Pakistan or Bangladesh to the Indian Ocean. In either case, the goal would be to connect with Sri Lanka, where a new, world-class harbor would open up one more entrepot in the Indian Ocean. ASEAN is the starting point of the maritime Silk Road proposed by China, but it is also the region most fraught with complexities, and where U.S. influence is most deeply rooted.

THE EU AND OBOR

The EU's response to OBOR has been similarly reactive, and even more disjointed. The EU only really began assessing the initiative in 2015 – though, to be fair, China's plans have been extremely vague. However, even on the much more concrete issue of the AIIB, the EU lacked a clear policy, and some member states joined the bank individually.In 2013, the EU and China agreed an "EU-China 2020 Strategic Agenda for Cooperation", which includes infrastructure, investment, and connectivity as areas of interest. The agenda expressed the desire on both sides to enhance security consultations on Central Asia, to negotiate a comprehensive EU-China Investment Agreement, to expand cooperation on infrastructure networks between Asia and Europe, and to explore models of infrastructure cooperation, but gave little clarity on how and when these goals should be pursued.

With the announcement of OBOR, however, some concrete steps did begin to crystallise. The EU-China Summit Joint Declaration 2015 highlights the two parties' mutual interest in the Chinese Silk Road projects, as well as the Chinese will to support Juncker's Investment Plan for Europe. The declaration introduces a range of tools to improve EU–China relations in several areas, namely the Connectivity Platform, EU-China High Level Economic and Trade Dialogue, cooperation in the AIIB, EU-China Economic and Financial Dialogue, and the possibility of an EU-China Investment Agreement. In September 2015, during the High Level Economic and Trade Dialogue, China announced its contribution to Juncker's plan – the first non-EU country to do so, followed by the inauguration of a joint working group to increase cooperation in all aspects of investment, including the Silk Road Fund and the European Investment Bank (EIB).

The countries of Central and Eastern Europe (CEE), in an attempt to catch up with the rest of the EU, are leading the way in terms of working with China along the Silk Road, with a huge interest in Chinese investment. In 2011, China launched the 16+1 format to promote cooperation and exchange in a region composed of both EU member states and non-EU states. The format has been controversial, as it bypasses the EU and makes it harder to achieve a common EU policy on China. China's engagement in CEE threatens to turn the region into a strong advocate for China within the EU, regardless of Beijing's record on issues such as human rights and democracy.

For smaller states, though, the 16+1 offers an opportunity to tap into Chinese investment – just as Germany, France, and the UK have strong bilateral economic ties with China – even if this is through regional clusters. To date, China's engagement in Eastern Europe has not been significant enough to change any minds. Beyond the rhetoric, China's top EU investment destinations have been the UK, Germany, and France. China sees CEE as a testing ground for a new approach to Europe, but also as an area with less political stability and greater risks than Western Europe. The CEE countries, in turn, are excited about the potential volume of investment. Hungary was the first country in the EU to start talks with China on OBOR and signed a memorandum of understanding with China in June 2015, followed by Poland (mainly on railway projects) shortly after. Other countries may well follow suit. If this engagement aims to close the infrastructure gap between China, Eurasia, and the EU, then it will strongly serve European interests by bringing connectivity to Europe's least interconnected region.

Overall, reactions in Europe to OBOR have been mixed. European interest, where it exists, has seemed to come from the Baltic countries, southern Europe, and central and east European countries. A common or strategic approach is distinctly lacking.

Recommendations: How should Europe respond?

All of the above will force Europe to consider its place in Eurasia. It is likely that both China and Russia – and the smaller post-Soviet Central Asian countries – will want to keep Europe and the US involved in the region, but each for their own distinct reasons. Europe will always have different stakes and approaches to the region than the US and cannot count on Washington to protect its interests. The EU must decide what its goals are in the region, and how it can best pursue them.

It is clear that Europe – both as a Union and as member states – can and should engage with both OBOR and the EEU, using the leverage that comes from its market its soft power, and its expertise to mould and even absorb them. A principled abstention or opposition will simply encourage greater cooperation between two powers that in fact have much that might otherwise push them apart.

The EU has a clear interest in maintaining competition between Russia and China in Eurasia. Ukraine and the resulting Western sanctions against Russia created an intense but limited rapprochement between China and Russia – most visible in the resumption of sales of sophisticated Russian arms to China (the S-400 missile defence system, and Su-35 planes). This rapprochement poses a challenge to the EU – regardless of whether it turns out to be a win-win arrangement for the two parties. Their cooperation could affect Europe's whole relationship with Russia: political ties, the treaty base, and trade structure. Europe – and the West in general – will still want to be in a position that allows it to set the global, universal rules of the game in both politics and economics. The Russia–China relationship, though far from a perfect match, could make that more problematic in the future.

Most of the countries covered in our research warmly welcome Chinese investment, largely because of the lack of normative strings attached, while there is an awareness of the costs of cooperation with Russia. Many of the case-study countries would prefer EU regulations and Chinese investment, without Russian interference. But despite Russia's unpopularity, efforts to shut it out are not viable. Lately, the EU has learned from hard experience that Russia reacts in harmful ways when it feels threatened. In this case, it is clear that intense pressure on Russia will simply drive it into China's arms as a junior partner, which from Europe's perspective would be a bad outcome.

To maintain Russian-Chinese competition, the EU needs to carve out a space and role for itself in Eurasia. The countries of the region value access to Europe's market and look to Europe to protect them from Russian – and to a lesser extent Chinese – control. More prosaically, the EU's knowledge and expertise is highly valued in Central Asia, often transferred bilaterally from single EU member states, notably Germany, to single Central Asian countries. These countries understand that both the EEU and OBOR would profit from more accountable institutions, better border controls, and lower corruption levels, and that European know-how will be essential for achieving those goals. Even the most corrupt leaders in these countries, who have happily ignored the rules to enhance their power and enrich themselves, understand their value once they become the weaker parties in any negotiation. The EU should make use of that leverage.

Europe's approach will depend on which problem it fears most: Russian political hegemony or Chinese economic hegemony. Should Europeans encourage Russia's security role in Eurasia, particularly to counter the rise of Islamic fundamentalism and reduce Chinese influence? Or does the danger that Russia could be tempted to reunify the post-Soviet space through a sphere of influence, or direct annexation, outweigh these merits?

Regarding the economy, should Europeans encourage a regional economic pact – which, at the very least, would facilitate trade, including for third parties, in the Eurasian space? Or is Chinese economic hegemony – imposed through bilateral relations, and largely without security undertakings – a preferable option that would reduce Russia's overall capacity for making itself a geopolitical nuisance, and force it to reconsider its relations with Europe in a more positive light? The two countries in which these questions are most acute are Uzbekistan (because of its fragile security situation) and Kazakhstan (where an economic tilt towards OBOR would provide a viable Silk Road, potentially bypassing Russia).

The stakes are also high for Europe itself, particularly when it comes to OBOR. Europe needs cheap Chinese capital to compete with other sources for large public projects, both inside and outside the EU (the Commission has been pushing Trans-European Transport Network corridors, particularly in the Balkans). China's participation in the Juncker plan (the European Commission's Investment Plan for Europe) and the

EIB has enormous domestic implications for Europeans. Given these competing considerations, the EU will want the flexibility to promote different levels of Russian and Chinese involvement in different countries depending on their individual circumstances. Engagement with both OBOR and the EEU offers Europe the opportunity to influence these projects at a detailed level – where the EU excels – and to tailor their approach in a given country depending on whether China or Russia represents the greatest challenge.

This engagement should occur principally in areas of Europe's greatest interest in Eurasia: energy, infrastructure, security, and migration. Here we recommend a few immediate steps to help this overall approach:

- Set a framework for bilateral investment with China: Push for finalisation of the comprehensive China-EU Investment Agreement, in order to institutionalise and regulate bilateral investment. Include provisions on cooperation in Eurasia in order to secure and expand continental trade and investment between the two entities.
- Enable and promote EU investment in OBOR: Enable EU member states, the EIB, and the European Bank for Reconstruction and Development (EBRD) to invest in OBOR through the Connectivity Platform in Eurasia and beyond.
- Ensure that Chinese investment meets European needs: Strengthen and expand the EU-China Connectivity Platform in order to coordinate Chinese investment in the EU with the European Investment Plan.
- Leverage EU investment and coordination to set standards: Create a set of rules and standards that ensure that Chinese investment through the Connectivity Platform complies with European standards and regulations. For the Chinese, corruption at Central Asia's borders is a major cost that significantly reduces the speed of transactions and therefore undermines connectivity.

- Ensure that the various EU instruments work in harmony: Develop a European-Eurasian connectivity strategy to coordinate cross-regional projects, investments, and policies between all related EU instruments and foreign policy fields. This implies better cooperation of financial instruments in the four policy areas: European Neighbourhood Policies, Enlargement Policies, Central Asia strategy, and internal EU development and investment programmes for Eastern and Central European member states.
- Leverage Europe's existing stake in the region: Increase Europe's visibility in Eurasia as the single biggest trading and investment partner of nearly all relevant countries, by promoting infrastructure and connectivity projects to develop trade relations.
- Support projects with Chinese involvement to reduce Russian leverage in Eurasia: For example, recognise the recent China-Kazakh-Azeri-Georgian-Turkish joint agreement on transport cooperation in Eurasia. The EU has lost leverage since 2009 when it stopped its financial assistance to the Transport Corridor Europe-Caucasus-Asia (TRACECA), the most important European infrastructure project in the region, which is now financed by member states.
- Create a platform for EU–EEU cooperation: Cooperate directly with the Eurasian Economic Commission and on a multilateral level. A joint working group on EU–EEU trade cooperation could be a starting point, coordinating cooperation in areas such as technical barriers to trade, sanitary and phytosanitary issues, and customs. This should involve not only Russia, but also the ENP states of Armenia and Belarus, and the Central Asia partners Kazakhstan and Kyrgyzstan – and might help strengthen their roles in the Eurasian Economic Commission.
- Ensure that no country controls all energy routes through Eurasia: This will require strengthening cooperation in

the field of energy trade and energy security between Central Asia and Europe. Azerbaijan is a crucial partner, since it provides the only means to bypass Iran and Russia, via the Caspian Sea. Therefore, Europe may have to develop its own pipeline projects in order to avoid future project failures like South Stream and the recently halted Turkish Stream.

- Support eastern export routes for Russian gas: This will reduce Russia's obsession with retaining a monopolistic position on European markets and routes leading to Europe – something that has been the source of much tension between Russia and its neighbours, and Russia and the EU. Combined with the reforms in Europe's energy policy, this will help to provide the whole continent with energy markets free of excessive geopolitical stress.
- Maintain the attractive power of EU membership: Develop a real prospect of accession for the Balkan candidate countries, especially Serbia. Increased assistance will be necessary to help Serbia meet the necessary conditions to join the EU in a reasonable time. This will create incentives for Serbia to develop its relations with Kosovo, and help the EU to counter Russian and Chinese influence on Belgrade.
- Develop deeper relations with key Eurasian countries, particularly Kazakhstan: Increase technical assistance to Kazakhstan, the key country of Central Asia, through new financial assistance mechanisms. Astana left the EU's Development Cooperation Instrument (DCI) in 2014 due to its middle-income status and will not receive any basic EU assistance that is comparable to Russia's and China's government-coordinated investments. However, European foreign direct investment (FDI) still amounts to 60 percent of FDI in Kazakhstan.
- Create a platform for EU–EEU–OBOR coordination: The EU should establish a trilateral mechanism for EU–EEU–OBOR coordination, once EU–Russia relations

normalise. There is already a mechanism for cooperation between the EU, Russia, and Ukraine on the DCFTA with Ukraine, which is intended to revise parts of the deal that Russia finds problematic. This platform has not been productive thus far, but it can be sustained and widened.

In the end, Eurasian integration remains a distant prospect, whether or not it is a desirable outcome for Europe. The political obstacles to Russia, China, or the EU realising their goals of integrating the region are daunting. Instability, historic rivalries, and corruption haunt both Russia and China – not to mention the competition between them. But the importance of the region means that progress towards a certain degree of Eurasian integration is both possible and in Europe's interests. The prospect of Chinese and Russian failures should not make Europe feel better about the region or about itself. Rather, European cooperation with both the Russian and Chinese projects is necessary for progress in Eurasia, and, if properly structured, can promote European interests.

EU instruments

The Eurasian landmass is currently subject to two major integration initiatives: China's "One Belt, One Road" (OBOR) and the Russian-led Eurasian Economic Union (EEU). These initiatives have emerged and taken shape in a relatively short period of time, and target, in a broad sense, all countries in Central Asia, the Caucasus, and Eastern Europe. At the same time, the European Union has various policies, instruments, and tools that guide its relations with the countries in these regions. With the EU's major foreign policy tools under revision – the European Neighbourhood Policy (ENP) and the Global Strategy – it is a good moment to ask what Europe's interests are in the neighbourhood it shares with Russia and China, and what resources it has to hand. What are Europe's choices in an environment where it is not the only game in town, and where it may have diverging interests, and limited resources to pursue them?

The EU has developed varying relations with the countries of Eurasia, depending on geographical proximity and its interests. Some are candidates for membership and subject to its enlargement policies (i.e. Turkey and Serbia), some are part of the ENP and the Eastern Partnership (Azerbaijan and Ukraine), others are part of Europe's Central Asia strategy (Kazakhstan), and a fourth category is EU member states. The EU has diverse interests in these different sets of countries, and, because of the dynamics vis-à-vis Russia and Syria, these change quite rapidly. The variation in EU policies towards the countries covered by our case studies points to the need to reassess the existing tools, and potentially work on a more coherent approach towards the countries targeted by the EEU and OBOR. The EU has no policy yet towards the EEU, but has made more progress towards a common approach to OBOR via the new Connectivity Platform with China.

The EU assists Eurasia through various policies and instruments, whose financial volume is larger than Russia's assistance to the region, but smaller than what China has announced it will invest through OBOR.

Between 2007 and 2013, the EU spent €13.4 billion on the ENP through its European Neighbourhood and Partnership Instrument (ENPI), of which €3.9 billion went to the Eastern Partnership. After the European Commission proposed in 2011 to increase ENP funding to €18.2 billion, the EU agreed to spend €15.4 billion, through its newly created European Neighbourhood Instrument (ENI), to finance the Southern and Eastern Partnerships between 2014 and 2020. From 2007 to 2013, the EU budget for bilateral and regional cooperation in Central Asia was €675 million, which increased to €1.028 billion for 2014 to 2020.

In terms of its enlargement policies, the EU spent €11.5 billion on its Instrument for Pre-accession Assistance (IPA) from 2007 to 2013, and its successor, the IPA-II, has a budget of €11.7 billion for 2014–2020. However, Russian and Chinese investments are directly targeted to single countries, while the EU takes issue-based bilateral and multilateral approaches.

The EU has allocated around €82.2 billion for 2014–2020 through nine funding instruments, seven of which are related to countries in Eurasia. These are:

1. The European Instrument for Democracy and Human Rights (EIDHR), with a budget of €1.3 billion.
2. The Instrument contributing to Stability and Peace (IcSP), with a budget of €2.3 billion.
3. The Partnership Instrument, with a budget of €954 million.
4. The Instrument for Nuclear Safety Cooperation (INSC), with a budget of €225 million.
5. The Development Cooperation Instrument (DCI), with a budget of €19.6 billion.
6. The European Neighbourhood Instrument (ENI), with a budget of €15.4 billion.
7. The Instrument for Pre-accession Assistance II (IPA-II), with a budget of €11.7 billion.

Only the Instrument for Greenland (IFG) and the European Development Fund (EDF) do not contribute to projects in the Eurasian landmass. The budget allocated to projects with Central Asia falls within ENI, and amounts to €1.028 billion.

The objectives of the instruments are highly diverse, as are the needs of the target countries. This is why it is key for the EU to establish common rules and principles with the China- and Russia-led projects.

CHINA'S DEVELOPMENT AND THE U.S. DOLLAR SYSTEM

In recent years, China has taken a leading role in the establishment of a new set of international economic institutions, including the New Development Bank, the BRICS Contingent Reserve Arrangement, the AIIB, and the Silk Road Fund, as well as the Shanghai Cooperation Organization. Together they represent a regional counterweight to Western-led entities like the International Monetary Fund (IMF) and the World Bank—and more recently, the European Central Bank—that have dominated the global financial order since the introduction of the Bretton Woods system after the Second World War. China is arguably only the third country in history, after Britain and the United States, with the capacity to shape and lead a global system of finance and trade. Of course, in the foreseeable future, China will not replace the U.S. dollar system; it could at most stand on equal footing. After the United States overtook the United Kingdom to lead the world in industrial production capacity in the late nineteenth century, it took another fifty years and two world wars before it could dominate global finance. China recognizes this reality, and has consistently promoted the AIIB and other organizations as complements, not competitors, of the World Bank and Asian Development Bank (ADB).

Over the next decade or so, as long as no major instability unsettles the Chinese economy, it seems inevitable that the renminbi will become one of the most important international currencies. Nevertheless, it is far from clear that the renminbi, even in twenty years' time, could challenge the hegemonic status of the U.S. dollar.

As a capitalist economy industrializes, the strength of its currency depends on the country's continued productive capacity, supported by the government and civil society. However, in the subsequent phase of financial capitalism, the main source of a currency's credibility is the political and military strength of a country. From this perspective, the impregnable position of the U.S. dollar as the world's credit currency arises foremost from the United States' enormous military strength. The United States accounts for 40 percent of global military spending, more than that of the next ten countries combined.

Of course, a continually expanding military hegemony has not been the only source of U.S. financial dominance. Since the Second World War, private firms and government agencies in the United States have led the world in technological innovation, not only in arms manufacturing, but in chemicals, semiconductors, film and television, aviation, computers, finance, communications, and information technology.

All of these innovations have facilitated the global expansion of capital's high value-added. The foundation of the U.S. dollar's value, besides American military and political strength, is thus the United States' monopolistic innovative capacity in raising the value-added of capital.

In China today, a spirit of utopian capitalism is rampant at all levels of the economy, driven by the belief that as long as state-owned enterprises continually withdraw or dissolve, to be replaced by private firms, then China will be blessed by some miraculous market power with an innovative capacity for high value-added. But without an enormous investment in systematic research and development, it is unclear how scattered concentrations of private capital in China could make such advances in the near future. Consequently, China's currency is unlikely to challenge the U.S. dollar, or even the Euro. Ironically, the single force that seems most likely to bring down the U.S. dollar is the increasingly virtualized U.S. financial system itself.

In exporting capital over the past decade, China lacked any overall planning for foreign investment and development, sometimes entangling it in geopolitical crises, as in Libya or Sudan, other times in bureaucratic morasses, as in its role in the Mexican high-speed rail and Sri Lanka harbor projects. This misdirection resulted from the lack of any strong support and coordination from financial organizations like the AIIB.

While China has become an important capital-exporting country, it has largely avoided entering into explicit political or financial alliances that might protect its large-scale foreign investments.

With the establishment of the New Development Bank and the AIIB, however, China's financial ties to neighboring nations have become more formal and far-reaching. From this perspective, they represent the kind of transnational institutional construction needed to give greater focus and strategic leverage to China's capital exports.

One goal of the Obama administration's "pivot" to the Asia-Pacific was to prevent the emergence of a mutually beneficial

Asian currency alliance among China, Japan, and South Korea, which would have threatened the primacy of U.S. currency in the region. Toward that end, the United States encouraged the right-wing restoration in Japan under Shinzo Abe, helping form a defensive Pacific ring to contain China. In addition, the United States has sponsored the Trans-Pacific Partnership (TPP), in part to ensure that the Asia-Pacific region will remain a dollar stronghold. The AIIB represents China's response.

Though the United States put strong pressure on its European and Asian allies not to join the bank, since its founding in 2015 the AIIB has already attracted a prominent international membership, including not only major developing economies such as Brazil, India, and Russia, but also France and the United Kingdom.

One reason for the slow progress of the TPP negotiations is that the agreement has been centered on U.S. interests, and the marginal returns gained from tariff reductions might prove minimal in comparison to the financial implications. However, the founding of the AIIB compelled the United States to both speed up these negotiations and to make significant concessions, finally reaching an agrreement in October 2015. (Though even now, after all these efforts, the election of Donald Trump has put the TPP's future in unforeseen jeopardy.)

Awkwardly for the United States—which launched the TPP with the original intent of blocking China—the AIIB marks the first time since before Bretton Woods that the United States has been excluded from an important international financial structure.

When trusted European allies like the United Kingdom, Germany, France, Italy, Switzerland, and others announced their participation, Obama called an emergency national security meeting. The reason is clear: the AIIB challenges, albeit still within an institutional framework, the U.S. financial hegemony that has prevailed since the Second World War.

Of course, these allies are not jumping ship from the U.S. dollar-dominated system just yet, but only hedging their bets, as that hegemony has shown clear signs of exhaustion. In setting up the AIIB, China has stressed shared interests and cooperation among member nations, the better to attract interested allies.

The first European country to join the AIIB was reportedly Switzerland. However, because Swiss officials wanted to keep their negotiations with China secret and postponed announcement of the decision, Britain was the first European country to officially announce its participation.

That both Switzerland and Luxemburg, strongholds of financial capital that have previously declined to join most international organizations, have now signed on with the AIIB, suggests that the Bretton Woods alliance faces deep internal fissures. We can call it the Bretton Woods system's Triffin Dilemma: the interests of the United States and those of its longtime allies are beginning to show potentially insuperable contradictions.

The institutional coherence of this alliance has been slipping for some time. A primary purpose of the Bretton Woods system was to facilitate exports of excess industrial capacity and capital from the United States.

The interests of postwar growth in the United States and recovery in Europe were in line. In 1971, when the Nixon administration unpegged the dollar from gold and the United States began to export liquidity on a large scale, these moves likewise seemed to serve the interests of European financial institutions.

However, over the last two decades the fundamental needs of the two have come into conflict. Reforms within the IMF have stalled, because the United States does not want to give up its veto power, while other international financial organizations long dominated by the United States have proven unable to accommodate the rapid rise of East Asian economies. The AIIB, led by China, is a clear outcome of these trends.

The liquidity swap alliance formed in October 2013 among six central banks—the Bank of Canada, the Bank of England, the Bank of Japan, the European Central Bank, the U.S. Federal Reserve, and the Swiss National Bank—is designed to prevent another large-scale liquidity crisis in Europe and North America like the one that precipitated the financial crisis of 2008–09. Yet it is only preventive.

The new global paradigm now needs new institutions and proactive propositions. The IMF and the World Bank (and its subsidiary, the ADB), constrained by U.S. interests, are not up to the task. Can China take this opportunity to oversee the development of a new global financial alliance? For a large industrial country just entering the phase of financial capitalism, increasingly roiled by domestic disturbances, the challenge is unprecedented and enormous.

CHINA'S INROADS INTO NEPAL: INDIA'S CONCERNS

The political crisis that triggered off in Nepal with Prime Minster Prachanda's resignation yet again indicates not only the trials and tribulations of a fledgling democratic process but also points to the geopolitical vulnerability of the country sandwiched as it is between the two Asian giants.

While India considers Nepal a part of its sphere of influence, it is increasingly being challenged by China's inroads into Nepal. In fact, the growing Nepal-China nexus should be seen in the context of India-China power competition in Asia. Essentially Nepal facilitates China's security interests in the South Asian region. This can be clearly glimpsed from Chinese ambassador, Zheng Xianglin's statement delivered at the Council of World Affairs in August 2008 that "Nepal is situated in a favourable geographical position in South Asia, and a passage linking China and South Asia."

Nepal constitutes an important element of China's South Asia policy. One may recall Mao Zedong's five finger policy in which Nepal constituted one of the five fingers along with Ladakh, Bhutan, Sikkim and Arunachal Pradesh. The five fingers were essentially meant to serve as a 'new buffer' zone between India and China after the 'old buffer' (Tibet) came under China's sovereign control in 1951. With growing tensions in Tibet, particularly after the March 2008 uprising, China's conception of Nepal as a new buffer acquired particular significance.

Its policy towards Nepal came to be driven by the need to curb the clandestine activities of some 20,000 Tibetan refugees (the second largest Tibetan refugee community in the world) in Nepal. Consequently, China has been increasingly playing a significant role in determining the future shape of Nepali politics. During each of the high-level meetings China has extracted assurances from Nepal that it adheres to the one-China principle, acknowledges Tibet as an inalienable part of China, and will ensure that no anti-China activity is allowed on its soil. Underscored in China's South Asia policy is the strategy to marginalize India's influence in Nepal. Marginalizing India would allow China not only to dominate South Asia but also provide easy access to Nepal's roughly 83,000 megawatts of hydroelectric potential. It is interesting to note that China pronounces its foreign policy towards Nepal in a manner which presents not only a benign image of itself but which also helps assuage Nepal's fears of a domineering India. For instance, the December 2008 Yang Jiechi's assurance to protect Nepal's "sovereignty and independence" not only strengthened Beijing's diplomacy but also sought to obviate India's influence. News reports from Nepal even go further to suggest that "China intended to develop relations with Nepal in a way that would serve as a role model for bilateral ties between big and small countries." China has, in fact, laid down a four-fold policy to strengthen its bilateral relations with Nepal: "First, accommodate each other's political concern. Second, enhance the economic cooperation on the basis of mutual benefit. Third, boost people-to-people and cultural exchanges. Fourth, strengthen the coordination and cooperation in international and regional affairs."

Apart from stating a clear policy towards Nepal, China has been systematically pursuing a multi-dimensional engagement with Nepal. There has been a flurry of visits between China and Nepal in recent times. According to one news report, about 38 Chinese delegations visited Nepal in 2008 alone. China has been cultivating ties with not only the Communist Party of Nepal-Maoist (CPN-M) but also with the Communist Party of Nepal-United Marxist-Leninist (CPN-UML) and the Madhesi People's Rights Forum.

Lately, China has begun taking interest in Terai politics. There are reports of a high level Chinese delegation visiting the General Convention of the Madhesi People's Rights Forum in early 2009. In April 2009, a CPN-UML delegation led by Jhala Nath Khanal visited Beijing when China had impressed upon the delegation that it wants "a new kind of relationship" with Nepal. Besides high level visits, China's inroads into Nepal are being greatly facilitated by the systematic promotion of China Study Centres (CSCs) which are completely funded by China.

The number of CSCs in Nepal has increased in recent times. According to the CSC website, there are ten local branches located in Butwal, Banepa, Sankhuwasabha, Pokhara, Biratnagar, Morang, Sunsari, Chitwan, Nepalgunj and Lumbini, besides the central organization of the CSC-Nepal in Kathmandu. According to Bhim Prasad Bhurtel, the executive director of the Nepal South Asia Centre, Kathmandu, "33 China Study Centres have been established in southern Nepal adjoining the Indian border." He also mentions that China Radio International has launched a local FM radio station in Kathmandu with the purpose of bringing China closer to Nepal. Besides CSCs, a Nepal-China Mutual Cooperation Society (NCMCS), funded by the Chinese Embassy in Nepal, was established in March 2005. The primary aim of NCMCS is to strengthen diplomatic relations between the two countries as well as to disseminate an image of a friendly China as opposed to hegemonic India. Besides, there are other associations like the Nepal-China Executives Council in Kathmandu, the Nepal-China Friendship Association in Lumbini and the Nepal-China Youth Friendship Association in Pokhara. Further, to promote bilateral cooperation and exchanges the Nepal-China bilateral consultation mechanism was constituted in 1996. Such multi-layered engagement enabled China to not only strengthen its diplomacy in the region but also project a benign and cooperative image. It may be noted that India does not have such multi-layered levels of contact and lacks innovative ways (cultural or diplomatic) of reaching out to the Nepali government and people. In fact, similar culture and traditions in Nepal create a kind of extended cultural zone for India and often therefore many of the natural linkages that exist between India and Nepal are taken for granted.

China's proactive policy in Nepal can also be discerned from the military assistance it has been providing. On December 7, 2008 during a meeting in Kathmandu between Nepal Defence Minister Ram Bahadur Thapa and the deputy commander of China's People Liberation Army, Lieutenant General Ma Xiaotian, China pledged to provide US $2.6 million as military assistance for Nepal's security sector. Earlier in September 2008, China had announced military aid worth $ 1.3 million, the first such assistance to the Maoist government in Nepal. It may be recalled that in 2006 China had provided clandestine military assistance to the Maoists in a bid to placate them. In recent times, Beijing has shown keen support for the Maoist governments' proposal to integrate some 19,000 Maoist guerrillas with the Nepal Army.

As part of economic assistance, ahead of Prachanda's now-cancelled second visit to China, China had announced a doubling of aid to Nepal amounting to $21.94 million. To attract Chinese investment in Nepal, on April 7, 2009, the Nepal-China Executives Council (NCEC) and the Chinese People's Association for Friendship with Foreign Countries (CPAFFC) signed a MoU. The trade volume between the two countries currently stands at $401 million with China selling goods worth about $386 million, and Nepal exporting a mere $15 million.

To bridge the trade deficit, China has agreed in April 2009 to provide duty free access to 497 Nepali goods in the Chinese market. There are also proposals for a second South Asian

Countries Commodity Fair to be held from 6 to 10th June 2009 at Kunming where 40 Nepali enterprises are slated to participate with 30 stalls. China is the third largest country to provide FDI to Nepal, India and the US being the first and second, respectively.

Also, not to forget, China's initiative in building a road link between Lhasa and Khasa, a border town located some 80 kilometres north of Kathmandu. China has also accepted Nepal's proposal in April 2009 to open up two more custom points in addition to the existing five.

China is also building a 65 km second road link, the Syafrubesi-Rasuwagadi road, which is the shortest route from Tibet to Kathmandu. As part of promoting Nepal's hydro-power projects, in 2008, China's Assistant Minister for Foreign Affairs, He Yafei, pledged to provide Nepal a loan of $125 million for Upper Trishuli 3 'A' and $62 million for Upper Trishuli 3 'B'.

The plants would start operating from 2012. There has thus evolved a multi-layered engagement between China and Nepal, causing considerable concern in the Indian establishment. Even if Prachanda's statement is to be believed that "not a single (Chinese) delegation came to Nepal on my invitation," it nonetheless does not rule out China's growing inroads into Nepal. China's growing ties with Nepal undoubtedly supports its wider South Asia policy, much to the concern of India.

More importantly, China's strategic interest has been facilitated by the rise of the Maoists in Nepal. In fact, the January 2008 speech of Prachanda which got leaked has fuelled India's concern about the possibility of Nepal inching towards a Maoist dictatorship. Indeed, ideological similarity with Communist China lends suspicion to the growing affinity between the two countries.

Unlike Royal Nepal, the Maoists under Prachanda have shown in no ambiguous terms their strategic goal of reducing dependence on India and increasing ties with China. In this context, it is worth noting the draft proposal for a China-Nepal friendship treaty submitted on February 27, 2009 by the visiting

Chinese delegation to Nepal led by Assistant Chinese Foreign Minister Liu Jieyi.

The official reason provided was the need for a fresh treaty to meet the changing political environment in Nepal after the Maoists came to power. For Nepal, signing a treaty with China on the lines of the 1950 India-Nepal treaty undoubtedly curtails India's special relations with Nepal. At the same time, by pledging to overhaul the 1950 treaty with India on the ground that it "does not represent the aspirations of the Nepalese people anymore" Maoist Nepal clearly seeks to reduce India's influence in Nepal. Prachanda's May 09, 2009 interview to the Times of India in which he asked, "Why should Nepal seek India's consent on its security?" seems to hint at the Maoist's search for independent foreign policy. And on the other hand are reports about China pledging support for Prachanda's decision to sack the army chief when India was trying hard to prevent it.

In sum, observing the growing trends of Nepal-China ties, it may be argued that Nepal under the Maoist government has been clearly seeking closer ties with China at the cost of India and is far from pursuing a policy of equidistance. Further, Nepal's geo-political location coupled with China's proactive South Asia policy has clearly accentuated the security dilemma in the region. At this juncture, when Nepal is in turmoil, a great deal of foreign policy dexterity is required on the part of the Indian establishment to preserve its influence in South Asia and at the same time ensure a democratic Nepal that would deter China's inroads into Nepal.

ONE BELT, ONE ROAD AND THE START OF A NEW INTERNATIONAL ORDER

The international order has changed: One Belt, One Road, which, in a paternalist embrace takes in almost all European countries, is presented as the Chinese alternative to the Western model that dominated the world until now. The USA has been replaced as the world's leading economy and is losing its political hegemony to Chinese domination. This is shown by the reaction of Washington's most loyal allies in Europe, London and Berlin, signing up to the One Belt, One Road initiative without great hesitation and despite strong US opposition.

By contrast, Sino-European relations are not dominated by geostrategic or ideological rivalries, a fundamental premise for establishing mutually beneficial cooperation: China proposes to create, alongside Europe, a new international economic and financial order (Xinhua). The most notable milestone in this close collaboration is the Chinese injection of up to €10bn into the EFSI, a decision agreed between Beijing and Brussels in April 2016, making China the largest investor in the so-called Juncker Plan.

Together, they can generate economic growth and job creation, building and modernising infrastructure networks that improve intra-European connectivity. This could facilitate European products and services being exported to new markets and improve their entry conditions to the Chinese market itself.

Bibliography

Alperovitz, Gar. *The Decision to Use the Atomic Bomb*. New York: Vintage Books, 1996.

Anil, K.C.: *Military and Democracy in South Asia : Challenges, Politics and Power*, Sumit Enterprises, Delhi, 2009.

Austin, Greg: *China's Ocean Frontier: International Law, Military Force and National Development*. St. Leonards: Allen & Unwin, 1998.

Chang, Felix K.: *'China's Naval Rise and the South China Sea: An Operational Assessment.'* 2012.

Clinton, William J. *A National Security Strategy for a New Century*. Washington, DC: Government Printing Office, 1998.

Digumarti Bhaskara Rao: *Military Conversion : Impact on Science and Technology*, Discovery, Delhi, 2003.

Donnan, H. and Wilson, T. M.: *Borders: Frontiers of Identity, Nation and State*, Oxford: Berg, 1999.

Elisseeff, Vadime: *The Silk Roads: Highways of Culture and Commerce*. UNESCO Publishing. Paris. 1998

Felix K. Chang: *'China's Naval Rise and the South China Sea: An Operational Assessment.'* 2012.

Forbes, Andrew ; Henley, David: *China's Ancient Tea Horse Road*. Chiang Mai: Cognoscenti Books. 2011.

Friedman, G.: *The Future of War: Power, Technology and Indian Army*, N.Y., Random House, 1996.

Gao, Mobo: *The Battle for China's Past: Mao and the Cultural Revolution,* London, Pluto Press, 2008.

Garver, John W.: *Face Off: China, the United States, and Taiwan's Democratization*. Seattle: University of Washington Press, 1997.

Gerald H.: *The Peaceful Management of Transboundary Resources*. London: Graham & Trotman, 1995.

Ghosh, Ajoy : *China-Pak Conflict : Threat to South Asian Security*, Reference Press, Delhi, 2003.

Gottlieb, Thomas M.: *Chinese Foreign Policy Factionalism and the Origins of the Strategic Triangle*. Santa Monica, CA: RAND Corporation, 1977.

Hansen, Valerie: *The Silk Road: A New History,* Oxford University Press; 2012.

Jackson, Major Donovan: *India's Navy*. Sampson Low. London, 1940.

John B.: *Britain and the Persian Gulf 1795-1880*, Oxford, Clarendon Press, 1968.

John W.: *Face Off: China, the United States, and Taiwan's Democratization*. Seattle: University of Washington Press, 1997.

Johnston, Douglas: *The Theory and History of Ocean Boundary Making*. Kingston: McGill-Queen's University Press, 1988.

Kevin R. Vienna: *Beyond the Law of the Sea*. New York: Praeger, 1997.

Laquer, Walter, *The New Terrorism: Fanaticism and the Arms of Mass Destruction*, Oxford: Oxford University Press, 1999.

Larsen, Jeanne: *Silk Road: A Novel of Eighth-Century China*. 2009.

Lo Chi-Kin: *China's Policy Towards Territorial Disputes. The Case of the South China Sea Islands*. London: Routledge, 1989.

Lowe, A.V.: *The Law of the Sea*. Manchester: Manchester University Press, 1983.

Namboodirim, P. : *Intervention in the Indian Ocean,* New Delhi: ABC Publishing House, 1982.

Neil Frank R.: *The Philippines and the South China Sea Islands: Overview and Documents*. Metro Manila: Foreign Service Institute, 1993.

Prabla, Dixit: *Communalism: A Struggle for Power*, New Delhi, Orient Longman, 1981.

Rhodes, Richard, *The Making of the Atomic Bomb*, New York: Simon and Schuster, 1988.

Stephen Bates : *Calming the Waters. Initiatives for Asia Pacific Maritime Cooperation*. Canberra Papers on Strategy and Defence, 1996.

Thubron, C.: *The Silk Road to China,* Hamlyn, 1989.

Wishnick, Elizabeth: *Mending Fences: The Evolution of Moscow's China Policy from Brezhnev to Yeltsin*. Seattle: University of Washington Press, 2001.

Xue Litai: *China's Strategic Seapower. The Politics of Force Modernization in the Nuclear Age*. Stanford Cal.: Stanford University Press, 1994.

Index

O

P

R

S

T

❑❑❑